Michael Vatikiotis is a graduate of the School of Oriental and African Studies in London and gained his doctorate from the University of Oxford. He is a member of the Asia Society's International Council and has a decade of experience working as a private diplomat and conflict mediator for the Geneva-based Centre for Humanitarian Dialogue. Prior to that he worked as a journalist in Asia for thirty years, living in Indonesia, Malaysia, Thailand and Hong Kong. He is the author of two previous books on the politics of Southeast Asia and is based in Singapore.

@jagowriter

By the same author

Political Change in Southeast Asia: Trimming the Banyan Tree
Indonesian Politics under Suharto

Praise for *Blood and Silk*

'Books on the rise of Asia tend to concentrate on China and India. Vatikiotis fills a gap by providing a lively and learned guide to the politics, personalities and conflicts that are shaping a dynamic group of countries, including Indonesia, Malaysia, Thailand and Burma'
Gideon Rachman, *Financial Times*, Summer Reads

'A fascinating and many-layered portrait of Southeast Asia, brimming with colourful characters, insights and anecdotes, *Blood and Silk* is a rich palimpsest as can only be written by a longstanding student and scholar of the region like Michael Vatikiotis'
Thant Myint-U, author of *The River of Lost Footsteps*

'Vatikiotis's arguments are fluent and convincing, and his writing is suffused with a deep knowledge of and affection for Southeast Asia and its peoples'   Richard Cockett, *Literary Review*

'*Blood and Silk* is not a dry sociopolitical analysis. Vatikiotis has an eye for quirky detail, whether it be the Thai crown prince's pet poodle commissioned as an air force officer and dressed in uniform, or the self-important Muslim separatist from southern Thailand who prayed with Osama bin Laden in Khartoum but found the terrorist mastermind uninspiring and unimpressive. In the end, though, the outlook is menacing ... We can hope that Vatikiotis is wrong, but I fear he is not'   Victor Mallet, *Financial Times*

'Vatikiotis offers a lucid portrait of this fascinating region by bringing together a student's sense of wonder and curiosity, a journalist's scepticism and diligence in making sense of reality, and a peacemaker's compassion for the vulnerable'
Salil Tripathi, *South China Morning Post*

'An ambitious and timely book'   *The Economist*

BLOOD
AND
SILK

**POWER AND CONFLICT
IN MODERN
SOUTHEAST ASIA**

MICHAEL VATIKIOTIS

WEIDENFELD & NICOLSON

First published in Great Britain in 2017
This paperback edition first published in 2018 by Weidenfeld & Nicolson
an imprint of The Orion Publishing Group Ltd
Carmelite House, 50 Victoria Embankment
London EC4Y 0DZ

An Hachette UK Company

1 3 5 7 9 10 8 6 4 2

A CIP catalogue record for this book is
available from the British Library.

ISBN (paperback) 978 1 4746 0203 7
ISBN (ebook) 978 1 4746 0202 0

Typeset by Input Data Services Ltd, Somerset

Printed and bound by CPI Group (UK) Ltd, Croydon, CR0 4YY

MIX
Paper from
responsible sources
FSC® C104740

www.orionbooks.co.uk

For Janick, Chloe and Stefan

'We – running dogs, hunting hounds – we get to see
Only a moment of time of this drama we play in.'

'Kita – andging diburu – hanja melihat
Sebagian dari sandiwara sekarang.'

Chairil Anwar
Notes for 1946

CONTENTS

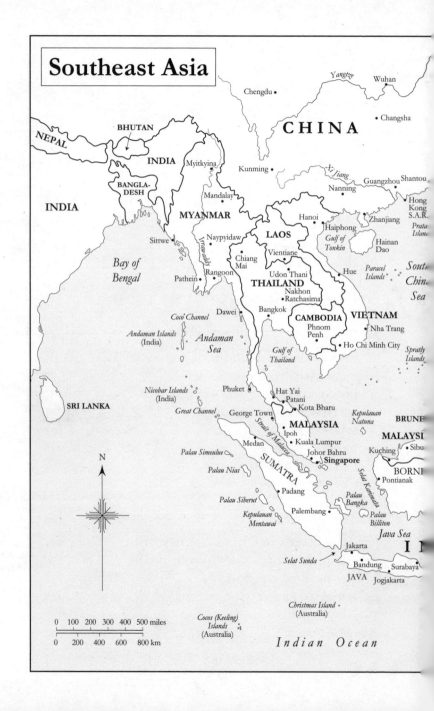

PREFACE

TO THE REVISED EDITION

When I began writing *Blood and Silk* I was concerned that my somewhat gloomy view of the social and political trajectory in Southeast Asia might be off. The region has a long history of not just surviving but of triumphing over adversity. The economies are growing at a healthy clip – averaging 5 per cent per year – and an air of stability pervades the region. But judging by what has happened in society and politics since the first edition was published in June 2017, I believe I was right to sound the alarm.

Across the region, respect for human rights, democracy and popular sovereignty has continued to diminish. In the Philippines, President Rodrigo Duterte's so-called war on drugs continues unabated; as of January 2018, there were an estimated 12,000 casualties, with some of the brutal killings caught on camera. To ensure a cover-up, the Philippine government tried – but has so far failed – to abolish the country's human rights commission. Meanwhile, Duterte's supporters were trying to persuade the maverick leader to extend his term of office beyond the six years imposed by the constitution, and hounding the independent media with threats of closure.

In Thailand, the military junta seemed to be in no hurry to hold an election and forbid political parties from meeting. Cambodia's Prime Minister Hun Sen reacted to a significant loss of support in the local elections of June 2017 by arresting the opposition leader on charges of treason and then banning his party altogether. Hun Sen's government, which ignored threats of sanctions by the country's principle western trade and investment partners, insisted it was acting 'within the rule of law'.

Tragically in Myanmar, an attack by a shadowy Rohingya insurgency at the end of August 2017 provoked a violent counter-move by the army, forcing more than 650,000 Rohingya to flee across the border into neighbouring Bangladesh in the space of four months. Currently two-thirds of the Rohingya population that lived in Myanmar before 2012 resides in Bangladesh, mostly in a sprawling, squalid collection of unhygienic temporary shelter that is now the largest refugee camp in the world.

The conflict trends were no better. Peace processes in the Philippines and Myanmar regressed. In the Philippines, failure to implement a 2014 peace agreement reached between the Moro Islamic Liberation Front and the government in Mindanao led to the splintering of the main armed group and the attraction of many young fighters to a brand of Islamic extremism popularised by the Islamic State in Syria and Iraq. For five months, a determined band of extremists led by a pair of brothers occupied the sizable town of Marawi, forcing its population of 200,000 to flee. More than 1,000 soldiers and civilians died before the Philippine army finally retook the city in November 2017.

The elected government of Aung San Suu Kyi in Myanmar pursued peace with more than twenty armed ethnic groups as a priority but, after a promising start, the peace process went into reverse and fighting resumed along the country's border with China. There are currently more than 150,000 displaced people in the Shan and Kachin States.

My focus on religious polarisation as a key driver of conflict in Southeast Asia was sadly prescient. Events in Rakhine State deepened a divide in Myanmar between the Buddhist majority and Muslim minority. The jailing of a Christian and Chinese governor in Jakarta on blasphemy charges, following mass protests by Islamic hard-line pressure groups, emboldened Islamic conservative forces with their exclusionary agenda. The result was to sow fear and discord in Indonesian society, and make it certain that politicians hoping to succeed in the 2019 elections would need to accommodate their demands.

Geopolitical trends pointed to an acceleration of China's dominance. Aided by the waning influence and effectiveness of United States foreign policy under President Donald Trump and driven by

Chinese President Xi Jinping's consolidation of power at the 19th Chinese Communist Party Congress held in October 2017, the country boldly pushed ahead with costly infrastructure development in Africa and across Asia under the umbrella of the ambitious Belt and Road initiative. Beijing demonstrated new confidence in its diplomatic posturing, indicating a firm intention, in the words of Chinese foreign minister, Wang Yi, 'to actively explore the Chinese way of helping find solutions to hot issues'. In late January 2018, the United States announced a new national security strategy that signalled a return to the containment policies of the Cold War; by targeting China, Washington increased the risks that Southeast Asia would become a battleground for great power rivalry.

It is important to know how Southeast Asia reflects and influences global politics, economics and power shifts, and I have aimed to give a good overview within these pages, as told from my personal experiences of places and people I have known and worked with for much of my life. Despite the setbacks and disappointments I have witnessed and recount here, I remain upbeat about the longer-term political prospects of Southeast Asia, primarily because of the resourcefulness and resilience of its people. I am grateful to hear from many readers that *Blood and Silk* has helped them understand the complexities of this fascinating part of the world, now more relevant than ever before to our daily lives.

Singapore, January 2018

INTRODUCTION

Behold a land perpetually wet, densely overgrown and always hot and humid. Then consider the impact of man, whose inimical habit is to sculpt and render landscapes both habitable and productive. The landscape is flat and cultivated, a patchwork of well-maintained earth bunds holding in the water-nourished rice, which feeds the people. Gently rising slopes hem the plains in a chaotic profusion of tangled green vegetation, giving way at the coast to endless stretches of soft, white-coral sand shaded by lines of windblown coconut trees, beyond which lies a calm turquoise sea glistening in the sunlight. Generic Southeast Asia: there are few parts of the world at once so benign and pleasing to the eye, yet so replete with a superabundance of life.

When I mention to people in Europe that I live in Southeast Asia they tend to respond by saying how privileged I am to enjoy a warm tropical climate, vibrant culture and exotic food. There is an enduring romanticism about Asia in the Western world. It grew from the awe with which early travellers, prisoners of coarse woven wool and strict religious injunctions, beheld the vivid coloured silks and promiscuous chaos of their first encounters. The impact has ranged from the influence of 'Oriental' religion and culture on the Enlightenment, to the stimulation of base instincts by the lush and lurid attractions of modern Bangkok. 'Everything is narrow in the West,' wrote the French historian Jules Michelet, 'Greece is small and I stifle; Judea is dry and I pant. Let me look a little towards lofty Asia, the profound East.'

Yet for me Southeast Asia is no romantic escape. I was thrown into the region first as a student and, later, as a professional. I learned over time of the Janus-faced aspect to modern Southeast Asia: one face projects astonishing social and material progress, the 'truly Asia' depicted in promotional material that is all five-star shopping and fine dining with a dash of local spice, attended by ever-polite smiling people speaking good English and wearing designer fashion. The other, facing inwards, is one of stern authoritarianism with no concern for the suffering of those left behind in the chaotic scramble to get rich and be glorious. It's hard to underestimate the value of the happy smiling mask, for all the income it earns, the security it provides: millions of tourists flock to Thailand despite the military government's bridling of dissent and postponement of elections. Singapore's insistence on strict rules limiting free speech, and prosecuting mosquito bloggers, hasn't stopped the world's major banks from occupying high-priced office space in the central business district, nor from making Changi Airport one of the busiest in the world, handling as many as 200,000 passengers in a day. Not even the risk of a return to military rule in Myanmar or of continuous violent warfare in parts of the country deters European tourists from sipping cocktails on luxury river cruises up the Irrawaddy River.

Behind the smiling mask of tropical abundance there lurks the reality of perennial threats to stability and survival, fuelled by rising levels of social and economic inequality and a chronic absence of the institutional safeguards and legal certainty we take (or at least used to take) for granted in the West. The Indonesian farmer who falls prey to creditors and climate change; the Cambodian teenager enslaved on a Thai fishing boat; the Muslim Rohingya migrant from Myanmar starving and beaten, then left for dead in a ditch by human traffickers along the Thai–Myanmar border. The countless women and girls condemned to prostitution; the innocent families trapped between insurgents and soldiers in conflict zones, their lives threatened and disrupted. This book seeks to dispel myopic myths of tropical Arcady, and for that matter the simplistic media narrative of heroic popular struggle against nasty authoritarian regimes. In the chapters that follow I aim to distil my own understanding of state and society based on decades of professional and personal engagement in the region. The arguments, although often captious, are heartfelt. Having lived and worked in four of Southeast Asia's primary cities and criss-crossed all ten of the countries as a traveller and writer as well as working professional, I hope to offer readers a more refined yet accessible explanation of what makes one of the world's most colourful regions tick.

This book is a journey through Southeast Asia, not in the conventional sense as a casual traveller might see the region. Instead it is a journey through a long experience of observation: my own experience over four decades as student, journalist, writer, and then as a mediator striving to end armed conflict. It's a journey in search of explanation. It takes us through the historical origins of state and society, the formative influences on modern nationhood and in turn how this has affected contemporary political trends and generated chronically high levels of popular struggle and violent conflict.

Southeast Asia lies at the heart of Asia, which for the first time in modern history now accounts for more private wealth and investment than Europe. The region's ten countries, covering almost two million square miles with a combined population of 650 million people, encompass cultures and peoples of considerable variety, complexity and historical significance. At one point in the medieval era, most of the civilised world derived enormous wealth from Southeast Asia's natural abundance. Chinese traders imported textiles and rice; Arabs, Indians and Europeans battled trade winds and each other over food-preserving spices. In turn, Southeast Asia was profoundly influenced by these trading influxes, which helped mould kingdoms and cultures that presented an open face to the world at a time when little was known of either the Americas or Africa. The Portuguese first conquered Malacca on the Malay Peninsula in 1511, three years before the Spanish established a settlement in Havana, Cuba.

Southeast Asia was therefore a region fated to be fought over and trampled on by major powers that forged enduring imperial edifices in the languid tropical climes of Java, Malaya and Indochina.

Five hundred years later, Southeast Asia remains a region of considerable strategic importance contested by outside powers. China vies with the United States for strategic primacy in the region, making it the main battlefront of a new global struggle for power. Corporate giants from China, Europe, the United States, Japan and Korea vie for consumer spending and big-ticket infrastructure deals, contesting its sizeable market. Southeast Asia's larger cities, Bangkok, Jakarta, Kuala Lumpur and Singapore, have become important beachheads for luxury brands and aspiring designer labels; Bangkok has twenty square kilometres of shopping mall space. Meanwhile, the meeting rooms of luxury hotels are filled with officials pressing schemes for closer cooperation, whether it's a free trade deal that opens up markets, or a defence cooperation agreement that binds nations to outside powers as they eye a part of the world that has always been a strategic highway connecting East and West. For much of its history Southeast Asia has endured ingression, and still does.

With three of its countries bordering China, Southeast Asia is the closest, most exposed region to what is now the world's largest economy. This is both a blessing and curse. China for centuries was more or less a benign neighbour, a source of trade, technology and legitimacy for Southeast Asian rulers who paid largely symbolic forms of tribute to the great neighbour to the north. Over the long centuries of European domination in Southeast Asia, China grew weaker and more insulated, and remained so until the last half of the twentieth century. Since then, China has steadily asserted its influence, at first by fomenting communist uprising, then offering financial inducements, and in recent years by using hard power projection. As the Western powers struggle to retain their global role and influence, Southeast Asia has become the fulcrum of a concerted effort to contest and contain Chinese power. In this book I argue that for all the perceived primacy of Western institutional and influence and military power, the dynamics of power and conflict in Southeast Asia makes it much harder for the West to sustain effective influence – and much easier for China to gain sway in the long run.

In the beginning, long before the Europeans came in the 1500s, waves of migrants, most of them from the north, established princely states in the lush valleys and jewel-like islands of the region. They planted rice and traded with wilder people of the forest margins.

They borrowed elements of the Hindu and Buddhist faith to shape systems of government and administration that bound people to kings and princes using powerful beliefs in cosmic centrality. Theirs was a network of principalities loosely connected by trade and bound by marriage, paying token tribute to distant kingdoms and enjoying a liberal form of autonomy before the era of centralised bureaucracies introduced by colonial rule. Pre-modern settlement was concentrated in valleys dotted with hamlets and fortified towns living off well-irrigated rice fields and fruit gardens. The surrounding hills were densely forested, the preserve of wild animals and malevolent spirits. When low cloud obscures the forested hills fringing these valleys, one can imagine how once man feared and venerated such intangible forms. For all beliefs are somewhat rooted in what we cannot see.

Huge swathes of Southeast Asia look pretty much the same today, although deforestation has taken its toll. The primary centres of power and authority, the cities where most people live, have changed beyond imagination. As they opened up to foreign trade and influence, they found themselves overrun by expanding European powers. By the end of the nineteenth century, colonial cities such as Rangoon, Batavia (as present-day Jakarta was known) and Hanoi, with their columned stone edifices and streetcars, rivalled their European peers in style and grandeur. When the colonial era ended in 1945, there were high hopes for the newly independent states that emerged from the Pacific War. Burma, Indonesia, Malaya and the Philippines were all granted independence as fledgling democracies. Not one stayed free and democratic for long.

By the mid-1950s the political landscape of Southeast Asia had become an ideological battleground. The forces of modernity and social awakening, allied with socialism and communism, were drawn to the ideology of redistribution and notional equality. They collided with traditional elites who had prospered under colonial rule and were fearful of losing power under the new democratic disposition. Faced with the paradox of undoing what they had wrought, the former colonial powers sided with the traditional elites, because at this point what they most feared was the spread of communism. This supported the advance of military-led regimes armed and bankrolled

by the West, which snuffed out the brief flickering light of freedom
in Southeast Asia. Democracy ended in Burma after a military
coup in 1962; with the quelling of a communist-backed coup in
Indonesia in 1965; and after the army intervened in Cambodia
in 1970. Waves of left-wing protest in Thailand in the mid-1970s
were ruthlessly suppressed by the military. Strong leaders like
Ferdinand Marcos in the Philippines and Mahathir Mohamad
in Malaysia used a mix of populist demagoguery and strong-arm
tactics to bypass the democratic institutions they inherited. By the
mid-1980s, authoritarian rule was the norm in Southeast Asia.

The world sat back as authoritarian styles of government evolved
and grew entrenched. It was easy to turn a blind eye because these
regimes tended to be benign in that they made efforts to feed and
clothe their people rather than jail or kill them – although they
did that too. Even instances of exceptional brutality were tolerated
because they kept the tide of communism at bay. The US and its
allies shut their eyes to the repression and nepotism of South Vietnamese President Ngo Dinh Diem in the mid-1950s because he was
fanatically anti-communist. As then US President Lyndon Johnson
observed: 'He's the only boy we got out there.' Not a single Western
power was ready to sanction Indonesia for killing around half a million people in the mid-1960s on the suspicion they were communist
sympathisers. This remains the case: there wasn't a murmur of indignation when in 2016 a panel of judges, convened by an Indonesian
people's tribunal in The Hague to investigate the events of 1965,
concluded that the United States, United Kingdom and Australia
should be held accountable for what they described as 'genocide'.

The Cold War in Southeast Asia heralded a dark period of repression and impunity, which the famous images of the period
convey well: a Vietcong suspect shot in the head on a roadside, a
self-immolating Buddhist monk in Saigon, and the senseless carpet
bombing of Cambodia. Ironically, it was a communist victory in
Vietnam, captured by an iconic photograph of the chaotic departure of Americans from the roof of their embassy in Saigon in
1975, which paved the way for the region's economic boom. Fear in
downtown Bangkok of an imminent communist invasion prompted scared Thais to sell land at rock-bottom prices to the city's Sikh

community, which led to an explosion of condominium and retail development.

The end of the wars in Indochina in the mid-1970s allowed pent-up economic forces to establish strong market-based outposts of trade and manufacturing that replicated some of the same advantages that had attracted the imperial powers a century or so earlier – a disciplined and plentiful workforce willing to work for less and an abundance of natural resources, as well as access to strategic seaports. From the mid-1980s Southeast Asia's incipient tiger economies grew so fast that at one point a decade later there was serious thinking in economist circles about a new model for global development. It was easy to be lulled into believing this was the new face of global growth; the steel-and-glass towers that sprouted in cities like Bangkok, Jakarta, Kuala Lumpur, Manila and Singapore projected prodigious wealth and industry. Leaders like Prime Minister Lee Kuan Yew of Singapore and Prime Minister Mahathir Mohamad of Malaysia thumbed their noses at the West and spoke about Asian values supplanting Western-style democracy. Investment bankers from Western financial centres all cheered and raked in their commission, making billions on emerging stock markets. It all seemed so permanent, until it came crashing down.

The financial crisis sparked by profligate and imprudent lending practices in 1997 revealed serious cracks in the edifice. The most dangerous shortcoming was in the realm of governance. Fast-growing as these economies were, they lacked basic elements of oversight; neither were they anchored very much to their own societies. Rapid economic growth in a semi-democratic or autocratic setting was seldom transparent or subject to checks and balances. The trickle-down was minimal and income inequalities ballooned. So when the markets crashed, huge amounts of money disappeared and people found themselves without jobs and safety nets. The result was social upheaval and protest, revealing an underdeveloped modern political superstructure and acutely divided societies.

Fifteen years on, democracy has made modest advances and government in the worst-affected countries tends to be a little more open and transparent as a result. The economies have on the whole recovered, and GDP growth rates were averaging 5 per cent by the end of the first decade of the twenty-first century. Once again South-east Asia had become a region of opportunity, with a $2.4 trillion economy making it currently the fifth-largest economy in the world after the United States, China, Japan and India. At a wine bar along Bangkok's Sukhumwit Road in 2015 the standing special offer of free-flowing wine and all you can eat for $15 drew a heaving crowd of European twenty-somethings. In 2015, the fastest-growing expatriate community in Singapore was from Italy, where 40 per cent of young people are unemployed. The dispirited and unemployed youth of Europe come to Southeast Asia in search of opportunity. A young Argentinian looking for work in Singapore lamented that South America, for all its stability and promise, was 'too far away from anywhere' while characterising Singapore as the centre of the world.

Yet for all the glamour, glitz and all-night clubbing, there is a dark underside. Argentina may be at the bottom end of the Southern Hemisphere, but it has put military rule and repression behind it. Across most of Southeast Asia, political progress and stability falls well short of what was anticipated in the late 1990s. The military plays either an overt or covert role in politics in three of the principal countries of the region; there have been two military coups in Thailand this side of the millennium. A draconian security law is back in force in Malaysia; Cambodia is threatened by a vicious vortex of political violence. And in the Philippines a popular strong-man president has turned a blind eye to the extra-judicial killing of thousands of suspected criminals since he was elected in May 2016. He said he 'didn't give a shit' when the United Nations registered concern.

Contemporary Southeast Asia is plagued by a state of demi-democracy. For the past four decades there has been something of a rolling transition. It started at the back end of the so-called third wave of democratisation in the mid-1970s and ultimately led to the People Power revolt in the Philippines a decade later. For different reasons and in different ways, this wave of political liberalisation stalled and then got started again after the Asian Financial Crisis in 1997. It has yet to deliver effective change. Hard-won freedom of expression has been diluted and often reversed by pernicious legal and security challenges. Whether it is new security and sedition laws in Malaysia, military coups in Thailand, or the rise of populists with scant regard for the rule of law or the autonomy of the judiciary, there would seem to be a perpetual drag on democratic progress. Making matters worse for the majority of people is the fact that the principal beneficiaries of growth and development are a thin sliver of society. The term oligarchy is nowadays used to describe the elite, which in turn uses endemic corruption and a monopoly on power to protect its privileged position. As Surin Pitsuwan, the late Thai foreign minister who served as Secretary General of the Association of Southeast Asian Nations once put it to me: as an advocate for freedom and equality, 'you can never afford to let your foot off the gas'.

As a result, little has been done to address the fundamental problems plaguing Southeast Asian societies. Profound inequalities of wealth and welfare have fuelled unending unrest and conflict within the ten countries, either involving non-state armed actors fighting for autonomy and local identity, or mass protest movements as seen in Thailand, Malaysia and Cambodia. Even more troubling, these inequalities provide tinder for the flames of religious extremism and conflict. Forty per cent of the population of the region professes the Islamic faith, which has been more successful in its spread throughout the region than Christianity. For almost a millennium, Muslims have lived peacefully alongside Hindus, Buddhists, Christians and animists, making Southeast Asia one of the most religiously diverse regions in the world. In recent times this equilibrium has been upset by the influence of conservative ideas on Islamic orthodoxy imported from the Middle East through other parts of South Asia. These narrow ideas, feeding off inequality and despair, have inculcated values of prejudice and hatred, which even if they influence a small minority of people, have been exploited and magnified for political ends. Just as Muslim Africa, the pastoral areas in particular, has seen ancient patterns of inter-religious coexistence disrupted and exposed to violent conflict, so there is a trend towards intolerance that is displacing traditional patterns of peaceful coexistence in Southeast Asia.

The stability of Southeast Asia therefore remains questionable, its politics unpredictable, its societies in flux. Understanding the reasons why Southeast Asian politics is so volatile and unprogressive is important for a global economy that is increasingly Asia-centred and that relies on trade that passes through Southeast Asia, as well as investment or manufacturing that serves its burgeoning consumer-driven economies.

This book examines the dynamics of power and the bewildering array of conflicts in Southeast Asia and offers a rather personal guide to understanding what makes this fascinating and strategically important part of the world tick. In addition to indulging my own desire to reflect on a lifetime of experience, my hope is that the larger powers who have spent centuries benefiting in one way or another from Southeast Asia's wealth of resources, whether as protectors, oppressors or benign overlords, derive some insight from what follows. Throughout the book I will return again and again to violent waypoints in the region's modern history that have had a magnified impact on society and cast a shadow over political progress: the 1965 communist killings in Indonesia, the Martial Law period of the early 1970s in the Philippines, the violent crackdown on student protesters in Thailand during the same period. And of course the genocide perpetrated by the Khmer Rouge in Cambodia after 1975. The scars of injustice and impunity persist and continue to influence modern trends of political change and stasis. The other recurrent theme is the threat to diversity and pluralism. Southeast Asian society is characterised by a dynamic diversity that has underpinned its stability for centuries. People of different races and religions mingling and coexisting in harmony are the hallmark of a society that has on the whole avoided the sectarian schisms of Europe and the Middle East. Modernisation and consequent inequalities have put pressure on this easy-going pattern of coexistence and for the first time in history there are strong centrifugal forces driving a wedge between different religious and racial communities with alarming effects on stability.

As Western governments struggle to retain influence in Asia, it is important they understand the contours of power and the stress points in society. Similarly, the flexing of China's new 'big country' muscles could do a lot of damage if its policymakers remain blinkered by archaic perceptions enshrined in the imperial archives. The frame for much of my analysis is the interplay of power, privilege and violent conflict. This stems from my experiences over four decades in Southeast Asia first as a journalist and later as a mediator. I have never run a business, built a refugee camp or taught at a school or university in the region. I plunged instead into the colourful labyrinth of politics and had a ringside seat, witnessing the changing fortunes of the powerful as well as the often-violent impact this had on the rest of society.

The book has long been urged, cajoled and encouraged by friends and colleagues. It has gestated for a very long time, and was written with trepidation: one of the first things I learnt about the part of Asia I have called home for the past thirty years is to be wary of explanations. To get too comfortable with explaining a certain trend or phenomena is to forget the exception lurking around the corner, to mistake change for continuity, and to assume that something discovered is a new phenomenon. Being an outsider opens up the possibility of being misleading, or misled. As a foreign devil and long-time barefoot reporter in these lands, I am conscious of the need to temper shrewd analysis with a healthy dose of scepticism. Therefore, to begin, it is apt to recall the late Richard Hughes, an Australian paragon of foreign devils and barefoot reporters. He once wrote as an introduction to one of his esteemed columns in the *Far Eastern Economic Review*: 'gallantry and gullibility are the contrasted themes of this week's intrusion'.

PART 1

POWER

CHAPTER ONE

JOURNEY INTO THE HEART
OF SOUTHEAST ASIA

'There it is before you – smiling, frowning, inviting, grand, mean, insipid, or savage, and always mute with an air of whispering, "Come and find out."'

Joseph Conrad, *Heart of Darkness*

Gullible and intrusive; that's just how I felt arriving for the first time in Southeast Asia in 1979. Disembarking from a Thai International Airways DC-10 at Bangkok's Don Muang Airport, a pungent organic odour and wet heat assailed me as I emerged at the door of the plane; it was like being slapped with a wet towel in a hot kitchen. The sensory trauma catapulted me out of the West and into the East. Driving from the airport into the city in the back of a sturdy Toyota Corolla, I soon left the rice fields and ornate temples, their cut-glass decoration glinting in the moonlight, and entered a corridor of grimy concrete shopfronts laced with sagging cables. The landscape looked disappointingly post-industrial, a bit like the wrong end of Los Angeles. I spent my first night at the Malaysia Hotel off Rama IV Road, a famous hostelry on the backpacker trail. The mattresses sagged and the sheets were stained. I strolled over to a nearby bar – the Blue Fox, I think it was called – and watched *The Deer Hunter* being played from a video recorder. Later, I lay awake listening to the roar of an exhausted air conditioner rattling in the window.

The Southeast Asia I saw for the first time that year was gripped by the trauma of the Cold War. The humiliating American military

retreat from Vietnam in 1975 spawned widespread fears of Vietnamese tanks trundling down Sukhumwit Road in central Bangkok
within forty-eight hours of reaching the Thai border. Cambodia was
convulsed in a murderous frenzy at the hands of the Khmer Rouge,
a diabolical regime that set out to exterminate intellectuals, emptied
the cities and put the remaining people to work in the rice fields.
Most other countries in the neighbourhood were ruled by repressive
military regimes, either installed or supported by the West to keep
communism at bay. These regimes, in turn, struggled to suppress
communist-led and Chinese-backed insurgencies on their dense
jungle margins. Yet despite all the fears of war and communist takeover, there was hope for a new era of prosperity and stability.

In the era before mass-market tourism and budget airlines, few
foreigners ventured very far beyond the big cities and beach resorts.
I wasn't a tourist – I was a second-year undergraduate studying
Southeast Asian languages and history at the University of London.
That summer I was keen to see as much as I could of a region I had
elected to study but never visited. So, soon after arriving in Thai-
land, I headed south to Indonesia. I flew into Medan at the tip of
North Sumatra. From there I endured a bone-shaking forty-eight-
hour journey across Sumatra to visit my university classmate Dewi
Fortuna Anwar in her ancestral village outside the district town of
Bukittinggi. The driver had never met a Westerner and insisted that
I occupy the front seat next to him in the rickety Mercedes coach.
Here in the front row, looking out of the flat expanse of fly-smudged
windscreen, I watched in horror as he steered the vehicle to the edge
of steep precipices, winding us up and down terrible roads. I travelled through a landscape dominated by violent hues of green lashed
fluorescent by rain punctuated by gashes of red laterite soil, like
open wounds in the earth. It was during this terrifying journey that
I developed a liking for the sweet clove cigarettes known as Kretek.
It was also during my week-long stay in West Sumatra that I first
became aware of the broad and seemingly unending tangle of family
ties that provides the essential matting of Southeast Asian societies.

A few weeks later, back in Thailand several thousand kilometres
to the north, I walked for miles with a local guide across hot laterite
roads and through dense jungle to the west of the little town of

Mae Sariang. After some hours, we reached a village inhabited by a hill-tribe people known as the Karen. An old man with a kind, wrinkled face smoking a pipe stared down at us from a split-bamboo terrace outside his thatched hut and called out: 'What took you so long?' I later learned that even though we were the first Europeans this particular village had ever seen, an old Karen myth had it that the book of knowledge would be brought by white-faced people, because when it had been distributed to everyone at the dawn of human existence by the creator, the Karen were too lazy to go and fetch a copy. I have a photograph of the man, but forget his name. He got it the wrong way around, of course. I was the one embarking on a journey that would become a lifetime of education.

My first impressions of Southeast Asia were infused with vivid tropical light and pungency framing glimpses of complex societies awkwardly embracing the modern world, yet bound by ancient traditions and conventions. Singapore in 1979 had been independent for less than twenty years. Although neat and tidy compared with Indonesia or Thailand, many streets were lined with two-storey shop-houses from which emanated smells of cinnamon and mace. The old colonial centre around the parade ground known as 'the Padang' was trimmed and in immaculate order, overlooked by the whitewashed stucco walls of the Cricket Club – still there today. In contrast, Bangkok was a mildewed-concrete jungle punctuated at random by tropical garden compounds protecting delicate wooden houses where bureaucrats with aristocratic titles fed leftover rice to their carp in the morning and later served up the crumbs of patronage to loyal retainers.

After some weeks of travel, I stayed with fellow students from London in the northern Thai capital of Chiang Mai, a city of such bucolic grace that I wondered, on warm and misty mornings or when the setting sun at the edge of twilight turned everything carnation pink, if it might be a model for paradise. The people of Chiang Mai were exquisitely mannered and polite, and with almost a hundred Buddhist temples within the crumbling city walls, riding around the city brought to mind an early seventeenth-century en-graving of the old Siamese capital of Ayudhya by some French Jesuit explorer. The city's accessible charm and bustle helped me begin to

One of many Buddhist temples within the city walls of Chang Mai.

understand the basic etymology of Southeast Asian society.

For all of Chiang Mai's charms, I was drawn to Indonesia, enchanted by the ideals of nationhood riotously played out with a blend of triumph and tragedy, and to the accompaniment of the discordant clashing of brass gongs and cymbals, where nothing was as it appeared. Back in London after completing my undergraduate studies, I applied to continue with doctoral research involving fieldwork in Indonesia. Unravelling the mysteries of Indonesia played to my own conflicted and complex identity as a Levantine polyglot transplanted to the West. I wrote my undergraduate history thesis on Sukarno, whose biographical details I devoured, recalling that my Greek auntie Zoe had once met him and received a signed portrait of the man when she worked as a secretary at the Indonesian legation in Rome in the early 1960s. There was a strangely subliminal impulse behind my attraction to Indonesia.

But it was not to be – at least, not yet. The authoritarian Suharto regime all but banned foreign research students, after attempts by an earlier generation of academics, notably the late Ben Anderson of Cornell University, to uncover the grisly details of Suharto's rise to power in the aftermath of a so-called communist-led putsch in 1965, following which around half a million suspected Communist Party members and sympathisers were murdered in a frenzy of state-backed killing. Instead, I joined the legion of social science post-grads who beat a path to the doors of the National Research Council in the more open, but no more democratic Thailand. The application cost fifty dollars, and my nominal proposal to study ethnicity in Chiang Mai landed me back in the magical city nestled like a cluster of jewels in the hills of northern Thailand in early 1982.

In the course of my research I encountered the uniquely Southeast Asian approach to confrontation and conflict: conflict is something to be avoided. In the Thai context, 'face' is everything; it is a manifestation of basic human dignity. In the West we talk of a person's soul giving form to the essence of being; across Asia, people have a more physical manifestation of self. To lose face is to suffer such an assault on dignity and self-esteem that a sudden, violent response is not only warranted, but expected. And so Thai society, in common with other Southeast Asian cultures, has developed a sophisticated array of conflict-avoidance mechanisms. These range from a pathological inability to say anything direct, in order to avoid giving offence, to a range of gestures and actions that outsiders interpret as a well-developed culture of manners, but which in fact are part of the suit of armour protecting against indignity. I learned to my cost that exposing reality in ways that offended or made others lose face prompted an irrationally over-the-top response. One day in the course of giving a public lecture at Chiang Mai University, I described a well-known scam involving the selling of Thai identity cards to illegal Burmese immigrants. This revelation so offended the local military commander that friends told me my life was in danger. To make amends, I visited a Buddhist temple to make a generous contribution to the abbot. Much as the Catholic Church sold indulgences to save souls, so too can face can be restored through a material exchange. It was a lesson that served me well in the coming years.

The mid-1980s were an inflection point in the politics of Southeast Asia. It all began in the Philippines, where the ageing dictator

Ferdinand Marcos held tight to the reins of power. But when the bumptious autocrat, who famously wore elevated shoes, ordered the public assassination of opposition leader Benigno Aquino in 1983, he lit the fuse of popular discontent. I covered the ensuing People Power movement from a cramped studio at the BBC World Service in London's Bush House, where, having joined the BBC after graduating, I was a trainee producer for the news and current-affairs programme unimaginatively named *24 Hours*. Most of the news broke out of the Philippines overnight, when I was on duty to produce what we called the 'dawns', or the morning edition.

These were the earliest days of perpetual cable coverage. The events unfolding in Manila were CNN's first global story. And there I was: huddled in a dark studio, in the bowels of Bush House in the middle of the night, seven thousand miles away from all the action. I could not have been more excited. I trawled for contacts to set up live interviews and stole sound-bites from the CNN feed. People Power dominated the fifteen-minute morning shows, which followed a bulletin of world news. At one point I found US Congressman Steve Solarz at home, and asked him down a scratchy phone line if I could patch him through to the studio. 'Fine,' he said, 'but I'm on the can.' Everyone hoped that People Power in Manila would act as a catalyst for liberal political awakenings in Jakarta, Rangoon and elsewhere. Events in Manila were amplified in the media and breathlessly projected as the end of history for Asia. It was a false dawn.

My real exposure to the realities of Southeast Asia politics began when the BBC appointed me their correspondent in Indonesia. I arrived in Jakarta in May 1987 on another long flight from London, received another wet slap in the face and was assaulted by an even more pungent odour. I carried with me a journalist visa issued at the Indonesian embassy in London, a high-end Sony cassette recorder, and an old pair of BBC cans, as we called headphones in those days. My first dispatch to London was a story about the launch of Indonesia's communications satellite.

And so, turning my back on the go-go eighties, all buttery Chardonnay and cocktails in Chiswick and Chelsea, I embarked on a career as foreign correspondent, a life in Southeast Asia. What did I know?

Not much. A few months learning some basic Indonesian plus what I could glean from the SOAS library reading room making notes from renowned Cornell University scholars of Southeast Asian politics and history Ben Anderson and Ruth McVey; didactic diversions into bound musty volumes of the *Journal of the Royal Asiatic Society* to read obscure articles about lost cultures; multiple viewings of *The Year of Living Dangerously*, and the odd plate of *satay* or *gado-gado* at the seedy Equatorial restaurant in Soho. This precarious patina of knowledge and experience barely equipped me to deal with the full-frontal assault of urban drama and sensuality spliced with unfathomable intrigue and bureaucratic obfuscation that was Jakarta in 1987.

'Authoritarian' and 'repressive' sound like technical terms; dry, remote and distant, they convey neither the physical pain nor mental suffering that the victims of autocratic governments suffer. Slamet Bratanata was my first real contact in Indonesia. I was told he was a dissident and that I must see him. I assumed that finding him would be hard, imagining some kind of underground movement, its leadership in hiding. So when I pulled up in front of a rambling Dutch villa on a leafy street in upscale Menteng by Saint Teresa's church, I was at first a little disappointed. The former Minister of Mines, who was dismissed for trying to introduce transparency and accountability into the contracts-tender process, smiled broadly as he greeted me on his veranda. He served tea in delicate Delft porcelain and spoke English softly but with a guttural Dutch accent. Slamet seemed less threatening than he was made out to be by Ministry of Information officials who had warned me not to speak to him.

Yet Slamet was no shrinking violet. Throughout the years I knew him, Slamet spoke plainly and expansively about the iniquity of President Suharto's authoritarian regime and his country's tragic history. As spokesman of an opposition group known as 'The Petition of 50', he wrote editorials and articles critical of the government. In conversation, Slamet brought alive the tableau of conflict that litters Indonesian history, marking time with successive bouts of killing. He introduced me to General Abdul Haris Nasution, the man who devised the Indonesian army's guerrilla strategy during the brief war of independence from the Dutch, who escaped with his life by climbing over his garden wall when rebel elements of the palace guard came looking for him on that fateful evening of 30 September 1965. Both men gave expression to the voiceless intellectuals who suffered the indignity of having to suppress the memories of these events and pretend they were the exaggerated delusions of foreign interlopers and fanatics. I was no fanatic, but it became obvious I was intruding. The Ministry of Information summoned me to explain following an article I had written that apparently showed my communist tendencies. Next question: 'Do you work for the CIA?'

I spent these early years revising the history I had been taught back in London, and grappling with the muted fear and apprehension of my friends and contacts. Much – too much – was not as it seemed. Slamet Bratanata could serve me tea in Dutch porcelain in a parlour adorned with silver and crystal, yet he could not open a bank account or leave the country. Nasution may have helped in a significant way to win freedom for his country, but he was exiled to a dilapidated house on a tree-lined street where he remained unrecognised, and uninvited to any official occasions. Ostracised, like some forlorn retired Field Marshal from a Gabriel García Márquez story, Nasution felt impotent and the army he built to win independence was now divided. 'The army is arrayed as on a chessboard,' the old general told me in his deep gravelly voice one hot afternoon in December 1990. 'They are no longer striving for unity, but playing one another off.' Here I learnt something else about Southeast Asian interaction. It isn't just a question of avoidance of conflict to save face, as I had discovered in Thailand. There is also suppression of conflict through fear and intimidation.

Over the next five years, I travelled the length and breadth of Indonesia, from mosquito-infested Merauke in Papua to the deep-water harbour of Sabang in Aceh. Everywhere I found evidence of the remarkable reach of the Suharto regime's development programmes; there were for example small clinics dispensing basic drugs and birth control in almost every village. Suharto, a portly man with silver hair and pudgy hands, was often seen interacting with peasant farmers wearing a simple straw hat and a broad smile; he made sure that financial aid for the farmers came from foundations established in his name. At the same time, I heard bitter complaints of how constrained and suffocated people felt because they could not express themselves. The military was omnipresent. Under what was termed the army's 'dual function', serving officers staffed all government departments, were members of parliament and provided stiff backbone to administration down to the village level. A good district officer – many of whom fit the profile of a relatively honest military man with fastidious parade-ground discipline – could become popular because he served the people. His office compound was swept and pruned; uniforms were starched and pressed, a flag-raising ceremony held every morning. The archetype was the lazy colonel who had slipped up somewhere in his career, and was assigned a position in some flyblown backwater where he tyrannised the people. Long before Susilo Bambang Yudhoyono became the first Indonesian president to be directly elected in 2004, I visited his office at Indonesian Armed Forces HQ in Cilangkap on the outskirts of Jakarta. Susilo was attached to the army information department; his office bare as his rotund face was smooth. He spent much of the time drawing circles with different-coloured marker pens on a whiteboard, describing what he called the mindset of the Indonesian people.

The army was everywhere, yes, but to be honest I seldom saw any military action. I made several visits to Aceh on the northern tip of Sumatra in search of the war, but saw only sullen faces lurking in coffee shops along empty streets. The war was fought in the shadows, in scattered skirmishes and in the souls of men. An Acehnese rebel group had been fighting for independence from Indonesia since 1976 and the army was accused of killing tens of thousands of innocent Acehnese, some by rolling tanks over their bodies according to a black book of alleged atrocities compiled by the Free Aceh Movement. Meanwhile the Acehnese rebel leadership lived in exile in Sweden, where they held menial civic jobs as postmen or city clerks and drew social security. The rebels had minimal firepower and held no territory but they were winning because the military abused the people it should have been protecting.

I saw that most clearly in East Timor. Indonesia invaded the neglected former Portuguese colony in 1975 and could have spent the next few decades developing its potential as a coffee-growing tourist attraction. Instead, the army decided to turn the small territory wedged between other remote and underdeveloped islands in the country's eastern region into a prison camp and source of income from trade and coffee exports. In 1989 I visited the capital Dili on the occasion of Pope John Paul II's visit. Just as the Polish pontiff had completed a turn of a huge field on the outskirts of the city in his white popemobile, the tearful, emotional crowd of thousands unfurled a banner demanding independence. Later, at the nearby home of then-Lieutenant Colonel Prabowo Subianto, who was to become commander of Indonesia's feared special forces and later to run as president in 2014, I met emaciated Timorese prisoners quaking with fear. Prabowo asked them to serve me tea and boasted how well they were treated. Yet tea spilled all over the table as they trembled uncontrollably. I'll never forget their blinking, red-rimmed eyes signalling their terror to me in silent semaphore.

I spent five years reporting in Indonesia, four of them as Jakarta bureau chief for the *Far Eastern Economic Review* (*FEER*), a weekly news magazine with a venerable status and reputation as a source of news on Asia, headquartered in Hong Kong. I had read the magazine as a student and jumped at the opportunity to join its ranks of journalists, many of whom were well known in the region. Working for the magazine allowed me to delve deeper and say more about the stories I was covering, which eventually prompted the government to make aggressive moves to terminate my journalist visa and expel me from the country. I gathered that it wasn't anything specific that I had reported; it was more that I had been there too long and perhaps knew too much. I appealed to the foreign ministry and the powerful defence minister, General Benny Murdani, whom I had gotten to know quite well. One day I was at a diplomatic cocktail party, which in those days served as the functional equivalent of social media today: the only way to find out what was going on was to cruise the buffet lines at embassy functions. Juggling a plate of crudités and a glass of wine, I ran into both Murdani and Foreign Minister Ali Alatas. 'How can they expel me?' I complained. 'Isn't this "Visit Indonesia" year?' Happily, they saw the logic and helped stave off the expulsion order, but in return I promised to move on.

*

My next posting was in Malaysia, superficially a more urbane, tranquil setting of incipient modernity sprouting from the trimmed lawns and black-and-white bungalows of the British colonial era. My first impressions of Kuala Lumpur were framed by visits to the Selangor Club and the racecourse that is now the site of the futuristic Petronas Twin Towers. The British bequeathed all the trappings of modern justice and political participation before they departed Malaya on 30 August 1957: high courts, bewigged judges on benches, a Westminster-style parliament complete with honourable speaker and mace. Beneath twirling, dust-caked fans at the Selangor Club's long bar, lugubrious Dravidian high court judges, called to the bar at Lincoln's Inn, downed whisky sodas and sparred with one another in Oxonian accents while watching test cricket. This clubbable idyll masked a deeper malaise; for the British also bequeathed the seeds of perpetual conflict by establishing an unequal society plagued with institutionalised racism.

Malaysia is a confounding confection of races – Malays, Chinese and Indians. The Malays, who constituted about half the population, were granted political supremacy before the British left in 1957, which put the 38 per cent of the country who were Chinese and the 11 per cent who were Indian at a distinct disadvantage. The basic dynamic was that of mainly rural Malay majority fears of being overrun by the better-educated urban-based Chinese minority. To ensure their dominance, the Malays engineered a crude system of patronage to ensure that the lion's share of the economy was in their hands, as well as supreme political power. 'Before there was one country,' the Malaysian novelist of Tamil origin K. S. Maniam wrote in his evocative novel *In a Far Country*. 'Now there were many countries inside that one country.'

Of all the iniquities of the colonial legacy in Southeast Asia, none was more corrosive than the racial division of labour pioneered by the British and emulated by the Dutch in Indonesia. The concept was fiendishly efficient: how to manage the costs of labour yet prevent empowerment of the native populace. The answer: import a labour force from afar, and control the degree of mobility in society by determining professional boundaries and levels of status in racial terms. A British colonial officer posted to Burma named John

Sydenham Furnivall captured the whole idea in his seminal work, *Colonial Policy and Practice*, published in 1948. I read Furnivall as a graduate student in Chiang Mai. His concept of a 'Plural Society' in which people 'mix but do not combine', hold on to their own religions and languages and meet only in the marketplace, helped explain the apparent passivity of native economies, controlled through mechanisms of divide and rule.

Unfortunately, these same mechanisms were passed on to the newly independent states of Malaya and Burma; ideals of nationhood and independence may have enshrined notions of one people, but in reality laws and conventions bequeathed by the British sustained and reinforced racial boundaries. This tragic legacy of strict delineation lies at the heart of the tragedy that has unfolded in Myanmar's Rakhine State since 2012: The Buddhist Rakhine insist that the Rohingya belong in Bangladesh, citing British colonial records that purportedly show they were imported as labour from what was then East Bengal. Above all, these divisions in society were politically convenient; majority Malays in Malaysia and Burmans in Burma used them to justify a pre-eminent role in their plural societies in which other races and linguistic groups, such as Chinese and Indians, and myriad highland minorities such as Shan and Karen in Burma, nonetheless made up significant proportions of the population. This set the stage for chronic social incoherence and tension – and violent conflict.

By the time I reached Malaysia, almost half a century after independence, the Malays continued to fear and resent the Chinese. A veteran journalist of Indian descent told me he once heard Tunku Abdul Rahman, the country's first prime minister, say of the Chinese: 'If they all piss at the same time, we would be drowned.' This fear in turn propelled Malay society towards interpretations of Islam that emphasised exclusive conservative mores to protect racial and religious boundaries. The law in Malaysia forbids Malays to convert to other religions, and violation of religious conventions such as eating during the fasting period of Ramadan incurs heavy fines. Muslim religious observance is strictly enforced and the Religious Affairs Department patrols public places to catch and punish offenders holding hands out of wedlock. It is a striking example of how pious religious observance has been deployed as a boundary marker in more complex social and economic settings. As I found elsewhere in the region, the short-term gain in terms of protecting identity is fast overcome by long-term damage to the fabric of tolerance and diversity that holds Southeast Asian societies together.

It is hard to underestimate the divisive forces in Malaysian society, where racial intermarriage is rare and political affiliation defined in racial terms – all this has grown far worse since I lived there in the mid-1990s. Successive governments have boasted of the achievements of multiracial harmony but have reinforced differences and turned a blind eye to absurd impulses such as banning Muslims from touching dogs, or suing ice-cream companies for allegedly using non-halal ingredients. A more recent absurdity is the accusation that Christians use Christmas to convert Muslims to their faith. 'Malaysian society is structurally unsound,' Malaysian Army General Johan Hew, himself a Chinese converted to Islam, told me soon after I arrived in 1991: 'So like the internal combustion engine it operates at only sixty per cent efficiency.' Although there was much about Malaysia that I grew fond of, the underlying atmosphere of racial discord was oppressive and I was somewhat relieved by the end of 1994 to move back to Thailand where, outwardly at least, society seemed more cohesive.

The continuity of tradition and culture is often valued as an attribute of stability. This was the barely concealed leitmotif of my secondary school history course in England, which glossed over all the unfortunate events that befell the British beyond the shores of the United Kingdom, highlighting instead the continuity of throne and parliament. Thailand suffers from much the same delusion. Returning to Thailand for the first time since my student days, I felt a curious ambivalence. At one level, the constant accommodation and tolerance aimed at avoiding conflict suggested a society well equipped to adapt to modernity. Yet at the same time there was an immovable rejection of modern mores and a stubborn resistance to inevitable social change. Among the friends I had made as a student in the early 1980s, I felt a baffling lack of concern about the outside world. Perhaps it was hard for me to grasp the Buddhist concept of impermanence, but I sensed something darker, more sinister, built around ignorance and a wilful rejection of modern values.

On my return to Bangkok in the mid-1990s, this time as a foreign correspondent, I found the city almost unrecognisable: a place bedazzled by newfound prosperity and paralysed by unchecked growth and extravagant consumption. Gone were the mouldy concrete facades that depressed me on my first visit at the end of the 1970s; they were covered over by tinted plate glass and billboards advertising expensive branded goods. Thais flaunted their wealth by purchasing ever-larger luxury motorcars and then slowly poisoned themselves sitting in gridlocked traffic jams. There was something inhuman about the way parents forced their exhausted children to eat and sleep in air-conditioned vehicles that took them to and from schools, sometimes spending six hours a day or more in their cars. My own two young children were no exception. They were woken at around 5 a.m. to begin the long journey through interminable traffic jams to their school. Our lives revolved around traffic; managing it, avoiding it and often just surrendering to sitting under a hot car roof trying not to count the hours.

Thais lived as if there were no tomorrow: money was made easily and more could be had on easy terms from banks living off profligate flows of foreign capital invested in the stock market without any caution. Forests of poorly financed and undersold condominiums sprouted across the city. The architecture was grand, employing stucco Corinthian columns and expensive marble. Habits changed and displaced traditional Thai ways with brash symbols of Western consumerism. Silk '*mor hom*' shirts and khaki safari suits were shed for sleek navy-blue Zegna and Yves St Laurent; goblets filled with vintage French claret replaced tumblers of rice-based *Mekhong* whisky. A profusion of Italian restaurants sprang up and populated the city with a colony of chefs fleeing recession-tightened Europe. It felt like the *belle époque* Lawrence Durrell described in colonial Alexandria. It didn't last.

On 2 July 1997 the Thai baht fell through the floor after the government devalued the currency and called in the International Monetary Fund. Suddenly the super-rich were very poor. Thailand's crisis became Southeast Asia's problem and before long the IMF turned its attention also to President Suharto of Indonesia. Banks and businesses collapsed, equity wasn't worth the paper it was printed on, and the legions of workers assembling those condominiums and tower blocks disappeared, leaving behind piles of rotting concrete and rusting steel. People who weeks earlier had owned banks started selling sandwiches or running thrift stores where cast-off luxuries went for a song. It wasn't just the collapse of an economic boom; Thailand's tough carapace of protection from the outside world shattered.

The financial crisis jolted Southeast Asia out of the fantasy world created by foreign investors and venture capitalists, in which relatively young nations catapulted from agricultural-based subsistence and poverty to sleek, modern, consumer-based so-called 'tiger economies'. The crisis precipitated the privileged elite's loss of legitimacy, and the erosion of social cohesion and control. Something snapped. After the Berlin Wall fell in 1989, Western commentators declared the triumph of universal values of democracy. In sharp contrast to the Cold War coddling of autocrats to keep them out of communist clutches, there was loud cheering in the West as once-stable pro-Western governments tottered amid clamours for reform. In Indonesia, thirty years of authoritarian rule came crashing down in a frenzy of looting and lynching in Jakarta.

In May 1998 I stood with a small group of journalists on a deserted main boulevard in the centre of Jakarta between a line of troops armed with automatic rifles and a noisy mob of students taunting the soldiers and calling for democracy. The students were angry, the troops nervous; at one point bullets started to whizz above our heads. Someone said they must be rubber bullets. Surely they were. I later learned that the soldiers had magazines loaded with both rubber and conventional ammunition and, although he was reluctant to recognise the situation, the game was up for Suharto. 'The President is divorced from reality,' Sarwono Kusumaatmadja, a former Suharto minister and a close confidant of mine, had told me a month earlier: 'Like the melting clock in a Salvador Dali painting.' Once the treacherous elite saw the wind blowing the other way they abandoned him, emerging the very next day as true believers in democratic process and reform.

However, it seemed to me that there were more profound, existential changes happening. Writing two years ahead of the 1997 financial crisis, I wondered whether wealth and progress, most of it fuelled by Western capital and technology, could be an effective agent of progressive change. Instead, I saw ruling elites adapting and cohabiting with modern forms of governance. 'Traditional models of power and authority have been recovered or reinvented to support strong forms of government authority and leadership,' I wrote, predicting that political culture in Southeast Asia was evolving in a direction that might diverge from trends apparent in society and generate conflict. Indeed, under pressure from rapid modernisation and the stress of economic hardship, societies had begun slipping their moorings and drifting into a sea of turmoil. The visionary American anthropologist James C. Scott writes that mass exodus, often coupled with rebellion and banditry, was the traditional response to catastrophe in Southeast Asia. But in the urbanised modern context, people have nowhere to run to; calamity must be endured with the threat of sanction. The tendency is either to capitulate, or resist.

Perhaps this explains the orgy of rioting, looting and murder that erupted in Jakarta with explosive force on 4 May 1998. The trigger was President Suharto's decision to increase the price of petrol by 70 per cent, although tensions had been simmering for months because of the economic hardship brought on by the financial crisis. What began with a few student protests escalated after shots were fired, and within a few hours large areas of Jakarta's northern districts, home to ethnic Chinese, were burning. Anyone who looked Chinese was dragged out and lynched. Joining the mob of foreign journalists who flocked to Jakarta in what looked like the Philippines in 1986 all over again, I was horrified by the footage streaming live via CNN and the BBC. The rioting eventually subsided after the army moved in, but these first few days set the scene for Suharto's eventual ousting. My colleague John McBeth and I struggled, taking turns at the keyboard of a computer in a small office on the eleventh floor of the Antara Building in downtown Jakarta, to distil these events into what we hoped was crisp, biting analysis that would rise above the torrent of daily coverage in a weekly magazine. Staring out at the city, its empty streets devoid of traffic save for the odd military vehicle; it was hard not to imagine an uncertain future for the country, while at the same time hoping for the best.

Indeed, as much as this marked the start of Indonesia's democratic transition, it also was the prelude to years of violent unrest. Over the next decade, conflicts began to surface, some stirred by elite political forces in a bid for power, others stemming from dormant separatist movements in marginal areas, or from harnessing religious dogma to disgruntled elements of society to train and unleash violent militancy and extremism.

Southeast Asia is home to almost one third of the world's Muslim population; it is also the hearth of Theravada Buddhism and hosts sizeable Hindu and Christian communities. By and large, Muslims and non-Muslims have coexisted harmoniously in situations where they are minorities or as a majority. Hand in hand with Southeast Asia's rapid development, Muslims adopted progressive ideas and helped spearhead new thinking about pluralism. In the mid-1990s, B. J. Habibie, a quirky German-trained engineer who was Suharto's technology minister (and later the man who succeeded him as president) teamed up with Anwar Ibrahim, then deputy prime minister of Malaysia, to launch a new intellectual platform for modern Muslims. I attended talks and seminars where there was much discussion around the idea of channelling faith towards science and technology: a new Alhambra. Anwar talked volubly about tolerance and multiculturalism, about building a new harmony in Southeast Asia based on a common cultural heritage, about liberal values and a commitment to human rights. He sponsored seminars on the Philippine nationalist José Rizal and the Bengali poet Rabindranath Tagore. This was his 'Asian Renaissance'. Anwar was also very good at firing up the crowds with traditional Islamic rhetoric. 'The ordinary people may be ignorant of the bigger issues, but they appreciate a man who knows Arabic – the language of Al Quran,' he thundered to a large crowd of supporters in the eastern Malaysia state of Kelantan one moonlit evening on the campaign trail in 1993. Worries about Anwar's Islamic activism as a student melted before his conviction that the modern Muslim was a tolerant, technically proficient aesthete who drove a BMW, not a Koran-thumping, limb-slashing cleric in flowing robes with a yen for stoning adulterers. Sadly for Anwar, and in my view for Southeast Asia, his views and driving ambition only served to reinforce envy and suspicion among his enemies, ending in his prosecution and jailing on charges of corruption. Replacing the rhetoric of Asian Renaissance was the vitriolic hate speech of Asian jihad.

I struggled with this sudden and unexpected change of course. One moment the Muslims of Southeast Asia were on course to replicate the scientific and social achievements of the Moors in Spain, the next they were seeking the establishment of seventh-century Arabia in a new Asian caliphate. The 11 September attacks on New York and Washington DC in 2001 unleashed a maelstrom of cleverly incited and directed violence, supported on shoestring budgets by social outcasts who used their often-inadequate knowledge of the scriptures to manipulate poor boys from the sticks with low self-esteem and time on their hands. It was one of the most effective strategies to fulminate conflict in societies made susceptible by decades of high growth with poorly distributed wealth and benefits.

At first there was a lethal convergence with the existing pockets of territorial conflict. Even before the global jihad exploded with such spectacular impact against the steel-and-glass frame of the World Trade Center's twin towers in New York, a plot to simultaneously explode bombs in eleven airliners crossing the Pacific to the US was hatched by Pakistani terrorists in the Philippines. If it had succeeded four thousand people might have been killed. In both the Philippines and Thailand, subnational conflict involved the struggle of Muslim minorities to free themselves from non-Muslim overlords. One of the most notorious of the region's Islamic extremists, Hambali, was arrested in 2003 and imprisoned in Guantanamo Bay. He envisaged a terrorist campaign to install an Islamic caliphate covering all Muslim lands in Southeast Asia, drawing on the grievances of Muslim youth in poor and marginal areas of Indonesia, Malaysia, Thailand and the Philippines. By now, I had left the field and been appointed Managing Editor of *FEER*. Moving to Hong Kong put me at the centre of the finest network of reporters and correspondents covering Asia. It was a distinct privilege to sift through weekly dispatches from so experienced and passionate a band of journalists. Reporters such as Bertil Lintner, John McBeth, Nate Thayer, Margot Cohen and Murray Hiebert were the finest witnesses and analysts of events in Southeast Asia. Although I could not know at the time, when on 11 September 2001 two airliners slammed into the Twin Towers in New York, a short distance from the offices of *FEER*'s owners, Dow Jones, the fallout delivered a death blow to the magazine; bringing to a close an era of Western hubris and ambition that forced Dow Jones to turn its gaze, and financial support, elsewhere.

Meanwhile, my world had changed. The Southeast Asia I confidently assumed was equipped with both the social and economic means to avoid becoming engulfed by the hatred and violence spewing out from the Middle East was now caught up in the maelstrom. My assumptions were wrong.

The final leg of my journey through Southeast Asia in place and time has been conducted over the past decade as a mediator in armed conflict. In 2004, after the closure of the redoubtable *Far Eastern Economic Review*, I received a call from a friend suggesting I meet the executive director of a Swiss organisation involved in engaging armed groups to negotiate peace agreements. Hard as it was to grasp how this worked, I was nonetheless intrigued, not to mention unemployed. So I jumped at the opportunity with alacrity. A few weeks later I moved to Singapore, where I established a regional office for the Geneva-based Centre for Humanitarian Dialogue (HDC).

Audacious as it seemed, the idea was to explore opportunities for mediation of the region's armed conflicts, of which there was no shortage. HDC pioneered the idea of a private mediation in Aceh, after Indonesia's bold but eccentric President Abdurrahman Wahid agreed to initiate talks with the Free Aceh Movement in 1999. The talks, involving suspicious foreign ministry officials and exiled members of the Free Aceh Movement, forged an early agreement on a humanitarian pause or temporary ceasefire monitored by an ASEAN-led team of observers. (Breakthrough as it was, the powerful Indonesian military teamed up with conservative political quarters in Jakarta to undermine these efforts and it wasn't long before talks were suspended and martial law was declared in the troubled province.)

For the past decade I have inhabited a strange world of marginal people and prohibited space, perpetually shadowed by violence and suffering. In a stark departure from covering the struggle for reform and progress across Southeast Asia that coloured my years as a journalist, I came face to face with yawning fissures in a society underpinned by ethnic and religious prejudice. I understood at last that people, no matter how elevated their level of responsibility, would stubbornly strive to protect their interests rather than sink differences in the pursuit of common progress. Following the path of violence and trying to talk people into peace has driven me to consider the region more realistically. There is a brutal pragmatism about the way politics is conducted and all the collateral damage left in its wake. Motives ascribed to lofty ideals or policy goals in government handouts or interviews disguise naked personal interests. Saving face drives a lot of people to extreme positions from which they will not budge. Violence ensues.

Throughout this last period of my long journey through Southeast Asia, I have confronted its darkest secret, which for all the progress made by these societies in material terms, is their profoundly frustrating capacity to perpetuate conflict at huge cost to society for rather mundane and selfish reasons. Whether a simple matter of face, or some interpersonal power struggle, there is seldom a let-up in the climate of menacing violent conflict. Political feuds fester and perpetuate hatred that in turn goes unreconciled, and which afflicts successive generations with heartfelt grievances. Violence leaves a trail of victims who are never recognised or compensated. No matter how progressive the outlook is in political or economic terms, no one seems committed to finding a just and lasting peace. Chronically conflicted and enduring elite factions have dominated government in Southeast Asia throughout the period I have lived and worked in the region, preventing the development of modern institutions to promote more open and transparent governance. In the following chapters I will attempt to explain why.

CHAPTER TWO

LANDS BELOW THE WINDS

This was the East of the ancient navigators, so old, so mysterious, resplendent and sombre, living and unchanged, full of danger and promise.

Joseph Conrad, 'Youth'

Geographically speaking, Southeast Asia sits like an enlarged appendix to the Asian continent. To the west it borders the Indian Ocean; to the east the Pacific. The mainland comprises the deltas of three major rivers – the Irrawaddy, the Chao Phraya and the mighty Mekong – each of these muddy waterways providing generous floodplains of alluvial silt on which the rice-growing societies of Burma, Thailand, Cambodia and Vietnam have been supported for over a millennium. In addition to an abundance of water and fertile silt, vast areas of forest offer a profusion of tropical hardwood and wildlife. Further south, islands hang like a string of beads from a long peninsula probing the warm waters of the Andaman Sea. Surrounded by warm water and blessed by moderate trade winds in both directions, these coastal areas supported trading centres that allowed an accretion of material and cultural influences from both East and West. In terms of scale, Southeast Asia comprises 'an area comparable to all Europe and its seas north of the African coast', wrote the British geographer E. H. G. Dobby in 1950.

The term 'Southeast Asia' originated from the military designation given the region by allied commanders based in Ceylon (now Sri Lanka) beyond the reach of the invading Japanese during the

Pacific War. European scholars of the nineteenth century referred to the region as Farther India (in other words, farther from the Western metropolitan centres of the world); the mainland was a place between India and China and so dubbed 'Indochina'; the peninsula and islands were the 'Indies'. The names reflect India's influence on the region, which was particularly apparent in the culture and beliefs of the pre-modern ruling class. Ancient seafarers knew Southeast Asia as the 'Land Below the Winds', sitting as it does below the tropical monsoon and beyond the typhoon belt, making sailing safer, the warm turquoise seas less treacherous.

This happy confluence of environmental factors made Southeast Asia a natural conduit for trade between India and China, which in turn heralded an infusion of cultural and technological influences that forged one of the great cosmopolitan crucibles in world history. Already one of the most ethnically diverse regions of the world with 1,000 of the world's 6,000 ethnolinguistic groups, trade brought distinct others from India and China. Whereas the Mediterranean embraced Islam and Christianity, Southeast Asia melded Hinduism, Buddhism, Islam and Christianity. This was reflected early on in the diversity of its populations. Maurice Collis, a twentieth-century Anglo-Irish writer of narrative history for the region, described the trading port of Mergui along the west coast of Burma bordering modern Thailand (then called Siam). His imagining of what it must have been like there in the seventeenth century is as accurate as it gets:

> . . . neither the Burmese nor the Siamese counted for much in the port . . . it was the Mahomedans, chiefly from India, who dominated the commercial situation. If Indian enterprise was the life of the place, the Mongolian inhabitants gave it an air. The atmosphere was Indo-Chinese and Buddhist, animated but polite; the crowd was brightly dressed and clean; Burmese and Siamese men sauntered and idled; the women, stout, downright and handsome, managed the bazaars; Malays, glowering and touchy, flitted by fingering their snaky daggers; and the Chinese, careful and smiling, made their profit.

Such diversity speaks of ease of access and a region so outward-looking and well connected with the wider world that it lends new meaning to the term cosmopolitan. Ancient Chinese and Indian philosophers, who only became known in Europe during the Enlightenment of the seventeenth century, were part of intellectual and spiritual discourse in Southeast Asia almost at the same time as they lived and taught. Traders from the Arab, Indian and Chinese worlds who looked exotic to the Venetians of the sixteenth century were roaming Southeast Asia three hundred years earlier and had established communities in all the region's trading ports and capitals. Long before the era of European domination, Southeast Asia was suffused with a web of connections involving trade and the movement of people. Pottery from the Sung dynasty in China sits on the dusty shelves of a museum in Cebu City in the central Philippines, where swords from India are also on display. They were probably used by local tribal warriors when the Portuguese explorer Ferdinand Magellan landed there in 1521 with three battered little ships and a scurvy-ridden crew. Chinese traders were living in the ancient Khmer capital Angkor in present-day Cambodia by the tenth century, which supported a population of around one million people at a time when London's population was no larger than 35,000. Arab traders sailing from the coast of India reached the Moluccan islands in the far eastern end of the Indonesian archipelago a century before the Europeans arrived in the 1500s. The Europeans came along and harnessed all this fecundity to enrich themselves. As Voltaire wrote: 'European princes and merchants in their voyages to the East have been in search not of wisdom, but of wealth.'

Today, Southeast Asia is just as accessible and accommodating as in centuries past. Its cities are meeting places of East and West, grand bazaars for cultural and material exchange – where women still dominate and the Chinese, 'careful and smiling', make their profit. Mingling with the pungent smell of spice, vast shiny emporiums in places like Bangkok, Kuala Lumpur and Singapore sell international branded goods (not all of them genuine) at discounted prices and draw consumers from all over the world. Passengers arriving at Singapore airport are greeted by signs declaring 'The Great Singapore Sale'; in Bangkok it's 'The Midnight Sale'. In Indonesian and Malay, the word for market, *pasar*, is derived from the old Persian word 'bazaar'.

Yet as this benign geography enabled a rich diversity of people to evolve sophisticated social and cultural frameworks drawing on outside influences, so it also invited waves of invasion and subjugation. The American historian Leonard Andaya argues that it was trade and the presence of foreign merchants and visitors that stimulated early state formation in the region: contributing to 'an intense awareness of self among local individuals and groups'. Confronted by waves of traders from more advanced societies, he argues, the locals needed to maximise their advantage. They did so by joining with others and forming numerically larger and more extensive networks, which afforded them some protection and made the trade more profitable. However, the natural flow of people down from the harsh dry plains and foothills of the Himalayas through lush green valleys to the sea drew successive Mongol Chinese invasions into Burma and Vietnam. Southeast Asia has long been conceived as a geographical region with cultural roots in southern and northeastern Asia. Hinduism and Buddhism were both imported from India, influencing statecraft and the organisation of society. Centuries before the widespread use of English, Sanskrit was the language of power and privilege. Islam arrived a little later from trading ports on the coast of India. Christianity arrived at the tip of a sword with the conquering Dutch and Portuguese. China was the source of material goods such as porcelain and scientific technology, as well as the tools of commerce and trade. To count in the Thai language is virtually the same as in Cantonese, reflecting a long trading connection to the south coast of China. Many of the words for ordinary objects such as tables and windows in modern Indonesian have their roots in Portuguese. The Malay language is suffused with Arabic loan words. The cultural underpinnings of Southeast Asia are all connected to somewhere else. While Latin and Greek lie at the root of most European languages, in Southeast Asia, Sanskrit, Chinese, Arabic, Portuguese and, more recently, English have all contributed to contemporary parlance across all the languages of the region.

Access to Southeast Asia's bustling coastal trading centres enabled the Western world to acquire the exotic spices to cure meats in the centuries before refrigeration. This in turn made tiny islands in the Molucca Sea, where the spices grew, prized acquisitions and drew nascent European trading powers into conflict over them. The microdot island of Run, about three kilometres long and less than one kilometre wide, was famously traded by the British with the Dutch in 1664 for the island of Manhattan. Run's principal asset was a rich grove of nutmeg trees, which at one time in the seventeenth century was almost worth its weight in gold.

Across Southeast Asia, the combination of ancient cultural synthesis lacquered by successive waves of invasion has left a durable legacy of colourful and creative diversity. Indeed, modern Southeast Asia has few parallels as a region. The Gulf States in the Arabian Peninsula have acquired today something of the centrality of ancient Southeast Asian trading centres through the connectivity of modern air travel – land above the wind, perhaps – but cannot rival them in terms of the numbers of people cities like Bangkok, Kuala Lumpur or Singapore support, and the richness of their societies.

The Strait of Malacca, a narrow 700-kilometre passage connecting the Indian and Pacific Oceans, opens up into the South China Sea through which the bulk of shipping between China and Europe must pass. It remains perhaps the world's most strategic natural sea lane. Something like $6 trillion worth of trade and a quarter of all oil carried by sea passes through the area each year. Perhaps this explains why China claims the South China Sea as its own, based on dubious historical arguments that the rest of the world challenges. Further south, the much deeper Lombok Strait offers an alternative route for larger ships – not to mention nuclear submarines. Being a prisoner of fortunate geography has promoted modern forms of invasion such as tourism and international finance, economic mainstays for many countries in the region. In 2015 32 million tourists visited Thailand. With assets worth $2 trillion, some 200 banks operate out of tiny Singapore, where some of the largest Swiss banks have moved their international banking departments.

Despite its history of presenting an open face to the world, the region harbours many dark secrets. Its people, a product of so much diversity, can be conservative and inward-looking. Countries that have long been exposed to foreign trade and adventure periodically close up and try to remain aloof. Southeast Asia attracts and repels in equal measure, and is not for the faint-hearted.

Arriving from the West, situated beside a ripple of forested hills that forms the border with India, the first country encountered is Burma (officially named Myanmar for now). Myanmar has a long and proud pre-colonial history that revolves around illustrious and not-so-great warrior kings, who bestowed on themselves modest titles such as the 'Arbiters of Existence' and 'Lords of the Rising Sun'. These kings struggled to unite the country under one dominion and, once they had done so, by about the eleventh century, proceeded to pillage and conquer well beyond, capturing and enslaving those who stood in their way. For a while they were subject to the marauding Mongol armies of Kublai Khan, who swept into Burma in the thirteenth century demanding tribute. However, by the sixteenth century King Bayinnaung ruled lands from the upland margins of northeast India across the Shan States in the north to the borders of China, including much of modern Thailand. The original mud walls of the old city of Chiang Mai in northern Thailand are said to have been built with the bones of slain soldiers from invading Burmese armies.

All the same, it took the British army, equipped with breech-loading rifles and accurate artillery, just two weeks to subdue the last Burmese kingdom at Mandalay in 1885. It was a moment of abject humiliation for the Burmese, as their last king, not yet aged thirty, was removed from the splendid moat-ringed palace in a bullock cart and sent into ignominious exile in India.

The new colony of Burma was governed from Calcutta, the centre of administration for British India, and developed into Southeast Asia's primary rice exporter. The capital at Rangoon became a bustling metropolitan centre with electric streetcars and imposing brick and stucco edifices flanked by columns, many of which still stand today, crumbling and overgrown with moss. The atmosphere of imperial grandeur with its seamy underside of racism and terror was admirably captured in the novel *Burmese Days* by George Orwell, who served as a junior officer in the Indian Imperial Police in the mid-1920s. In his compelling essay, 'Shooting an Elephant', Orwell describes what he calls 'the dirty work of Empire': 'The wretched prisoners huddling in the stinking cages of the lock-ups, the grey, cowed faces of the long-term convicts, the scarred buttocks of the men who had been flogged with bamboos – all these oppressed me with an intolerable sense of guilt.'

The Burmese can be more forthright than neighbouring Thais or Malays and Javanese further south. Perhaps that's why, as Norman Lewis noted, their myths are conveyed by nearly life-size puppets rather than the shadows of puppets, as with the Indonesian Wayang. And although the Burmese can be stubbornly emphatic, they are given to kindness; perhaps a result of the extended periods that every Burman spends as a novice in the village Buddhist pagoda.

Modern Burma's history (the country's military rulers renamed the country Myanmar in 1989) is a tragic trajectory from democracy to tyranny, followed by decades of often violent struggle to restore democracy. A nationalist movement led by student firebrand Aung San thrived during the Japanese occupation, forcing the reluctant British to agree to independence. However, Aung San was gunned down in a hail of bullets during a cabinet meeting in 1947 – almost certainly a plot by rivals in association with some British officers acting without London's approval. A series of weak, fractious governments led by avuncular, well-educated

Myanmar still boasts some of the imposing edfices of the colonial era.

and well-meaning politicians assumed the reins of power after independence was formally granted in 1949. But faced with mounting challenges from ethnic minorities on the periphery and a strong Communist Party insurgency backed by neighbouring China, it wasn't long before the army emerged as the unifying force. A coup in 1962 led by the army commander Ne Win inaugurated a period of harsh military rule from which the country has yet to completely escape.

The people of neighbouring Thailand, by contrast with the Burmese, are supple in their interactions. The Burmese like to characterise the Thai, their ancient adversaries, as amoral and unprincipled; the Thai point out that their ability to wriggle out of commitments allowed them to escape the colonial yoke. Thais are a fiercely independent people who migrated from an area in southern China, where Thai-speaking people still live today. Early Thai society revolved around rice cultivation, with village relations centred on a local chief or 'Chao'. As Chinese imperial rule expanded, the Thai moved south and occupied lowland areas where more rice could be grown, more labour organised and larger political entities established. Aided by a distinctive Buddhist faith carried by monks from the island of Ceylon, the Thai gradually asserted their independence.

Thailand emerged as a notionally unified kingdom in the thirteenth century, having won independence from the once-powerful Khmer empire to the east. Situated first at Sukhothai in the central plains region in the middle of the country, then further down the Chao Phraya River at Ayudhya, the Kingdom of Siam flourished, drawing on well-organised corvée labour to grow rice and equally well-managed commerce to export rice and hardwood in junks, trading as far as China and Japan.

Freedom was a key aspect of this emerging Thai polity. A late thirteenth-century stone inscription found in Sukhothai, and said to have been the edict of King Ramkhamhaeng, declares: 'There are fish in the water and rice in the fields. The lord of the realm does not levy tolls on his subjects for travelling the roads. They lead their cattle to trade or ride their horses to sell. Whoever wants to trade elephants does so . . .' In reality, Thais were free to grow rice and trade their cattle and horses so long as the profits flowed to the court, which established an elaborate system of trade monopolies and labour management through which all able-bodied men owed a portion of their time and profit to the king. Little wonder that in the mid-seventeenth century, a Dutch visitor to Ayudhya described King Prasat Tong as 'one of the richest princes of India'.

As Europeans began to arrive from the start of the sixteenth century, eventually occupying Burma, Malaya and much of Indochina, there were repeated attempts to subjugate the Thai kingdom. Early European expansion into Southeast Asia was spearheaded by small bands of adventurous traders in rickety, waterlogged ships manned by malodorous and malnourished men. There were no massive armies at their back, no flotillas of men-of-war. Using a combination of audacious deal-making and missionary zeal, they somehow established beachheads in the grimy outskirts of royal capitals, such as the seat of the Siamese kingdom in Ayudhya. But neither the imposition of unequal trade treaties nor attempted conversion to the Christian faith were of any use. The Thais remained stubbornly free. Or did they? Thongchai Winichakul, a progressive, left-leaning Thai scholar, argues that Thailand didn't quite escape colonisation as its economy became subject to the same nineteenth-century forces that governed neighbouring territories held by the British and the French. In any case, Thai kings fashioned their own form of internal colonisation, using European-style bureaucratic reforms introduced in the early twentieth century to harness people to centralised government, which at that time was regarded as modern and progressive – the hallmark of a modern state.

When Japan invaded the country in 1941, Thailand used subterfuge to keep both the Allied and Axis powers onside; a Japanese demand to declare war on the United States was never met after the Thai ambassador in Washington refused to deliver the letter. As a result, when the British argued for the occupation of Thailand after the Japanese were defeated, Washington defended Thai sovereignty. Thailand's historical continuity has been both a blessing and a curse. While it has helped foster a rich culture and unique identity, it has sheltered the country from social progress. Respect for monarchy, which sits at the apex of the system of government, has built an imposing if arcane edifice of power and cultivated a conservative mindset that has prevented the devolution of power and autonomy to the people. Modern Malaysia is a federation, while contemporary Indonesia and the Philippines have devolved government authority to provinces and districts governed by elected officials. Yet Thailand's interior ministry appoints every one of its ninety or so provincial governors from Bangkok. Attempted popular challenges to the entrenched conservative establishment, centred on the royal court, met with stiff resistance and sparked the political crisis that has gripped the country for two decades. The grim determination of the establishment to cling to power explains why the military, after seventeen coups, remains in the political saddle.

Further east across the mighty Mekong River, modern Cambodia, Laos and Vietnam constitute what used to be known as Indochina. Squeezed between the depredations of marauding Chinese armies and European trader-adventurers, ancient Vietnam eventually succumbed to French rule, which spread westward into the lands of the Khmer and Lao. The French ran tidy colonies under a paradoxical regime that managed to exploit and cultivate the natives at the same time. The notion of *mission civilisatrice* implied that colonial rule must be both profitable and civilised; thus, the people of Indochina were encouraged to learn French, wear French fashion and convert to Christianity. At the same time, ordinary people were taxed on everything, forced to give up land to French-owned estates and serve as indentured labourers.

The end of the Pacific War saw stirrings of nationalism inspired by the march of communism in Russia and China. Ho Chi Minh was the son of a local magistrate who used his education at a local French lycée to earn his passage to Europe as a cook's steward and later a pastry chef. While working in France at the end of the First World War, Ho was drawn initially to Woodrow Wilson's high-minded rhetoric on self-determination, and even sought to meet the US president when he was in Paris to sign the Treaty of Versailles. Disappointed at being spurned by the West, Ho was drawn to socialism and later joined the Comintern in Soviet Russia, where he was trained in communist agitation and sent to China. There he started organising expatriate Vietnamese, and laid the foundation of the Communist Party and its associated black-shirted Viet Minh armed movement that would eventually win the war of independence against the French. The 1954 Geneva Accords divided Vietnam in two, and it was only a matter of time before communist agitation from the North, which was looking for a means to unify the fractured party, threatened the Western-backed puppet government of the anti-communist South. The ensuing struggle inaugurated another two decades of war that engulfed Laos and Cambodia, dragged in first France then the United States, and cost around 1.5 million lives. The war ended with the fall of Saigon in 1975 to the North Vietnamese army, unifying Vietnam.

Cambodia is the only Southeast Asian country that was effectively rescued and rebuilt with external intervention in the post-colonial era. It was in some ways a reprise. The French colonised the country for almost a century, having rescued it from virtual extinction in the 1840s. The newly independent kingdom stepped out on to the new post-colonial stage under the leadership of the flamboyant King Norodom Sihanouk in the 1950s. Sihanouk, with his French education and native Khmer sensibilities, confused everyone by playing the Western playboy and Hindu–Buddhist god king at one and the same time. A succession of coups and counter-coups destabilised the country, and drew it into the Indochina conflict. The emergence of the Khmer Rouge in Cambodia at the end of the Vietnam War heralded almost five years of spectacular mass savagery as the extremist communist movement, which started as an offshoot of the Viet Cong, ordered the evacuation of cities and, in a bid to forge a classless society, the murder of intellectuals in a frenzy that resulted in the death of around two million people. Yet the legacy of so much death and destruction has been surprisingly peaceful. The Paris Peace Accords signed in 1991 established a United Nations-led recovery and reconstruction effort that shepherded a return to notionally democratic government.

Though the trauma of civil war in Vietnam appears to have been absorbed, the untold cost in terms of human life continues. Since the end of the war 42,000 people have been killed as a result of unexploded ordnance littering the land. In Cambodia, a United Nations-backed tribunal has spent over a decade seeking justice for the victims. Just a handful of ageing Khmer Rouge leaders have been successfully indicted; the Khmer Rouge leader, Pol Pot, died in 1998 before he could be arrested or brought to trial. Every year in May, Cambodia commemorates what is called a 'day of anger', an ambiguous reference to the fact that the Khmer Rouge reign of terror was ended only after Vietnam invaded the country. Rising out of the ashes of war, then civil war, Cambodia's present leader, Hun Sen, is a man of humble rural origins. He rose through the ranks of the Khmer Rouge, before defecting to Vietnam to avoid one of the movement's incessant internal purges. Today, Hun Sen is Southeast Asia's longest-serving prime minister, having assumed the job in 1985 while still in his thirties.

The long narrow Malay peninsula that extends down from Thailand to almost touch the tip of Sumatra served for centuries as an antenna of sorts, picking up and transmitting the external influences that wafted through the region on favourable winds. Hinduism then Theravada Buddhism first came to the region via the shores of the Malay peninsula in the eighth and ninth centuries; Islam soon followed. The Portuguese who occupied Malacca in 1511 on the west coast of the peninsula were the first Europeans to settle. Malacca had been a substantial trading empire in its own right, ruled by a Malay sultan converted to Islam, and early European visitors described it as a thriving, polyglot trading centre. One Portuguese visitor wrote that Malacca was 'at the end of the Monsoons and the beginnings of other . . . every hand must come to Malacca'.

By the early nineteenth century the British had occupied strategic waypoints in Penang, an island off the west coast facing the Andaman Sea, and then Singapore, a muddy island perched at the southern tip of the peninsula. The British turned these mosquito-infested low-lying swamps into profitable trading centres which became known as the Straits Settlements. To serve as a labour force, the British imported tens of thousands of indentured Indian and Chinese labourers, who also settled in tin-mining and rubber-producing towns up and down the Malay peninsula like Ipoh, Taiping and Mersing. By the end of the nineteenth century, a complex plural society evolved in which each ethnic component recognised and respected the other's space and role in the colonial pecking order. Meanwhile, the British in their solar topis and khaki shorts, downing pegs of whisky or 'stengahs' in club bars, benefited from the total absence of any unified sense of nationhood. In stark contrast to India, popular uprisings were unheard of in British colonial Malaya.

The end of empire was relatively smooth and tranquil for Malaya. As in India, the British crept out at midnight on the appointed day, leaving in place a form of government and people in power virtually indistinguishable from the mother of parliaments and the clubbable types in tweeds and soft caps who dominated the benches of Westminster. The avuncular, whisky-loving father of the nation, Tunku Abdul Rahman, was a British-educated Malay aristocrat inclined towards moderation. His underlings quarrelled around him and, despite the trappings of English civility, politics eventually became ugly. The early years of independence were marred by a determined communist insurgency centred on the ethnic Chinese community, which was suppressed by 1960 using brutal tactics of violence and repression with the assistance of the British army. What was quaintly called 'The Emergency' bequeathed the government a suite of sinister internal security laws that have helped keep a lid on dissent ever since. The principally Chinese membership of the Communist Party of Malaysia reinforced the fears of the Muslim Malay majority, which contributed eventually to mainly Chinese-populated Singapore's separation from the Federation in 1965. As a result, race and religion became the pronounced markers of Malaysian politics in the years after race riots in 1969. Successive governments ever since have talked idealistically about racial integration and a 'Malaysian' identity, but have instead steered the country towards a more divided, racially defined future.

Across the Malacca Strait, the Dutch East Indies was one of the most successful colonial enterprises ever conceived. The original company was a private venture, founded on the back of the spice trade at the start of the seventeenth century in the distant Moluccan-island chain. 'Despair not, spare your enemies not, for God is with us,' was how one of the companies' early merchant leaders, Jan Pieterszoon Coen, described his mission as he ruthlessly carved out a huge share of trade across the spice islands. A strict Calvinist, he killed all those who crossed him; at one stage almost wiping out the entire population of Banda Island, famed for its nutmeg, because the natives were selling spice to the English. The ruins of Coen's factory can still be seen in Banda Neira, where they are overgrown and the Dutch government is reluctant to push for their preservation – even though a statue of the man was erected in his home town of Hoorn in the Netherlands. Huge profits were to be had from nutmeg and mace, which grew on these islands exclusively and in abundance. The history of Southeast Asia might have been completely different if Europeans did not need these tropical spices to mask the pungent smell of unrefrigerated, rotting meat.

By the end of the nineteenth century, the Dutch ruled much of Indonesia in a manner they considered benevolent and paternalistic, but in reality subjected the natives to violence and hardship. That Indonesians died in their tens of thousands building roads and harvesting rice and sugar cane did not seem to bother their Dutch masters, who derived huge profits and did not even consider asking for local help when the Japanese invaded in 1941. As in Burma and Malaya, Japan formally promised Indonesia its independence, but at the same time used the machinery of colonial administration to run the country and exploited millions of workers as forced labour, many of whom died overseas for the Japanese war effort.

Indonesia's revolution was short and scrappy. It began with a hastily assembled group of nationalists at a small rented house in central Jakarta where the leading revolutionary, a charismatic, Dutch-educated engineer named Sukarno, drew up a rather simple, four-line declaration of independence. After proclaiming freedom from Dutch rule, Sukarno added with charming politeness, perhaps because a Japanese military officer was present, that 'matters which concern the transfer of powers and other things will be executed by careful means in the shortest possible time'. Independence was won four years later. The Dutch initially put up fierce resistance, often involving harsh measures to repress the Indonesian freedom fighters whose commanders pioneered hit-and-run guerrilla tactics later adopted by other insurgencies in the region. The Dutch enlisted British military help to effectively invade their colonial possession after the Japanese surrendered. Indonesia's fledgling army was a rag-tag assembly of former Japanese-trained militia, student hotheads and local brigands. Its leader, General Sudirman, was a composed, consumptive Javanese schoolteacher who still remains something of an enigma. His lean frame, cloaked incongruously for the tropical climate in a long heavy overcoat, graces the main thoroughfare named after him in downtown Jakarta. The British came to the aid of the Dutch at first, but with the post-colonial era well under way, Indian troops fighting in the British army were unhappy about opposing Indonesian nationalists. The United Nations, backed by India and the United States, intervened and the Dutch were prevailed upon to acquiesce to reality. Indonesia was born.

As in Burma, the early years of nation building in Indonesia were marked by upheaval. Indonesia was already home to a large communist movement that rebelled even before the revolution was won and was ruthlessly put down in 1948. The Dutch had offered a form of federalism, which Indonesia's founding fathers suspected was a bid to divide and rule the new nation, which somewhat improbably embraced a far-flung cluster of islands with disparate cultures and distinct languages. So a unitary republic was established. However, some regions outside the main island of Java were unhappy with the centralised form of government, as were some parts of the country that favoured Islamic statehood. The resulting regional rebellions forged a lasting preoccupation with unity and fears of centrifugal forces that has made it hard for governments, even in the post-1998 reformist era, to tolerate demands for autonomy.

Indonesia was governed by a pluralistic, democratic system for the first decade of its existence, but regional rebellion and fractious politics lured founding President Sukarno into applying autocratic measures he styled 'Guided Democracy'. Yet at the same time his penchant for the politics of mass mobilisation allowed the communists to develop a huge following. By the early 1960s the Partai Komunis Indonesia (PKI), with its three million members, was the third-largest Communist Party in the world. With China and the Soviet Union already backing people's revolutions in Indochina and in Malaya, there were fears in the West that another domino would fall. The army, growing uneasy by this stage and almost certainly encouraged by Western intelligence agencies to challenge Sukarno's power, came up with a doctrine to justify its intervention in politics:

the 'Dual Function'. The resulting tense standoff amid appalling levels of poverty and social tension is well captured in Christopher Koch's novel *The Year of Living Dangerously*. The situation reached a climax in 1965, when an attempted coup, the explanation for which remains murky, resulted in the deaths of six army generals in the early hours of 30 September. The alleged plotters, some of whom were identified as members of the presidential guard, were accused of having had links to the PKI. More likely, as the late Indonesian scholar Ben Anderson argued in a seminal paper he wrote with Ruth McVey and published in 1971, it was an internal army putsch cloaked in a communist carapace to disguise a bid for power.

The subsequent backlash against the PKI resulted in a mass killing spree that ended in the deaths of around half a million – there are no precise numbers and there has been no accountability. As a result, one of Asia's most appalling modern human tragedies remains cloaked in mystery. Sukarno, ailing and politically compromised, languished in power for another three years before a smiling, chubby-faced general no one knew very much about called Suharto assumed the presidency in 1968 after a rigged vote in the National Assembly. President Suharto ruled Indonesia for the next thirty years under a soft form of military-backed autocracy that helped the country achieve rice self-sufficiency and high levels of literacy but which emasculated freedom of expression and popular sovereignty until his fall in 1998.

Northward across the Sulu Sea sits the Philippine archipelago, another necklace of islands seized and colonised in the sixteenth century, this time by Spain. Unlike the rest of Southeast Asia, the Philippines faced the Pacific, and its ties to Europe were via Mexico, then known as New Spain, which administered the islands until 1821. The Spanish galleon trade was built on the back of silver coin mined and minted in the New World, which paid for goods from China and Southeast Asia such as silk, porcelain, spice and exotic wood sent to Europe on galleons via Mexico. It was a lucrative closed circuit of commerce that lasted three hundred years. The thriving Spanish community swiftly converted the native population to Catholicism, while the church acquired land as well as souls and grew very rich, thanks to a system of administration that allowed Spanish friars to raise taxes.

Even though Spanish colonial rule devolved some authority to natives, and many Filipinos were educated and rose to prominence through inter-marriage or induction through the church, it remained a fundamentally exploitative system. A fiery spirit of nationalism emerged among a clique of educated Filipinos from educated, middle-class families exposed to war and revolution in nineteenth-century Europe. Among them was a multi-talented ophthalmologist, José Rizal. Singularly gifted and effective as an essayist, poet and novelist, Rizal used the power of writing, mostly from abroad, to launch a reform movement that snowballed into rebellion. Rhetorical and at times dreamy, his writing offered simple epithets that mobilised feelings: 'Men are born equal, naked and without chains. They were not created by God to be enslaved.' As simple a sentiment as this seems, it would have been a revelation to many Filipinos taught by the friars to regard the Catholic Church as the sole intercessor. The power of his writing angered the Church as much as the Spanish colonial administration – where in fact he had many liberal sympathisers. He was arrested in 1892 and executed a few months later for rebellion.

Alas, the Philippine Republic was declared just as Spain lost its Philippine possessions to the United States as a result of the Spanish–American War in 1898. Although barely a century had passed since the United States won freedom from British colonial overlords, the American government showed no hesitation in acquiring a new colony of its own and crushed the fledgling republic, setting the stage for a forever prickly and ambivalent relationship towards the United States in the contemporary period. In the museum that occupies the former prison in Cebu, the city of the renowned Spanish seafaring conquerors Magellan and Legazpi, the tattered and rotting remains of a Spanish flag lies at the bottom of a glass-topped box, around which are displayed old photographs of public buildings edged by trimmed lawns over which flies the Stars and Stripes, a reminder that the country that calls itself the leader of the free world was, not that long ago, a colonial power that suppressed the very freedoms upon which it was founded. It was only in 1935 that the US granted the Philippine islands commonwealth status, just in time for another occupation by the Japanese a decade later.

The long struggle for freedom has instilled in Filipinos a strong sense of national longing that manifests itself at times with hot-blooded Latin zeal. Despite this long struggle for freedom, it took barely two decades for demagoguery and dictatorship to supplant the institutions of democracy carbon-copied from the United States. Ferdinand Marcos was a small-town lawyer and politician from the northern province of Ilocos Norte who combined intellectual ability with a pugnacious personality, and was given to using force to get his way. Elected president in 1965, he and his shoe-loving wife, Imelda, were accused of amassing wealth through corrupt practices. To cling to power, Marcos declared martial law in 1972 and was only ousted after the police and the army rebelled in 1986 in what became known as the region's first people-power uprising. The people may have spoken when hundreds of thousands marched along the main EDSA highway in Manila, but the army acquired a taste for power as well. In subsequent years there were several attempted coups led by disgruntled officers. One group even occupied the lavish Peninsula Hotel in 2007, which left government-backed troops no choice but to send an armoured fighting vehicle crashing through the glass doors of the hotel.

Ferdinand Marcos denied that he had plundered his country's wealth and considered the corruption charges levelled at him during the 1986 election campaign part of a smear campaign orchestrated by the opposition. Four years later a court in the US found his wife Imelda not guilty of charges that she raided the country's treasury and invested the money in the US. However, the Philippine government did manage to freeze some $630 million held in Marcos's Swiss bank account and later filed corruption charges against Imelda Marcos in the Philippines. A Presidential commission is still working on tracing and recovering the allegedly stolen assets.

Filipinos are among the best-educated, most talented and versatile people of Southeast Asia. Formal education in English from primary-school level has endowed them with mobility to escape the paucity of opportunities at home; almost 12 million Filipinos work overseas, sending home remittances in 2014 worth $24 billion – almost 15 per cent of GDP.

Often overlooked in overviews of Southeast Asia is the world's third-largest island of Borneo, where Indonesia and Malaysia have far-flung provinces and states, sandwiched between which is the pocket sultanate of Brunei. Blessed with offshore oil and gas reserves, tiny Brunei is ruled by a Malay sultan whose passion for the high life has steadily been dampened by age and a sense of guilty piety. In the past two years, Islamic Shariah law has been implemented and the celebration of Christmas declared illegal. Borneo was until quite recently one of the least developed, least spoiled parts of Southeast Asia. The island's 140-million-year-old tropical rainforest is one of the most important green lungs in the world, though estate development and the price of palm oil have been responsible for deforestation on a vast scale. Reliance on primary resources has left Borneo's tribal societies exploited and marginalised, which makes the region one of the most likely to be restive in the second half of the twenty-first century unless meaningful autonomy is granted.

By the end of the twentieth century most of the ten nations of Southeast Asia had achieved remarkable levels of development and admirable stability set against comparable states in Africa. When Ghana and Malaysia won independence in 1957, both countries had about the same level of development; they inherited the same British legal and administrative systems and relied on the export of primary resources such as rubber and palm oil. Half a century later, Malaysia had pulled way ahead of Ghana, with a GDP of around $300 billion compared with Ghana's $40 billion and per capita GDP of $18,000 compared with Ghana's $3,500. Most economists attribute this striking contrast to the high levels of foreign direct investment attracted to Southeast Asia's relatively open, well-educated and stable societies.

Vietnam, Malaysia, the Philippines, Indonesia and Thailand today have per capita GDPs above $3,000, placing them in the middle-income category. Increasing numbers of Southeast Asians live in cities with access to social services – the populations of Indonesia and the Philippines are 50 per cent urban. In these same countries the proportion of people working in agriculture is well below 40 per cent. One third of the region's population have a disposable income of between $16 and $100 a day.

Yet remarkable economic growth and much-improved social indicators have not for the most part translated in Southeast Asia into
substantial political progress, defined in a broad sense as pluralistic
democratic government. Nor has a constant average rate of as much
as 10 per cent growth per annum for much of this time translated
into a more equitable distribution of income and wealth. In fact,
while overall rates of poverty have declined across Southeast Asia,
the startling reality is that the gap between rich and poor and the
share of income earned by the very rich has increased at an alarming
rate. The main reason this has come about is that all the investment
fuelling economic growth has favoured those who own the capital,
rather than the labour working for it. There have been high returns
on capital, while wages have been kept as low as possible to maximise those returns. Not surprisingly, this has generated a discordant
chorus of protest and upheaval. Southeast Asia in the time I have
known it – since the late 1970s – has experienced perpetual turmoil
that has inflicted real suffering at ordinary levels of society.

Sizeable GDP figures and the modern infrastructure of commerce and industry masks a dark underside that keeps 40 per cent
of Indonesians clustered around a poverty line of around $2 dollars
a day. In a recent survey, the World Bank reported that fifteen years
of sustained economic growth in Indonesia have helped to reduce
poverty and create a growing middle class. However, growth over
the past decade has primarily benefited only the richest 20 per cent
and left behind the remaining 80 per cent of the population: that's
around 205 million people. Thailand's overall poverty rate has come
down from close to 14 per cent of the population to less than 10
per cent in the past five years, but spectacular income inequality
gives Thailand one of the most skewed wealth-distribution profiles
in the region. Less than 20 per cent of Thais earn over 60 per cent
of income in the country. The problem is especially acute for an
estimated 5 million migrant workers from neighbouring Myanmar
who subsist in Thailand on wages well below the official minimum.

One of the central questions asked throughout this book is why
so much capital investment and productivity has not translated into
greater degrees of social or economic equality, justice and freedom.
In the following chapters I will endeavour to explain why.

CHAPTER THREE

DIVINE KINGS AND DARK PRINCES

'It appears that His Majesty cannot consider himself rich until he has gathered all the treasures into his treasury and has everything squeezed out of the community.'

Description of King Prasat Thong of Siam,
Jeremias van Vliet (1640)

Not long after I arrived in Indonesia to work as a correspondent in the mid-1980s, I was introduced to the charmingly arcane world of Javanese aristocracy. The longer I lived in the country, the less I took it for granted. The majority of Indonesians are Javanese – almost 100 million of them. They speak a language distinctive from mainstream Indonesian and belong to a refined culture that draws on stratifying and spiritual Hindu and Buddhist influences, which reached the island sometime in the eighth century. On a visit to Java's cultural hearth, Jogjakarta, a charming city about three hundred kilometres southeast of Jakarta, I toured the sprawling grounds of the royal palace that belonged to Sultan Hamengku Buwono IX, whose name translates somewhat immodestly as 'the one who holds the world'. With my Western sense of these things, it wasn't at all clear to me why the proud republic of Indonesia would harbour a reigning sultan retaining feudal titles and accompanying powers. In the dusty outer courtyards of the sultan's rather dishevelled palace, parts of which were covered by rusting corrugated iron, older men wearing dark long-sleeved jackets made of cotton and brown batik sarongs padded barefoot to and fro, their heads covered with *blangkon*, starched turbans hugging the skull and ending in a knot at the nape of the neck. I was told they were palace servants who had volunteered their service to the throne for a minimal wage. I became even more confused when I learned that the sultan was also a hero of the republican revolution. I learned it was his refusal to strike a bargain with the Dutch colonial authorities, and his subsequent financing of republican forces battling Dutch soldiers trying to recapture the city – which served as the revolutionary capital of Indonesia – that earned him the nation's undying love. In fact, the sultan served as vice president of the republic from 1973–8.

When the old sultan died of a heart attack in October 1988 I attended his funeral. It was an extraordinary spectacle. At least a million people, ignoring the rain, converged on the palace and lined the seventeen-kilometre stretch of road leading out of the city to the royal graves at a clump of hills named Imogiri. As the sultan's draped coffin passed, borne on an ornate catafalque drawn by eight horses and tended by retainers in colourful court livery, a mass of people surged forward and rubbed pieces of their clothing against it, in an effort to obtain one last vestige of the old sultan's mystical protection. They called him 'Our King', and for a brief moment the spotlight was on the feudal past, in a country forged as a modern republic. For the funeral I was obliged to wear Javanese court dress – a batik sarong, *blangkon* and velvet slippers. I followed the cortège in a bus filled with other mourners. Perched in the front seat a close relative of the sultan's sat motionless for the entire three-hour ride. Meanwhile, the city filled with rumours of mystical happenings: the night before the funeral, clocks had stopped ticking and the cocks didn't crow before sunrise; one of two large banyan trees planted in the middle of the field adjacent to the palace disappeared (today a new, much smaller tree grows in its place). Many said the sultanate would end. Hamengku Buwono had no appointed heir, and it was whispered that the country's authoritarian president, Suharto, considered himself the rightful inheritor of the crown.

The Javanese culture is a confounding synthesis of waves of outside cultural influences that have washed over the island of Java's volcano-studded landscape. Today, the majority of Javanese are Muslims, but there is also a sizeable Roman Catholic community. Many also believe at the same time in a superstitious mysticism rooted in the earliest beliefs of this ancient people, who submitted to deities they believed controlled their volatile but fertile environment, along the stormy sea shore and atop active volcanoes. Binding them all is an attachment to the ancient Hindu tales of the Ramayana and Mahabharata, which have been told for countless generations using elaborate forms of dance and puppetry, supported and promoted by a long line of kings. This was not something modern progress and development could easily supplant.

In the event, Hamengku Buwono's son, Prince Mangkubumi, was crowned Hamengku Buwono X. I attended his coronation a year after his father's death, a splendid display of Javanese pomp and ceremony set to the semi-tonal clash of brass gamelan cymbals in the shade of the old palace pavilions. At one point, while conversing with the late sultan's brother, Puroboyo, who was dressed in an exquisite hand-painted batik sarong, the old man's underwear fell around his ankles. Without missing a beat, the elderly prince clung to a nearby guest and stepped casually out of them. An observant retainer appeared in order to remove them. I was reminded of the old portraits hanging in the palace museum, depicting sultans

Coronation of Sultan Hamengku Buwono X in Jogjakarta, 1989.

precariously perched on the arms of Dutch colonial governor generals. Although seemingly a pose of submission, there was nonetheless an air of dignity about these men that suggested they could not be taken for granted. Indeed, not only does the incumbent Hamengku Buwono serve as governor of the Jogjakarta special district, he has even considered making a run for president. Remarkably, for all their collusion with the Dutch, the Javanese princes survived the republican revolution and transition to independence.

The paradox of Javanese royalty can be baffling: on the one hand the modern monarch acts as governor of a city of a million people and advocates modern democratic government; on the other, he is a traditional ruler considered to possess supernatural powers by communing with Nyai Roro Kidul, an ancient goddess of the Southern Seas. As a recent taxi journey took me past a new convention centre in Jogjakarta, my driver remarked on the speed with which it had been built: just a few months. Oh, I replied; how was that? 'Why, the Sultan used his magic, of course,' he responded, a look of wonderment in his eyes.

Understanding the role of monarchs and princes, both in the past and the present, is one of the keys to understanding how power is wielded today in Southeast Asia. This sounds like a preposterous statement in the face of modern trends towards democratic government underpinned by popular sovereignty, rendering the whole idea of monarchy an anachronism. Yet my own experience of Southeast Asian power and politics suggests otherwise. I very much agree with the late British scholar Michael Liefer, who argued that while conventional wisdom suggested that monarchy has become an anomaly, 'in the case of Southeast Asia, this axiom is only valid up to a point'. The lingering memory and role of monarchy has had a marked influence on contemporary governance in the region, and not just from the monarchs themselves, where they are present. This culture of princely power and privilege assumed by governing elites, in turn fosters a paternalistic culture that breeds enduring impunity and corruption. As Roger Kershaw put it in his book on monarchy in Southeast Asia, the culture of monarchy is 'manipulated by elites (even by monarchs themselves), in order to pre-empt the destructive or destabilising effects of modernisation'.

Monarchy survived the colonial era because it was a useful means of reinforcing colonial control over society. The Dutch enlisted the Javanese princes and other local sultans to enforce the system of corvée labour; the English elevated and pampered the Malay Sultans so they could legitimise British rule. Then, when the colonial period ended, monarchy was again seen as a useful asset – primarily as a bulwark against communism. The enduring appeal of trappings of monarchy to modern elites demonstrates the failure of early nationalist leanings towards a more egalitarian socialist order. The power structures of Southeast Asia might have looked very different if, for example, Tan Malaka, Indonesia's charismatic communist leader, had not been murdered in 1949, or if Chin Peng, leader of the Malayan Communist Party, had not been ruthlessly suppressed with the aid of British troops in 1960. Instead, modern nation building, aided by determined Western efforts to prevent the spread of communism during the Cold War, promoted and reinvigorated traditional forms of princely rule.

As a result of this reliance on archaic models of power, Southeast Asia has struggled to balance the inexorable opening of government to democratically elected officials with an entrenched culture of leadership derived from the 'Devaraja' or god-king culture of the ancients. The distinctive style of this leadership draws on the anachronistic trappings of patronage and immunity, derived from pre-colonial patterns of princely rule. These vestiges of arcane princely power have paradoxically strengthened with the passing of an earlier generation of nationalist leaders imbued with more modern, often revolutionary notions of popular sovereignty. They have hindered the cause of freedom and, therefore, bear close scrutiny as a key to understanding the region's contemporary power dynamics.

Monarchy still thrives in five of the ten countries of Southeast Asia, blending traditions of kingship from the pre-colonial era with more modern forms of constitutional rule. Brunei, Thailand, Malaysia and Cambodia all have monarchs as titular heads of state. Indonesia uniquely has forms of monarchy thriving in a republican context at the regional level. These two traditions, one archaic and the other modern, coexist uneasily – all the more so in times of stress, whether because of succession or political instability. The end of the colonial era in Southeast Asia was marked by the adoption of modern forms of statehood modelled on the democracies of the departing colonial rulers. Thailand was never colonised, but its absolute monarchy initially modernised in response to pressure for bureaucratic efficiency at the start of the twentieth century, and then eventually democratic reform in the 1930s. A constitutional monarchy was established with limits on royal power. Old photographs of the last absolute king of Thailand, Chulalongkorn (1868–1910), show him on a visit to several European capitals wearing topcoat and tails, rubbing shoulders with his peers and studying modern forms of administration. He sent his numerous sons to British public schools. This exposure convinced the Thai king to reduce the power of the nobles, appoint an official heir, and introduce far-reaching bureaucratic reforms. To some extent, as we shall see, this modernising trend was reversed under King Bhumibol Adulyadej, who when he died in October 2016, was the longest-reigning monarch in the world.

To help underwrite their legitimacy in Malaya, the British found it convenient to patronise traditional local rulers. They observed that Malay society was deferential to legitimate princes, to whom people brought grievances and expected judgement, or their daughters and expected largesse. Eventually, the nine rulers of the Malay states constituting the core of the new Malaysia federation were enshrined as keepers of Malay tradition and defenders of Islam as the division of powers evolved. One of their number serves as the Malaysian king – or Yang di-Pertuan Agong – on a revolving basis. Cambodia's King Norodom Sihanouk, like Hamengku Buwono IX in central Java, was both traditional ruler and modern nationalist, leading his country to independence from France in 1953, before abdicating to go into politics. In much the same way, the Sultan of Jogjakarta assisted in the establishment of the Indonesian republic and at one stage may even have been considered a potential head of state. He served for a period as vice president and finance minister, and won the preservation of his realm as a special administrative area that his son and heir still governs. Someone who knew him well, a European, told me that Sihanouk was fond of saying: 'I was an absolute monarch reigning in the twentieth century!'

Their capacity to adapt and regenerate helped the monarchies of Southeast Asia not just survive but also sustain their power and influence. This wasn't simply the result of modernisation, which in the normal scheme of things would have resulted in their fading significance. The residual power of monarchy is in part explained by the continuity of its archaic sacred and cultural symbolism, which the monarchs themselves – and the elites around them – have perpetuated along with the patronage derived from their considerable wealth. In other words, a benefit derived from both the sacred and the temporal dimension of monarchy. What was the nature of this power, how did it come about, and how is it used today?

For almost all the ancient societies of Southeast Asia, the king was believed to harmonise the world of profane, human existence with the sacred cosmic order. Ancient forms of kingship in Southeast Asia draw on inclusive Buddhist traditions embodied by the Dharma, the religious and moral law governing individual conduct, combined with the more exclusive caste-driven distinctions of Hindu tradition. A twelfth-century inscription from a temple wall in Pagan, an early Buddhist state, has one early Burmese king declaring: 'Greed, hate, delusion, rooted all in self. Oh, may they die, whenever born in me. Won not by oppression, may my wealth remain.' Perhaps this is not quite as specific as the Magna Carta, which committed English nobles to an elementary social contract, but the Pagan inscription is in fact decades older. Hinduism, much like Christianity for pre-enlightenment European monarchs, provided justification for imposing legitimately centralised rule, deploying symbols of the Hindu gods Siva and Vishnu, thereby endowing the kings with supernatural powers. Note the built-in contradiction: as Buddhists, kings were meant to embody the fair and just ideals of the Dharma; yet they could only effectively rule and amass power if they held themselves above and apart from society and maintained strict Hindu caste cleavages.

This power–values paradox is seen most clearly in Thailand. King Bhumibol Adulyadej was born in 1927 in the United States, the son of an aristocratic medical doctor. He grew up and was educated in Switzerland, and spent seventy years on the throne espousing

Dharma values of providing justice and welfare for his people until his death in 2016. Although notionally a constitutional monarch, at the height of his reign King Bhumibol had acquired near-sacred status among his subjects – albeit underpinned by a frequently used *lèse majesté* law. The throne King Bhumibol inherited in 1946 was much weaker than it is today. The absolute monarchy ended after a coup led by democratic-reform-minded civilians and military officers in 1932. Some scholars argue they were more concerned about protecting Siam, as it was called, from colonial depredations than about liberating the people. What followed was a long period of military-backed strongman rule. When King Bhumibol ascended the throne in 1946, following the death of his elder brother Ananda Mahidol in mysterious circumstances (a gunshot to the head, deemed accidental), the new king hardly seemed a prospect for a strong monarch. Reed-thin and short-sighted, the nineteen-year-old had spent most of his life growing up in Switzerland on the shores of Lake Leman, where he enjoyed water sports and fast cars. Yet by the mid-1970s he had essentially reinvented the monarchy as the core of the Thai state and extended its influence across vast areas of society and development infrastructure.

For those worried about the march of communism in Indochina, in particular the United States, a strong monarch seemed the ideal means to keep totalitarian socialism at bay. For the strictly authoritarian Field Marshal Sarit Thanarat, who seized power in a military coup in 1957, the monarchy was a powerful ally in the war against communism and what he saw as inappropriate Western values of democracy. Over time, beginning under Sarit's tutelage, King Bhumibol exercised enormous influence on the body politic using an elite network of officials, soldiers and business people who believed that untrammelled democracy was a threat to the core values of their society. Using the king's name, they supported periodic conservative military coups that unseated uppity democratically elected governments, and placed the virtues of a conservative judiciary high above any principled constitution. In King Bhumibol's view, as my former *Far Eastern Economic Review* colleague Paul Handley writes in his superb biography of the king, constitutions were 'impermanent, mutable and not worth fighting over'.

That this staunchly reactionary stance brooked almost no effective opposition says much about the power of the monarchy as an institution, along with its battery of social and legal sanctions enforcing *lèse majesté* – a criminal offence in Thailand that carries a lengthy prison sentence. The impact on Thai society has been profound, a mixture of genuine respect and also obedience. The majority of Thais stand still in public places when the clock chimes eight in the morning, as the royal anthem resounds across the nation's public address systems. They do so again at six in the evening. In addressing royalty, Thais are obliged to use an elaborate version of the personal pronoun 'I' that translates into 'I who am but dust under your feet', and in the presence of the king or queen, and their children, Thais are required to prostrate themselves. Oddly, and many of my Thai friends say auspiciously, I observed King Bhumibol officiate at a Buddhist Lent ceremony on my very first day in Bangkok back in 1979. I recall being asked by a gruff royal household officer to crouch down so low on the marble steps of the emerald Buddha temple (where I was coincidentally visiting as a tourist) that my knees ached for hours afterwards.

The Thai monarchy's imposing edifice rests on the Royal Household Bureau, an elaborate bureaucracy which is nominally controlled by the government, but in reality comprised of officials appointed by the monarch. This machinery is in turn partially funded by the Crown Property Bureau, with assets of at least $40 billion. Through revenue from land ownership and investments in key state enterprises, the bureau earns in excess of $300 million a year and is not obliged to pay tax on these earnings. In theory, these assets are available to the king to spend at his pleasure; in reality, the royal household has become an expensive, top-heavy crucible of patronage comprised of competing factions of retainers who derive undeclared benefits from royal favour. Members of the royal family not only enjoy the privileges and protocol of their position, but also varying degrees of protection under *lèse majesté* laws that impose lengthy jail sentences on those accused of criticising the king and his immediate family, making it – in effect – impossible to question anything about the institution of the monarchy in Thailand.

Around the palace there grew concentric circles of power and patronage, including the military, and in particular the elite regiments of the king and queen's guard. By the start of the twenty-first century, these palace guards officers dominated the army command structure, and carried out the military coups of both 2006 and 2014. An influential courtier told me: 'You have to understand that these officers grew up serving the king or queen, staying up all night during their soirées and literally sleeping at their door.' There is something absurd about the adulation: a stray dog adopted by King Bhumibol was revered as a national hero and became the subject of an animated movie; the crown prince's pet poodle was commissioned as an air force officer and dressed in uniform. When one evening at a diplomatic dinner hosted by then US ambassador Ralph Boyce the poodle, named Fu Fu, jumped up to the dining table and started eating from startled guests' plates, no one moved or thought to shoo the dog away. The scene, related by Boyce in an official cable later released on WikiLeaks, was reminiscent of Ryszard Kapuscinski surreal description of the court of Ethiopian Emperor Haile Selassie.

King Bhumibol's incomparable charisma and popularity was undergirded by his strong personal commitment to the development of Thailand and its people. He is credited with helping to develop advanced agricultural techniques to increase productivity, including irrigation, cloud seeding, fish and livestock breeding. In terms of scale and impact, these efforts may have been modest, but they nevertheless helped weave an image of the king as a generous benefactor and benevolent ruler. The king himself saw these efforts as beyond the symbolic. In his view, Thailand's survival rested on careful economic and environmental management of the realm. Later this was formally defined as his concept of a sufficiency economy and has become part of official development orthodoxy. Even if it is unclear exactly what this means today, King Bhumibol's own views were clear. 'Development must respect different regions' geographies and people's different ways of life,' he told a group of journalists in 1987. 'We cannot impose our ideas on the people. We can only suggest. We must go to meet them, find out what their needs are, and then fully explain to them what can be done.'

In his later years, crippled by strokes and a degenerative disease that inhibited his movement, King Bhumibol withdrew to a hospital room and seldom emerged. He used public addresses on the occasion of his birthday to advise his subjects on issues such as the rule of law and democracy. Some argue that his public endorsement of the use of the courts to underpin the rule of law emboldened the judges and paved the way for a number of rulings that affected the course of the country's political development in the past decade. Contemporary political conflict in Thailand is seen as pitting the courtly conservative establishment against a populist movement that draws on the charisma (and deep pockets) of a commoner. Former Prime Minister Thaksin Shinawatra's Pheu Thai Party (formerly called the 'Thai Love Thai' Party) is led in part by politicians formerly associated with left-wing movements that the palace establishment opposed and which were crushed by the army in the 1970s. As a result, the monarchy was dragged into the political conflict, resulting in a sharp increase in the number of *lèse majesté* cases. This was almost certainly less about the king himself, who was ill for the last seven years of his life, and more about conservative palace elite manoeuvring around the succession to preserve their power.

The end of King Bhumibol's long and successful reign, when it came on 13 October 2016, generated high anxiety in Thai society. Tens of thousands of people thronged the route to Bangkok's grand palace where the king's body lay in state at the start of a period of mourning. Wearing black or white, the traditional funerary colours, people quietly sobbed or looked on with tears in their eyes, some holding portraits of a monarch who was loved by all. The palace authorites reported that as many as 12 million Thais from all parts of the country thronged the palace grounds for the entire year before the royal cremation on 26 October 2017. This outpouring of grief was marred by a few ugly incidents in which those perceived not to be sufficiently aggrieved were victimised.

As he grew more infirm, King Bhumibol was seen less and less, appearing once a year to give an audience to senior officials where, speaking plainly in a halting voice, he exhorted people to abide by the rule of law and respect democracy. Thai politicians are bad at reconciling their own issues because they are used to relying on their king as an intermediary, even if his preference was for weak coalition governments populated by cautious conservatives. And although he is credited with taming the military after soldiers fired on student protesters in 1992, there were other instances before then and afterwards, when he endorsed military action against his people and supported military coups. Towards the end of King Bhumibol's life, speculation intensified about the succession. Crown Prince Maha Vajiralongkorn was first confirmed as heir to the throne in 1972. Following King Bhumibol's death, Vajiralongkorn reportedly ordered an initial delay in his proclamation as King Rama X, having requested a period in which he could mourn with the rest of the country. It is also possible that the court astronomers were searching for an auspicious date, or that a short symbolic gap in the line of succession was deemed prudent to avert a well-known prediction that the Chakri dynasty would only last nine reigns.

The new king, who came to the throne at the age of sixty-four, was faced with considerable challenges. Thais felt uncertain about the future without a much-loved king whose immense moral charisma meant that people relied on him to resolve their problems. There were those who hoped to see the monarchy weakened, in particular because of the way it was seen as supportive of the military's intervention in politics. The political upheaval of the past decade has thrown up new political forces in the north and northeast of the country that feel less bound to the centralising, unifying ideology of the throne. These feelings are magnified in the deep south of the country where a violent insurgency representing the Malay Muslim community seeks secession. King Bhumibol's departure therefore left Thailand without a strong source of unifying leadership at a critical juncture for the country. Neither the military, wielding power through a council of generals and a rubber-stamp legislature stacked with military officers, nor the fractured political elite, could hope to provide popular or legitimate leadership. No one expected the new monarch to be in a position to manage these fissures on his accession. Perhaps that is a good thing. In fact, there were those in conservative circles who wished to see the monarchy retreat from its central role in Thai society – to help Thais resolve problems for themselves. As one senior politician and statesman put it: 'King Bhumibol's legacy should be that Thai people can now govern themselves in a truly democratic manner.'

*

It hasn't just been monarchs themselves who have wielded effective princely power. Former President Suharto of Indonesia (in power from 1966–98) was a towering figure in the modern history of his country who benefited from the symbolism of the ideal ruler providing for his people. Although not actually a king, many Indonesians treated him as one. Suharto was born in 1921 in Central Java, the (possibly illegitimate) son of a minor irrigation official. He was given a basic education in the home of a relative, where he was raised as a foster child. His rise to power is still somewhat shrouded in mystery and puzzles many who knew him and the milieu in which he developed. He was no charismatic orator like Sukarno, the modernist leader of the Indonesian revolution whom he effectively deposed after a silent coup. Suharto lacked a formal education and the intellectual capacity to dominate his fellow veterans of the independence struggle, with their Dutch-educated backgrounds and socialist ideals. Although many rumours circulated of his aristocratic lineage, he was born far from the palace in Jogjakarta – though he did marry into minor nobility from the neighbouring royal city of Solo. Yet this orphaned son was cunning and ruthless. Suharto seized an opportunity to assume power in the midst of a confused

President Suharto of Indonesia in 1989, at the height of his power.

and messy purge of army ranks that left six senior generals dead at the end of September 1965. He held on to power by building on the lucrative business partnerships between ethnic Chinese entrepreneurs and senior army officers from which the Indonesian army's quartermastering needs were derived, thus benefiting from the dependent forms of patronage by which the overseas Chinese immigrants traditionally survived.

Suharto also honed and exploited native Javanese methods of managing power and patronage, the details of which were distilled and compiled in a short book by his daughter, Siti Rukamana. Amongst other things, Suharto's homespun Javanese wisdom justified the use of mendacity and subterfuge to hold on to power. He was a man of few words, aiming perhaps to live up to the Javanese tradition that a wise king uses his words carefully because he can't take them back. Above all, Suharto was a master of ensuring that everything depended on him – even development aid down to the village level. In this sense, he more closely resembled the classical Hindu–Buddhist ruler than even King Bhumibol of Thailand, who perhaps because of his Western upbringing and education avoided direct political intervention to uphold the notion of his role as a constitutional monarch.

The Javanese kings derived their legitimacy from concepts of power couched in the realm of the supernatural; birth or selection was a secondary element. The divine inspiration, charisma or aura (*wahyu*), combined with supernatural power (*sekti*) that radiated out from the royal palace to cover the realm. This power diminished over distance, and was transitory in nature – so should the king's policies fall short, or some misfortune befall the realm, the king could be considered to have lost his *wahyu*. The late Indonesian scholar of Javanese history Ong Hok Ham loved to point out that Javanese kingship was unstable. The primary basis for succession of power lay not in hereditary right but rather a reincarnated spiritual phenomenon. Royal power was absolute but also fluid and susceptible to rivalries both from within the royal family and the layers of royal bureaucracy and administration without.

This concept of power as a fluid, finite resource perhaps helps explain why Suharto expended so much energy on demonstrating his *wahyu* by providing effective development and also ensuring that his potential rivals were kept off balance. Echoing the Javanese kings of old, Suharto expended considerable resources in demonstrating support for the farmers. He built a huge ranch on the outskirts of Jakarta to develop cattle-breeding techniques. And just as King Bhumibol was frequently photographed with map or plan in hand, directing officials in the execution of hydraulic works and reforestation, so too did Suharto regularly appear on television speaking with farmers about rice cultivation and cattle rearing, wearing a straw farmer's hat and waving sheaves of rice. Here was a president who liked nothing better than to tell farmers what to do – he would become animated when talking about new techniques for bovine artificial insemination, and on the national broadcasts one could see the look of adulation on the faces of poor farmers ushered before him to hear these pearls of agronomic wisdom. Suharto was born the son of an irrigation official but was never a farmer.

Suharto was conscious of the utility of traditional Javanese manifestations of power to enhance his legitimacy. One of the most revered legends of Javanese kingship revolves around King Jayabaya (or Joyoboyo), who ruled the East Javanese Kingdom of Kediri in the mid-twelfth century. He was considered the archetypal wise king or '*ratu adil*', who reunited the kingdom and heralded an era of prosperity. Like the *ratu adil*, Suharto carefully cultivated an image of humility to mask his monopoly on power and his family's fabulous wealth. He wore a drab safari suit and kept punctual office hours. He shunned the grand stuccoed presidential palace for a plain, single-storey house located in a central Jakarta suburb and filled with cheap cut-glass kitsch. He had no weakness for fast cars or women, and preferred to go fishing. However, unlike King Joyoboyo, Suharto did not abdicate and retire to meditate.

Both President Suharto and King Bhumibol used symbols of agrarian sufficiency – sowing rice or ploughing fields – to embellish their image as ideal rulers and demonstrate their apparent selflessness. One of Suharto's proudest moments was when he received a Food and Agriculture Organisation Award from the United Nations in 1985, celebrating Indonesia's achievement of rice self-sufficiency.

King Bhumibol preferred to highlight his achievements more modestly – by sponsoring his own international award for scientific achievements, known as the Mahidol Awards – yet local hagiography attributes novel forms of cloud seeding and hydraulic management to the king. Echoing old King Ramkhamhaeng from the Sukhothai era, King Bhumibol literally made sure there was rice in the fields and fish in the water.

While it could also be said that both men were conscious of the need in a modern context to reinforce their legitimacy through good works, the societies they presided over were susceptible to the traditional symbolism of leadership, especially at the elite level, because it served their own selfish ends of power. So, these men – two of Southeast Asia's longest-serving rulers in the modern period – consciously deployed Hindu–Buddhist ideals of the just, beneficent ruler. These largely symbolic strategies helped them concentrate immense power by making it hard for rivals to question their legitimacy. As mentioned previously, Suharto ensured that he was the source of village-level funds for building schools and clinics, roads and bridges – amounting to almost 20 per cent of state developments funds; the funds came directly from him via a special presidential-instruction mechanism that had an Orwellian ring to it: *Inpres*. As the country's 'father of development', he was never going to allow anyone else to take credit for Indonesia's progress.

Yet, in both cases, these archaic paternalistic approaches to rule hobbled the country's political progress. Suharto's micromanagement and the centralisation of decision-making stunted Indonesia's institutional and bureaucratic development and left it wholly unprepared for democracy. His three sons and three daughters were given carte blanche to build corporate empires covering lucrative areas of the economy, which in turn foreign investors were required to do business with. Under licensing and monopolistic practices fashioned by the army to fund itself after Dutch colonial rule, Suharto allocated to his family the enterprises in choice areas of economic growth and then ordered state-run banks to lend them money. He used an arcane foundation law, which had been enacted to provide a loophole for the independence movement to acquire funds, to stash away billions of dollars, and forced poorly paid civil servants to make donations.

Whether to bolster their positions or to ensure enrichment, both President Suharto and King Bhumibol presided over societies that developed profoundly unequal, unusually rich and often repressive hierarchies of officialdom in support of their peerless leadership. As much as critics point to both men as obstacles to effective popular sovereignty, it is important to highlight the role of their bagmen and gatekeepers whose extraordinary power made them chiefly responsible for perpetuating chronic corruption and for holding up reform. This trend drew nourishment from another of the historical roots of leadership and power in the region: patronage and the management of followers by petty princes.

Southeast Asian states evolved from agrarian, village-based societies where the ideals of the Dharma sat well with the need for transparency and equality when it came to working the land and sharing resources. But as society evolved, and populations multiplied in lowland areas where irrigated rice cultivation flourished, strong, successful leadership was that which harnessed the most effective strategies for centralising power and maintaining social partition. One of the earliest detailed records of state organisation in Thailand, for example, is the thirteenth-century *Mangraisat*, describing the laws and conventions of the northern Thai state of Chiang Mai. Chiang Mai at that time would have been a small town of a few thousand people situated along the Ping River, which irrigated a long narrow valley of rice fields ringed by forbidding, forest-covered, spirit-inhabited hills. One of the central articles of the *Mangraisat* is the establishment of a hierarchy of officials:

> For every ten citizens let there be one *Nay Sip* (literally in charge of ten), and one foreman to act as an intermediary and make known the tasks assigned. For each five *Nay Sip* let there be one *Nay Ha-Sip* (in charge of fifty) and two foremen, one for the left side and one for the right side. For two *Nay Ha Sip*, let there be one *Nay Roy* (in charge of one hundred) . . .

And so on. Over this basic form of hierarchy, which allowed for the organisation of agricultural manpower, was laid a rich covering of

Hindu caste-based statecraft, developed by the Khmer kings from the ninth century, in what is now modern-day Cambodia. Thus was forged a tradition of courtly rule steeped in the Indic–Brahmanic traditions of caste privilege, which Thailand, as well as Cambodia in the earlier Angkor period of Khmer civilisation, adapted and turned into a complex hierarchy. The successful king was the one who controlled the most manpower. Possession and the efficient organisation of labour in these early princely states were far more valuable than land ownership. People enjoyed a surprising degree of mobility, and if a king or prince in one place treated his subjects badly, they could simply move to another. A king without subjects had no power at all. Little wonder then that the Malay word for wealth (*makmur*) is the same word used to denote an abundance of population.

In order for rulers to sustain and keep their subjects loyal, a means needed to be found to reward them. In return, people accepted the notion that rulers were of higher status, on account of their sacred position, and therefore those who worked in close proximity would be rewarded with rank and status. We have a very detailed account of Khmer civilisation and society handed down by the observant Chinese scholar Chou Ta Kuan, who travelled to the Khmer capital in the late thirteenth century. Chou describes a society differentiated in terms of how many slaves an individual possessed, with the king at the apex and to whom the most beautiful women in the land were sent to serve. He also includes a short description of Chinese merchants living in the region. In the pre-Mongol period, before much of China's external trade with the world came under strict control, the emerging kingdoms of Southeast Asia relied on Chinese merchants for the import of precious metals, in return for which they bartered rare woods, gems and other natural items considered luxuries in China. After the collapse of the Qing Dynasty, towards the end of the nineteenth century, the number of Chinese traders grew and they used royally endowed commercial privileges and tax farming to shore up competing factions at the court.

All this gave rise to one of the most characteristic features of social and political organisation in Southeast Asia: the strong role played by patronage in determining the size and composition of groups and factions, the basic unit of a political organisation based more on command over manpower rather than on possession of land and goods. Slavery was for the most part institutionalised, the prime source of slaves being prisoners of war. The victorious ruler wasn't interested in occupation of the defeated ruler's land and territory; the victor seized not just the defeated ruler's army but also the entire population to work as slaves. That's why even today there are communities of former Thai slaves in Myanmar, and Burmese slaves in Thailand with folk memories of their forced migration. No record has ever been found of the privation and suffering ordinary subjects experienced as their kings battled one another atop war elephants. From my research of historical communities in and around Chiang Mai in northern Thailand, I heard folk memories of groups of people carted about as booty and forcibly resettled. With this form of warfare, mass killings or massacres were rare, since manpower was the primary spoil of war.

For those fortunate to serve the princely ruler at court, much like Elizabethan England, title and status were easily won and lost at the whim of a divine ruler who could summarily dismiss or execute anyone deemed disloyal or dangerous. The notable observer of nineteenth-century Burmese society, Sir James George Scott, related a story about King Mindon Min, who, on hearing in 1874 that Gladstone had lost the premiership to Disraeli in the British parliamentary elections, reacted by saying he supposed poor Gladstone would be in prison. Much as then, power is regarded as an absolute attribute in contemporary Southeast Asian societies: you either have it, or you don't. And your life is worth far less if you don't. This vestigial concept of power as a physical attribute, as opposed to something ephemeral or institutional, perhaps also helps explain why people are so reluctant to give up or transfer power, and why democratic rules are often flouted. In the modern context, it seems scarcely plausible that such notions continue to exist, but they do.

As easy as it is to denigrate the manner in which Hindu–Buddhist traditions of kingship have underpinned the modern management of power in Southeast Asia, these traditions have also helped achieve balance in situations where men with guns would otherwise rule the roost. King Bhumibol of Thailand may have been regarded as innately conservative as well as personally powerful and wealthy, but he was credited with interceding at critical moments in modern Thai history to mediate between warring military and civilian factions. His intercession in the first bout of student agitation that caused violence in 1973 and then again very publicly in 1992 was styled by foreign as well as domestic observers as the intervention of a wise king with only the interests of his people at heart – even though the marginalisation of radical elements that ensued was very much to the advantage of the conservative elite. At other times, such as the most recent bout of street violence and protest in 2010, Bhumibol maintained an astonishing silence, and the army was sent in, resulting in bloodshed. Suharto was himself an army general, but as his power and stature grew he marginalised the army as a source of power and placed key civilian technocrats in charge of the economy – to the point where the army began plotting against him in the late 1980s. Modern Myanmar, on the other hand, is a singularly interesting case of what happens when the monarchy disappears.

By far the most important fulcrum of Burmese history was the sudden and undignified removal of Thibaw Min, the last king of what was then called Burma after the fall of Mandalay to British

Prince Taw Phaya, last surviving grandson of King Thibaw of Burma, with his sister in 2017.

forces in 1885. Failure to restore the monarchy, something the British colonial rulers considered but casually rejected, created a cultural vacuum that arguably condemned Burmese society to its modern fate of perpetual military rule. 'Burma without a king,' observed Thant Myint-U in *The River of Lost Footsteps*, his elegantly written history of the country, 'would be a Burma entirely different from anything before, a break with the ideas and institutions that had underpinned society in the Irrawaddy valley since before medieval times.' Thant's rather personal and passionate account helps us understand that the roots of Burma's malaise lie in a wounded historical psyche. Burma after 1885, he writes, was adrift, 'suddenly pushed into the modern world without an anchor to the past, rummaging around for new inspirations, sustained by a more sour nationalist sentiment'. Thant, the grandson of former UN Secretary General U Thant, drives at the heart of modern Burmese: their fruitless search for missing pieces of history.

The old palace walls and wide moat still dominate Mandalay, haunted by fading memories of a once-revered leadership long ago trampled by the same foreigners who today champion Aung San Suu Kyi, daughter of the founder of the Burmese army, Bogyoke Aung San, who won the country independence. In fact, much of the palace was rebuilt in the 1990s. It was bombed by the Royal Air Force during the Japanese occupation – an act of utter perfidy in the eyes of the Burmese. Against this background, one day in 2014, I attended a talk in Mandalay about 'Old King Thibaw' at a literary festival organised by the Irish wife of the former British ambassador. There was Thibaw's grandson, Prince Taw Phaya, sitting quietly in the audience listening to Indian author Sudha Shah talk about her book, *The King in Exile*. The presence of the prince made it painfully sad to hear of the deposed king's reduced circumstances in Ratnagiri, southwest India, of the last few jewels he gave away as favours, of the poverty his descendants endure as auto-rickshaw drivers and mechanics in India. Asked at the end of the talk to say a few words, the old prince, then aged ninety, was speechless at first.

'You don't want to hear an old man's gibberings,' he said, just managing to hold back his emotions. For it was clear that old wounds had been opened by this story, and by the pictures of the once-splendid court and the scattering of its wealth. And then it came, something taken, never found: The Burma Ruby. Had someone slipped it into his pocket as the family were exiled? Is it the same stone that sits today in the British imperial crown?

'Yes, it's the same stone,' declared the old prince, rising to his feet excitedly and addressing the audience. 'A stone the size of a pigeon's egg!' (British officials deny this is the case – but that hasn't stopped a junior member of the old royal family, Soe Myint, from travelling to London to ask for the stone back.)

Modern Myanmar is often considered in isolation from other mainland Southeast Asian states such as Thailand and Cambodia, a legacy of the fact that the British ruled what was then called Burma as a part of British India. In fact, the traditions and cultures governing the organisation of these societies spring from the same root. The modern-day presidential palace in the newly created Myanmar capital of Naypyidaw – the name translates as 'abode of kings' – resembles the old royal palace at Mandalay, complete with a moat. The president receives dignitaries in something that resembles a throne room, replete with gold gilt trimmings, and the army parades in the shadow of giant statues of Burma's three most important kings.

Mainland Southeast Asian Buddhist societies are anchored in a blend of animistic and Buddhist beliefs layered and ordered by rituals of kingship derived from Brahmanical Hinduism. Neither element on its own provides quite enough social stability. Thailand at the end of the eighteenth century was disorientated following the sacking of their glorious capital of Ayudhya by the Burmese army in 1767. For decades the countryside was plagued with banditry as organised rice cultivation manned by corvée labour broke down and people preyed on one another to survive. These were dark, chaotic years, hardly remembered in Thai history because they were succeeded by the establishment of a new royal line, the current Chakri dynasty, which built a shiny new capital at Bangkok on the banks of the Chao Phraya River, restoring the old ritual and order of the kingdom, symbolically re-using bricks from the ruined former capital.

Fast-forward to 1990 and Cambodia, and the end of a long civil war; who knows what the final death toll was after the 1975–9 period of Khmer Rouge tyranny? Perhaps as many as two million people perished in the killing fields, as a self-styled peasant government moved to erase Cambodian history through its ill-conceived utopian policy of forcibly relocating everyone from towns and cities to the countryside. Here they would work the land, as illiterate Khmer Rouge cadres weeded out intellectuals and professionals, whom they executed. Significantly, and despite such a wrenching and bloody break with the past, there was little hesitation about restoring Cambodia's ancient Hindu–Buddhist monarchy when the resulting civil war was at long last settled. And like a talisman the monarchy, though lacking in power, helped repair and restore a centre of gravity to Cambodian culture, with its religious rituals and exquisite royal ballet somehow masking the inexplicable Khmer Rouge past but also, at least when King Norodom Sihanouk was on the throne, tempering to some extent the monopoly of power exercised by Prime Minister Hun Sen.

King Norodom Sihanouk, who ruled from the early period of Cambodian independence in the 1950s until his death in 2012, was a canny and charismatic figure; he used the monarchy at once to underpin modern nationalism and reinforce a submissive feudal mentality. His successor King Sihamouni is more interested in music and dancing; he presides over weak institutions with little power and by all accounts is completely beholden to Hun Sen. After almost four decades in power, Hun Sen, the son of an impoverished peasant smallholder, projects power much as the ancient Khmer kings at Angkor did: a vision of society cast in his name and dependent on his munificence. Over the past decade or more, Hun Sen has built four thousand schools that carry his name or that of his wife Bun Rany. Hun Sen, who began his career as a Khmer Rouge cadre, has also revived the practice of conferring noble titles, which can be obtained in return for contributing to the party that he controls. The size of his government – running to several hundred ministers and secretaries of state – speaks of the kind of retinue that ancient Khmer kings had at court. Instead of the security detail of a few dozen special police that leaders normally have in the region, Hun Sen has equipped a military force of over five thousand men with modern weaponry and labelled them the Prime Minister's Bodyguard Unit. This kind of power is unassailable by democratic means. In May 2016, Prime Minister Hun Sen ordered all Cambodians to refer to him as 'Glorious Supreme Prime Minister and Powerful Commander'.

Modern Myanmar has had no experience of the balance of bureaucratic and military power that lay at the heart of Southeast Asian princely statecraft. At one point in *River of Lost Footsteps* Thant Myint-U wonders: if King Thibaw had lived longer, would he have become king again after the British left? He goes on to relate several forgotten, half-hearted and ill-fated attempts by minor princes to restore some of the former Konbaung dynasty glory. Independence, when it finally came in 1948, was driven by young army officers imbued with strident Japanese martial values and by politicians fired up by socialism. It is also important to understand the profound impact of the emasculation of Burmese pride and culture. As Thant Myint-U points out: Burma was made an adjunct of British India, never a colony in its own right; Indian workers were brought in to fill all the coveted new jobs in the civil service. 'What had been urban and cosmopolitan in old Burma had vanished. And what was modern in the new Burma was alien.' It's hard to capture the prevailing patronising tone of British colonial officials from the period. One fragment I found in an Oxford library years ago, from a former British colonial official's personal papers, quotes a typical view from the 1920s: 'All this talk of promoting Burmans – how can it be done? Have you ever met a Burman fit to be a commissioner? As to having Burman ministers, why, just try to visualise it – can you see a Burman minister attending office and dealing with files, and being called "Sir"?'

All the same, unlike Thailand, with its unbroken tradition of bureaucracy serving the monarchy, or for that matter Malaysia, with its pampered but socially dominant Malay rulers, Myanmar without the monarchy was pretty much a ship at sea without a captain or cultural anchor. The result is a country still dominated by a 400,000-strong army (the fifteenth-largest in the world) and no figure or institution of comparable strength or reputation to balance or countermand its power. Unless of course Aung San Suu Kyi's eventual ascendancy to the presidency changes the equation. For all the suffering she endured in her struggle to win democratic elections in Myanmar, there are those concerned about her own leadership style now that she has won a majority in parliament and secured an effective state counselor's position in lieu of the presidency. The impulse to rely on a single focus of power was evident. On a visit to Myanmar six months after she was elected, almost every minister or official I met was already deferring to her decisions. 'All matters will be decided by the State Counsellor,' one deputy minister told me repeatedly. Aung San Suu Kyi is considered an imperious leader who brooks no dissent or opposition within her party. One photograph posted on social media showed her party officials kneeling before her while she sat on a chair. Perhaps she will have the courage to ask the British government, which claims a close relationship with the former Oxford student, for the return of King Thibaw's ruby.

Aung San Suu Kyi is the most prominent of only a handful of women who have risen to high office in modern Southeast Asia, offering a distinct counterpoint to the male-dominated ruling tradition of the region. Others include Corazon 'Cory' Aquino, who was propelled to the Philippine presidency on a wave of popular protest after the murder of her husband, leading opposition figure Benigno Aquino, in 1983. Megawati Sukarnoputri led the first organised political opposition to Suharto in the early 1990s under the banner of the Indonesian Democratic Party (PDI). The daughter of founding President Sukarno, Megawati was selected as the second reform era president in 2001. Gloria Macapagal Arroyo served as president of the Philippines from 2001 to 2010, while Yingluck Shinawatra was elected prime minister of Thailand in 2011. What these women have in common is links to leading nationalist figures, either as daughters or wives – in Yingluck's case, younger sister. Political leadership is very much a male-dominated field in Southeast Asia. Women have traditionally wielded extensive influence behind the scenes. Thrust into leadership roles, however, they are formidable opponents and their influence is if anything stronger. Aung San Suu Kyi's two-decade-long struggle for freedom, including fifteen years of house arrest, made her an unbeatable opponent to the powerful military establishment after her release in 2010. Aquino's presidency was buffeted by the threat of military takeover in the mid-1980s, but when she died in 2009, the emotional impact on the nation was so profound that her rather ineffectual son rode to power as president on the sympathy vote. Megawati still wields considerable influence in Indonesian politics because the incumbent President Joko Widodo was elected under the banner of her Democratic Party of Struggle. In the coming years it will be interesting to watch the political career of Nurul Izzah Anwar, the daughter of the jailed former Malaysian deputy prime minister, who has inherited something of her father's gift for oratory and personal charisma. But as she herself has admitted; it is hard to craft a distinctive leadership platform as a woman when you are seen as representing a powerful political dynasty.

Today, Southeast Asia's remaining monarchs are regarded by some scholars and critics as anachronistic barriers to progressive change. A rich literature of criticism of Thailand's monarchy with its archaic demands on unquestioned adulation, the strict legal sanction imposed on resisters, and the cover it provides repressive conservative forces in the country, thrives outside of Thailand. Critical posts on social media have earned the unsuspecting jail time at home under a broad computer crimes act; and exile abroad. But the case of Malaysia presents monarchy in a somewhat different light. As in Thailand, the nine reigning Malay rulers (one for each of the Malay states) are regarded as the pinnacle of the establishment – in this case, majority Malay society. This imbues them with the role of arbiter in times of stress and conflict. In matters of religion, in the face of the manipulation of Islamic dogma, Malay rulers can be a force for moderation. Constitutionally, they are above politics but play a limited role through the Conference of Rulers. The main function of this body is to elect the king once every five years, but it also notionally has a role in safeguarding the constitution when it comes to Malay rights and privileges. In the past, there were rumblings in ruler circles about matters such as the imposition of Islamic 'Hudud' criminal law, or the degree to which the government limited freedoms. As political tensions rose over a financial scandal that appeared to implicate Prime Minister Najib Razak in 2015, the rulers stepped up their muted expressions of concern about unity and stability. At the Conference of Rulers in mid-2015 they called for measures to safeguard moderation, while the well-regarded and popular Sultan of Perak, Nazrin Shah, spoke out about the need to foster a culture of tolerance in Islam and respect differences of opinion for the sake of unity. These recent interventions by some rulers took many by surprise because they called into question whether the Malay rulers could stay above politics in times of crisis.

In August 2015, Sultan Ibrahim Ibni Almarhum Sultan Iskandar of Johor made a public statement advising the prime minister to pay more attention to the value of the currency, which had at that point plumbed eighteen-year lows in value. In what could be taken as a strong rebuke infringing on political issues, the sultan said: 'I would also like to remind representatives elected by the people to shoulder public responsibilities entrusted to them, and to set aside personal interests.' The young crown prince of Johor, Tunku Ismail Sultan Ibrahim, has more boldly used social media to express concerns. And as tens of thousands of people gathered in downtown Kuala Lumpur to protest against the government at the end of August, banners appeared quoting the Sultan of Johor's speech. Ironically, the colour yellow chosen by the Bersih protest movement – for clean and fair elections – is the traditional colour of Malay royalty. In a recent interview, the Johor Sultan made no bones about his royal prerogatives when it came to politics:

> I am not a puppet in Johor. I have the right to call my *mentri besar* [chief minister] to *tegur* [advise] him at any time and others in my government as well. I am the one who appoints the state government. I have always put my *rakyat*'s [people's] interest first.

In both Thailand and Malaysia, protracted political uncertainty and instability have dragged the monarchy into politics primarily because it remains an institution of considerable power and influence despite constitutional limitations. The effect, however, is double-edged: it allows people in situations where freedom of expression is limited to have their grievances aired, as in the case of Malaysia; but, as the case of Thailand shows, the power of patronage and legal sanction protecting the throne can also act as a considerable obstacle to free speech. In August 2015, a Thai man was jailed for thirty years for allegedly insulting the monarchy on Facebook. In a sign that little was about to change in terms of the primacy of royal power under the new reign, one of the first orders issued by the new king Rama X early in 2017 was for an amendment to the constitution with regard to the power to appoint a regent. The fact that this and other changes asked for will reinforce the power of the monarchy suggests that the new king fully intended to reign, rendering both politicians and the army dependent on his patronage and support.

It is clear that monarchy remains a fundamental player in the Southeast Asian political spectrum. As arcane and outmoded as monarchy may seem to those advocating a more egalitarian order, power relationships across the region are either rooted in or derived from the indigenous traditions of leadership from an era when kings and princes were the focal point of power and authority. Many people still welcome the monarchy's role as arbiter in times of political stress or crisis – such as when the current king of Cambodia sought, unsuccessfully as it turned out, to broker an agreement between the government led by Prime Minister Hun Sen and the opposition in 2014. Malaysians in the second decade of the twenty-first century are heartened by the strong defence of the values of tolerance and pluralism struck by their traditional rulers, set against the racial po-larisation and religious hatred provoked by their elected politicians. Yet because power and patronage flow from the apex of society in Southeast Asia, monarchs, no matter how virtuous or above politics they appear to be, can do little to deter the manipulation of their authority without damaging their own prospects for survival.

What does this say about ordinary people and their relationship with rulers, both traditional and modern? Ahead of the 2014 presiden-tial elections in Indonesia, I engaged a group of voters underneath the shade of an elderly ficus tree by the palace gates in Jogjakarta. One of the voters, Mas Tiarno, a driver of one of the city's myriad trishaws, expounded on who he thought would win. 'Everyone here in Central Java will vote for Jokowi,' he said confidently, referring to Joko Widodo, the popular governor of Jakarta (who was in fact successful). Tiarno went on to give the usual reasons: Jokowi, the man of the people, the son of the soil, clean and professional. 'When Jokowi came to Jogjakarta the other day he rode around in a horse and cart! Isn't that something?' But for Tiarno the clincher was that Jokowi had held a very special meeting with the Sultan. 'In there,' he said, nodding his head discreetly in the direction of the palace gates behind him. 'Four eyes only, and for two hours,' he said, his eyes growing wide. 'Normal people only get to see Sri Sultan for about an hour, and never in there.' The spiritual reference was implicit, for the sultan normally communes with Nyai Roro Kidul in special places, the inner sanctum of the palace being one of them. For those sceptical of the potency of Javanese culture and tradition in Indonesian politics, Tiarno was quick to point out that after the incumbent President Susilo Bambang Yudhoyono, himself a central Javanese, had floated the idea of eliminating the sultan's role as governor, there was uproar in the city and the president's own Democrat Party was defeated in local elections.

All this is not to say that people are willing to blindly accept the authority of their rulers. There were many examples in the pre-colonial chronicles of princely rulers who lost the support of their people if their rule was inept or unjust. Nor do ordinary people in the region consider the realm of power and privilege exclusive. As I will show in the next chapter, the callous and selfish behaviour of privileged elites is often the source of violent conflict in the region.

CHAPTER FOUR

ELEPHANTS AND LONG GRASS

'Large fish ate small ones.'

F. A. Swettenham (1907)

One day in 2013 I found myself sitting around a table in Bangkok with the relatives of people killed during the violent eruptions in the city between the red-shirt-wearing supporters of ousted Prime Minister Thaksin Shinawatra and the yellow-attired supporters of the conservative royalist opposition. Thailand's colour-coded protests over the past decade grew out of the failure to reconcile expressions of support for a popular elected government with fears in conservative circles that Thaksin was bent on overturning the social order and supplanting the monarchy with a popular dictatorship. The point of the meeting was to bring politicians from both sides of the divide, including a deputy prime minister, face to face with the victims of the violence.

Nicha, the widow of a senior army officer killed on 10 April 2010, stunned the government side by saying this was the first time in the three years since her husband's death that she had been allowed to meet with the government to demand an explanation. Cautiously at first, and then in an avalanche of emotion, the victims opened up and laid their concerns on the table. The government, which was at that time led by Thaksin's sister, Yingluck, was hard pressed to address them. Officials from the Interior Ministry, the Welfare Department and the prime minister's office were ill-prepared, and had nothing to offer, not even a word of condolence. At one point an

Interior Ministry official remarked glibly that details for obtaining compensation were available on a government website. Perhaps the most anguishing moment was when several of the relatives appealed to the government to prevent renewed violence. The sentiment was summed up by Phayao, the mother of a nurse shot dead while tending to victims inside a Buddhist temple, close to the protest site in 2010. She looked directly at the deputy prime minister, and said: 'It's like you're killing us for a second time. I don't want to swallow the blood of my daughter – I need to know the truth.'

This particular meeting was something of an epiphany for me. Despite decades of observing Southeast Asian politics at close proximity, I had always hoped that something good would emerge from the violence and mayhem that punctuates the region's history with alarming regularity, and which I have often found myself in the middle of. In the three decades I have lived in Southeast Asia, almost every year has been marked by the shadow of political violence. This has seen a succession of leaders seize power either by force or through rigged and dodgy elections. Since the mid-1980s there have been three military coups in Thailand, violent army crackdowns on popular protests in Myanmar and Cambodia, outbreaks of civil unrest and religious or ethnic violence in Indonesia, detentions and arrests of opposition politicians in Malaysia, legal action taken against critics of the government in Singapore, and two popular-protest movements interspersed by failed military coups in the Philippines. That's rather a lot of upheaval for a region of half a billion souls within a single generation.

In all this, the victims of political violence are often the least recognised. As a tentative democratic transition got under way in Myanmar after elections in 2015, there was little recognition of – much less accountability for – the thousands of students and other people who died during the May 1988 uprising that heralded thirty years of darkness in the country. In fact, some of the dissidents who believed the time was right to return and engage in open politics as the country's transition got under way found they were spurned by the very forces of freedom and democracy their comrades had died for. In neighbouring Thailand, it was only in 2014 that a memorial was finally erected in Bangkok to the fifty people killed in 1992, when

the army mowed down student demonstrators protesting against
a military government. How ironic in any case that the memorial
was raised in a country still enduring military rule. In Indonesia,
there is nothing to commemorate the half million or so people who
were killed in the anti-communist pogrom in the mid-1960s. Despite promises to consider a transitional justice process by successive
democratically elected governments over the past decade, it was left
to a people's tribunal convened in The Hague by members of Indonesian civil society in 2015 to generate a non-binding ruling by an
informal panel of judges that indeed genocide had been committed.
And by what standard of human dignity has the Myanmar government decided that 1.3 million Muslim inhabitants of the far western
Rakhine State cannot obtain citizenship and basic security?

You sometimes hear people blame the colonial legacy – problems
of unresolved or unwanted identity and integration that were the
result of colonial whims. Thailand, a country which escaped the
predations of colonial rule and the upheaval of a violent transition
to independence, nonetheless has a long history of political violence.
Student protests in 1973 and 1976 were ruthlessly suppressed. News
film of the October 1976 crackdown on students demonstrating at
Bangkok's Thammasat University shows soldiers and police casually
firing automatic weapons and bazookas into a crowded campus.
One of the students, Thongchai Winichakul, recalled many years
later how he cowered behind a stage and screamed 'unarmed, unarmed . . . don't shoot' to no avail. I have always wanted believe
there was a point to protest and resistance against military force,
which has so often played out on the streets of Southeast Asian
capitals – that some measure of social and political progress would
ensue. Yet on that day in 2013, as I sat watching, listening to Nicha
and Phayao, victims from both sides of the divide, crying across the
table from the dark-suited, blank-faced politicians nervously finger-
ing their expensive Swiss watches – the same political actors lionised
by democratic Western nations for standing up to the army-backed
conservative royalists – I realised: *Actually, no*. Too much of the
violence associated with politics in Southeast Asia stems from elite
power struggles of one sort or another – elephants trampling those
in their path.

These elites couldn't care less how much the masses suffer or die each time they quarrel among themselves. At the height of the clashes in central Bangkok between red-shirted supporters of the former Thai Prime Minister Thaksin Shinawatra and the unelected royalist government led by Abhisit Vejjajiva in 2010, I got on the phone with Prime Minister Abhisit to appeal for a ceasefire so that loss of life could be avoided. It was clear that, once the army moved in and crossed the bamboo and old rubber-tyre barricades, blood would be spilt. On purely humanitarian grounds, I argued, a respite was justified. But all he could say at the end of his mobile phone was that it was too late. His voice sounded strained, but detached. Meanwhile, sitting comfortably in exile, Thaksin was also reluctant to be drawn into a deal. Brinkmanship was the order of the day. The next day, as I watched the armoured troop carriers roll over the barricades, it hit me: perhaps there is no struggle for the greater good, only a scramble by a few to keep their positions and stay in power by any means possible. There is something egregiously callous about the casual disregard competing political actors appear to have for the deaths they leave in their trail. It was the same in Indonesia, even as a democratic transition got under way. In November 1998, after Suharto's fall, I watched soldiers shooting at students registering their disappointment with early reforms of the purportedly post-authoritarian era. I knew that some of the leading reformist parliamentarians had gathered at a nearby hotel, so I left the gruesome scene and rushed over. 'They're shooting at students,' I railed in front of a group of politicians sipping coffee in the lounge. 'Can't you go and do something?' The thought hadn't occurred to them.

Even during periods of relative calm, there is little ordinary citizens can do to protect themselves from the power of the state. What is it like to have one of your close relatives simply disappear? How do you live with the possibility that one of your loved ones has met a sudden, violent end, without knowing where, or when or how, and with no legal recourse to find out? If you want to know, ask the families of Sombath Somphone, Somchai Neelapaijit, or Por Cha Lee Rakchongcharoen, three citizens of Laos and Thailand who were trying in a modest way to make a difference by campaigning for their rights or the rights of others. In the case of Sombath, it was sustainable development – for which he was awarded a prestigious Magsaysay Prize from the Philippines; Somchai was a human-rights lawyer struggling to protect detainees in the conflict-plagued deep south of Thailand; Por Cha Lee, also known as 'Billy', was an environmental activist working along the Thai–Burma border. These are just three of the thousands of people over the past thirty years who have vanished – presumably murdered – in Southeast Asia, after they angered the authorities in the course of their work. According to Protection International, an NGO monitoring human rights, something like fifty land- and environmental-rights activists have been killed in Thailand alone in the past decade.

Across Southeast Asia, ordinary citizens of no importance or status have given up their lives struggling for justice and freedom. Their families have no recourse to justice, the victims often just bundled away in the dark and murdered in cold blood, their bodies disposed of like rubbish. One of the more frequently used metaphors in Southeast Asia is that when elephants fight, stay out of the long grass – an apt reference to the manner in which political elites clash and leave suffering and tragedy in their wake. Sadly, those who get trampled are the ordinary, nameless people, like the victims of political violence in Thailand, or the countless millions who lost parents, brothers, sisters, friends and other relatives in the senseless orgy of anti-communist purges across Java and Bali in the mid-1960s. Often these people have been aroused to protest by shallow, empty and rhetorical promises of a better future. They matter because they stand up and refuse to allow tyranny and impunity to prevail. Almost always, their hopes are dashed, beaten to a bloody pulp and left by the side of a road somewhere with no hope of justice for the victims: a tragic mandala of perpetual violence. And always, there is wishful thinking that after the death and destruction is tallied and the guns are laid down, lessons will have been learned and peace will prevail. Nothing could be further from the truth. Politics is a nasty, often brutal business in Southeast Asia, a key driver of conflict.

Politics everywhere is arguably the pursuit of power by those with narrow interests; Southeast Asia's chronic political uncertainty and unrest stems from the region's perpetually unsuccessful struggle for genuine popular sovereignty. In the three decades I have covered political developments in the region, the economies have grown, education and other social indicators have vastly improved, and cities like Bangkok, Singapore and Kuala Lumpur have become among the most globally connected, modern and sophisticated places in the world. Yet beneath these sleek metropolitan glass-and-steel carapaces lurks an enduring and seething underbelly of unmet popular aspiration suppressed by the effective concentration of power in the hands of a privileged few. The more people have prospered and advanced, the more they comprehend how badly their leaders serve them. Where, for example, corruption and the abuse of power was once rampant behind a veil of secrecy and ignorance, today a small online UK-based news site has helped to uncover the largest corruption scandal Malaysia has ever confronted, with allegations that Prime Minister Najib Tun Razak channelled almost $700 million, he claims from an anonymous donor, into his personal bank account. He denies any wrongdoing.

Such seemingly rampantly selfish, rent-seeking behaviour by those in power – and the frustration and tension it generates – has been a constant companion on my journey through Southeast Asia. It dominates my interactions with people, it is a thread common to all the relationships I have developed, and it is the root cause of the spectacular upheavals I have witnessed. There isn't a country I know in Southeast Asia where the struggle for freedom and justice has been conclusively won, where the journey to meet the goals of national aspiration and identity has run its course. In this chapter I will try to unravel the complexities of the socio-cultural and historical context that presents challenges to freedom, kills so many of its advocates, and which prevents lasting peace and genuine democracy from flourishing.

For historical reasons already touched upon in the preceding chapter, the politics of Southeast Asia is characterised by the baffling interplay of factions and circles of individuals. The American ethnologist Lucien Mason Hanks, who studied political behaviour in Burma, first observed this as a phenomenon in the 1960s. All human populations tend to divide into groups based on factors

such as age, class and experience. But in Southeast Asia the effect
is attenuated by what the pioneering English scholar of the region
O. W. Wolters calls 'a cultural emphasis on person and achievement, rather than on group and hereditary status'. This may seem
surprising in the face of modern Western perceptions of Asian societies as deficient when it comes to respect for individual rights and
achievements, but in the West norms and institutions have developed that impose reasonable constraints on individual behaviour. In
the Southeast Asian context, this is not so. The emphasis instead is
on the management of groups centred on men of achievement and
the power derived from personal status rather than caste, lineage,
or indeed any kind of defined professional boundaries. This means
two things: first, that the formal institutions governing political
activity, be they parties or parliaments, cabinets or departments,
don't adhere to operating principles or overarching goals based on
abstract ideals for the common good. The people in them tend
not to observe rules or regulations unless these serve their own
personal interests, thus creating an environment where corruption
and nepotism thrives. Second, patronage trumps meritocracy. To
get ahead, a person serves the leader of the faction or circle they
belong to, not the wider interests of the state or the people. This
uniquely person-centric pattern of political behaviour tends to
militate against placing faith in modern institutions and reinforces traditional concepts of power already elaborated on in the
previous chapter. These being relatively static, narrow-based and
non-inclusive, power-holders seek to concentrate and perpetuate
their power, not transfer it, or modify it based on feedback or demands
from below.

This points to one of the fundamental weaknesses of governance
in Southeast Asia, which is the lack of importance attached to institutions. Power is wielded by personalities primarily for their own
material benefit, rather than a greater good. Anyone who tries to
challenge those in power is deemed illegitimate and their ill treatment can thus be justified in terms of treachery. The challengers
cry foul, citing universal norms and values of freedom, justice and
human rights. Then, once the tables are turned, these same people
forget all about the principles they once embraced, and become

equally repressive. This instils in the general population either fear or a lack of respect for power holders, who tend to be perceived as corrupt and self-serving.

Remarkable as it may seem, this unchanging pattern of destructive competition for power has sustained significant advances in material prosperity for many Southeast Asians and brought the region far closer to developed world standards of income than many parts of Africa or the Middle East. Real GDP growth in the ten countries of Southeast Asia averaged 5.1 per cent in the first dozen years of the twenty-first century, compared with under 2 per cent for the United States and the United Kingdom in the same period. Yet despite high levels of growth, generating higher incomes and standards of living, politics in Southeast Asia rarely rises above selfish, narrowly based personal or family-centric interests, which in turn are pursued relentlessly, often through use of force or violence – which explains why in so many instances it is a military or police-backed elite that sits atop the pile, and why mass killings and disappearances happen with impunity. Why is this so different from other regions of the world? And why is it so important to understand?

The first thing to grasp is that much of the behaviour in Southeast Asia is governed by a personal, selfish impulse without any compulsion to take responsibility for one's actions. Unlike the totalitarian or democratic world of East Asia there is no overriding disciplinarian impulse in Southeast Asia injected by a Confucian sense of filial piety, or the conformity imposed by dynastic or lineage-based social systems. Conformity is a baffling aspect of Chinese political behaviour that in large part explains the enduring control exercised by the Chinese Communist Party, despite its inability to always deliver what people want or need. Factionalism is present in China, of course, but scholars have argued it is very much in tension with an overall impetus towards conformity. South Korea is an outwardly a free society where political behaviour is influenced by Confucian values of conformity and collective responsibility, so that when a Korean leader fails, he or she bows publicly in a show of humility and abject apology, an act that would be considered outlandish by Southeast Asian elites. When, for example, in 2015 the Indonesian speaker of parliament, Setya Novanto, was caught on tape demanding a 20 per cent stake from a major foreign mining company in return for supporting a renewal of its concession, instead of resigning in shame he brashly told the media he had only been joking. A political ally said the person who had made the recording, a state intelligence official, should be charged with slander instead. Novanto was eventually forced to resign as speaker, but in return his political party demanded power concessions from the government – turning Novanto's sins into a tradable commodity. Novanto subsequently won the leadership of the Golkar Party in 2016, but has since been arrested and charged with corruption over the alleged misuse of funds for an electronic identity card system. The sense of shame is absent when leadership is built on largesse to fuel patronage rather than ideals to mobilise genuine popular support. 'We are so accustomed to tolerating the extraordinary wealth of our leaders,' remarked Malaysian writer and activist Marina Mahathir, the daughter of Malaysia's most successful Prime Minister Mahathir Mohamad. 'That's because we consider they deserve these riches in return for looking after us.' As a member of the elite herself, this is perhaps as much a justification as an explanation.

What of moral compulsions or safeguards? Unlike in the West, there is no sense of guilt or shame in pursuing individual or family ambition in Southeast Asia. Buddhism, Christianity and Islam have infused the region for centuries, but the moral guidance offered by any faith has had little influence on the core values of the political culture. Rather, the dogma of the Holy Scriptures is used to enforce discipline and conformity at the lower levels of society, leaving the elite to enjoy a privileged place of exception. Across the region, elite political behaviour is untrammelled by collective cultural constraint and uninhibited by religious dogma. Almost anything goes.

One of the most egregious examples of this chronic degree of impunity in recent years was the 2009 massacre of 58, including 34 journalists and media workers, on a lonely stretch of road in the Maguindanao region of Mindanao in the southern Philippines. The victims were all part of a convoy of vehicles supporting the candidate in a small-town mayoral election to file his papers with the local election commission. The candidate, Deputy Mayor Esmael Mangudadatu, had a feeling that going up against the incumbent, Mayor

Andal Ampatuan, the son of the powerful governor of the province, might be risky because Ampatuan had threatened to chop him into pieces if he filed. So the deputy mayor asked the media to witness the filing, which family members in the convoy planned to carry out on his behalf, believing this would act as a deterrent. Before reaching the town, the convoy was stopped by about a hundred armed men, who proceeded to slaughter everyone. The methods used were unspeakably barbarous: women were raped before being shot in the genitals; a nearby mechanical excavator was used to hastily dig mass graves to deposit the victims, some of whom may have been alive. Afterwards, several members of the Ampatuan clan were arrested, but their trial has been hampered by lengthy procedural delays and not a single suspect has been convicted. Impunity is a feature of political behaviour we shall examine in more depth in a later chapter, but of relevance here is the callous disregard for the lives of those lost in the face of the larger elite interests – for the widely embraced assumption is that punishing the Ampatuans would have risked upsetting ties of patronage that Manila politicians need to win votes in Maguindanao.

The primacy of ties of patronage, and the protection this affords, stems from Southeast Asia's phenomenal reliance on interpersonal networks rather than on institutions with predictable or objective behavioural aspects governed by rules. The more individual assertion of patronage involves reciprocal obligations that evolved long ago into a hierarchically structured society to avoid friction and ensure the efficient management of manpower. In their traditional form, these obligations existed between influential, powerful people and their followers: a chief and his kinsmen, a noble and his retainers, all the way up to the level of kings and courtiers. In the modern context, these ancient bonds of patronage infuse all institutions, and supersede formal rules or laws that are meant to govern, but which in reality tend to be weak and poorly observed. So when people have problems they don't call the police, or rely on the rule of law; instead, they turn first to relationships with access to power. Very often the safest network of relationships is the family, which also explains why Southeast Asia is littered with political dynasties and afflicted with chronic nepotism: elected representatives install their

spouses and children to replace them; officials arrange the promotion of family members, and of course in business who would you
trust other than family? When the elected Governor of Sulu in the
southern Philippines reached the end of the limit of two terms in
office, he simply engineered the election of his son as governor and
appointed himself vice governor. Tragically, as old and well attested
as these concepts are – derived from academic studies of the region
going back to the 1950s – this doesn't undermine their saliency today.

Set against this bleak background, it has been my fate over a long
career to follow the meandering course of political development
in Southeast Asia. Although never a dull pursuit, and replete with
popular pageantry and larger-than-life figures, a certain monotony
blankets the perennial disappointment of leadership that ends up
betraying sweeping promises ostensibly based on idealistic principles and yet always serving the interests of a narrow, selfish elite.
This seems surprising, given the roots of modern Southeast Asian
nationalism in the Marxist or socialist liberal internationalism of the
late colonial era. Sukarno of Indonesia, Ho Chi Minh of Vietnam,
U Nu of Burma, and Sihanouk of Cambodia – all the great early nationalists – espoused visions of freedom and prosperity for all. This
produced what the New Zealand-born scholar Anthony Reid calls
the high modernism of the immediate post-colonial period: leaders
who cast their national struggles as popular social revolutions, mo-
bilising the masses, and ordering monumental public works.

At the start of my career as a journalist in Southeast Asia I met
some of these 'modern' idealists in the autumn of their lives. Men
like Slamet Bratanata, the Dutch-trained engineer in Jakarta, mentioned earlier, who was sacked as a minister because he refused to take
bribes, and others such as General A. H. Nasution and General T. B.
Simatupang, two of Indonesia's most highly regarded revolutionary
heroes, who believed it to be fundamentally wrong for the military
to monopolise political power – but right all the same for the army
to safeguard the values of the revolution. Although he died twenty
years before I arrived in Indonesia, many of my early contacts in
the country spoke admiringly of Sutan Sjahrir, the Dutch-educated
lawyer who was appointed the country's first prime minister in 1945.
Sjahrir was a socialist union leader trained at Amsterdam and later

Leiden University. On his return to Indonesia, he was appalled by the racism and prejudice that nativist nationalism had awakened in Indonesians and appealed for adherence to principles – socialist ideals, for the most part. In his ground-breaking pamphlet, *Our Struggle*, he wrote: 'A national revolution is only the result of a democratic revolution, and nationalism should be second to democracy.'

Later, in Malaysia, I met veteran journalist Veerasingam Kukathas, better known as K. Das, who was imbued with somewhat Fabian notions of nationalism. To this tall and lanky Tamil who chain-smoked Kent cigarettes, all races were equally Malaysian and joined together in a modern nationalist endeavour defined as a Malaysia for all Malaysians. They were members of the same clubs and drank the same whisky together, whatever their creed or race. People of Das's generation revered the country's founding father, Tunku Abdul Rahman, a Malay Muslim of princely heritage who famously drank and gambled all his life. The Tunku told Das in an interview that his main belief was in the pursuit of happiness, and that his duty as leader of the country was to make the people happy. (Not perhaps all that different from the traditional ideology of Southeast Asian princes, of which the Tunku was one, whose legitimacy depended less on the equality and more on the happiness of their subjects.) Before he died in 1990, sadly the year before I moved to Malaysia, the Tunku frequently expressed disdain for the manner in which the country was being turned into an incipient Islamic state. 'How could this be?' he asked incredulously. 'People, not states, must choose on their own to become Muslim . . . It is entirely up to the people to choose.'

From my conversations in this period, I could sense the idealism of the early nationalists that powered the establishment of nations and laid the foundations of modern, progressive society. Yet I felt very much like someone who arrived late at a theatre and missed the main act. Sadly, the ideals these early nationalist leaders had of popular sovereignty – and the 'modern' values associated with checks and balances on executive power – gave way under their successors to the hard-nosed quest for legitimacy and the concentration of power in a few hands. By the time I had settled in the stalls as a spectator, most of the advocates of the old, clubbable model of government by elected representatives who share power had died. Gone, too, were their ideas of benign democratic rule, drawing on concepts and ideas gleaned at distant Western universities or at the feet of patronising pipe-smoking, topi-wearing colonial administrators. And just as popular aspirations started to flower, as the economies of Southeast Asia prospered, the political culture regressed and found refuge in pre-colonial models of power. For me, the shift was noticeable in the late 1980s, a changing of the guard as the older generation of nationalist leaders with a 'modern' view of governance gave way to a new generation of leaders, less schooled in universal ideas of democratic government, human rights and free speech. In Jakarta today, a study has shown, someone with a bachelor's degree from a local university has the literacy equivalence of a Greek or a Dane who completed only lower secondary school. And so, unlike the generation that first embarked on nation building in the 1950s, the current generation of leaders is more parochial, equipped with knowledge acquired in poorly funded schools and universities.

As a result of this dysfunctional generational transition, leadership and elite composition is out of synch with the rise of popular aspiration fuelled by decades of material progress. This presents us with something of an orientalist dilemma – or trap. Are we to assume that it is only a matter of time before the old archaic structures crumble and give way to genuine popular sovereignty? This is the perennial refrain of brave human rights activists in the region: there is hope for the future. But the record of the past three decades is not encouraging; an endless cycle of violent repression, punctuated by forms of stable benign dictatorship that has kept people reasonably well off and provided for, but which has constrained mass action and bottled up popular frustration. In fact, the high modernism of the early independence era has been replaced with reassertions of traditional social and cultural behaviour, more rooted in the pre-colonial Hindu–Buddhist past.

It was a trend I observed in my earlier study of Southeast Asian politics in the mid-1990s. Struggling to understand how authoritarian leaders of the period like Suharto of Indonesia, Lee Kuan Yew of Singapore and Mahathir Mohamad of Malaysia managed to legitimise their strongman rule in ostensibly democratic settings,

I noted a tendency to revive traditional relationships between pre-colonial rulers and their people, wherein rights and duties were cast in more rigid, hierarchical frameworks involving obligations and unquestioning obedience. 'In the East the main object is to have a well-ordered society so that everybody can have maximum enjoyment of his freedoms,' Singapore's Lee Kuan Yew told the US-based *Foreign Affairs* magazine in 1994. 'This freedom can only exist in an ordered state and not in a natural state of contention and anarchy.' Rather than a natural trend towards more open, democratic government with accountability, I saw an adaptation of traditional models of divine kingship that involved strict, uncritical allegiance in return for largely symbolic and often self-enriching performance of good works. Instead of broadening, the power base grew narrower, which inevitably meant that challenges were countered and emasculated by force. At the time I realised I was flying in the face of a wave of global optimism unleashed after the fall of the Berlin Wall and the end of the Cold War – the 'End of History' moment described so eloquently, albeit prematurely, by Francis Fukuyama.

Much later, it seemed as if Southeast Asia woke up to the need for a set of values more congruent with the emerging global norms, based on universal human rights and standards of human security. In 2005, a group of eminent persons, many of them former leaders – and all of them incidentally men – huddled to draft a Charter for the Association of Southeast Asian Nations. Established in 1967 at the height of the Cold War, ASEAN was primarily designed as a security mechanism, allowing its five original member states a forum for consultation to forestall conflicts between them and also speak with a stronger voice to the outside world. For a while, ASEAN was pretty much an informal talk shop; its primary function was to balance the forces in Southeast Asia and address lingering suspicions, which was mostly done with polite jocularity on the golf course. But ASEAN soon acquired institutional legs, a secretariat in Jakarta, and a framework for addressing, with some reluctance, barriers to trade. The major powers pressed ASEAN to formalise security arrangements and a regional forum for discussing security was established. But the larger question remained: what kind of community and society does ASEAN, by now embracing all ten states of the region, represent? In the end, the Charter, which was agreed upon and endorsed at the leadership level in 2008, was heavy on protecting the integrity of states, defining principles of sovereignty and non-interference, and light on promoting individual rights. One of the purposes of the Charter, according to Article 1 paragraph 7, is to 'strengthen democracy, enhance good governance and the rule of law, and to promote and protect human rights and fundamental freedoms with due regard to the fundamental rights and responsibilities of the Member States of ASEAN'. The stress throughout is on the rights of Member States as opposed to individual citizens of the region, and a human rights body set up by the Charter has done nothing for the victims of violence and repression carried out in the name of the state.

Throughout my journey in Southeast Asia, I have been dogged by a troubling dilemma. While the destructive culture of absolute power and its perpetuation by selfish elites is a manifestation of archaic continuity, the people of Southeast Asia have clearly progressed in spite of their leaders and equipped themselves with the means to battle anachronistic limits on popular sovereignty. In material terms, per capita income provides the means to acquire property and spend on providing for a family, a sizeable middle class has evolved in large modern metropolitan centres that rival many cities of the developed world in the level of services and amenities they provide their citizens. In rural areas levels of literacy are high across the region, basic health services are provided, no one really starves – although pockets of relative deprivation persist. Set against this palpable extent of social and material progress, there is a kind of virtual reality inhabited by the state which considers that citizens are subject to the bridling imposition of centralised government, a system that decides what measure of truth is allowed into school curricula, or how much land can be owned, or what can be printed in a newspaper. The embrace of the internet and widespread use of social media has not yet managed to overcome these sanctions; a harsh computer crimes act in Thailand allows the police to arrest people for postings on Facebook or Twitter pages; in Malaysia the police have detained people for tweets and postings considered offensive, and in Indonesia a gay couple was arrested for posting that they loved each other on Facebook. Set against these constraints, it is indeed hard to imagine much progress in the democratic sphere. Indeed, the central challenge for the people of Southeast Asia is that it is hard to register their concerns: freedom of expression and popular sovereignty remain bridled and constrained.

But people are not fooled. They manage to live in a parallel world, one where they can, with hard work, escape the folly of their rulers and sometimes overcome the chronic inequality that plagues Southeast Asia. From the fruits of their enterprise they can watch their children transcend the drudgery of subsistence agriculture and make their way in the city. These same sons and daughters of poor farmers can either choose to earn their way to a better life with relatively little interference, or equipped with better education contribute to society in less material ways. Both economic and social enterprise are alive and well and insulated to a surprising degree from the suffocating blight of bad government and headline-grabbing intra-elite squabbling. Those who would impose an orientalist paradigm of perpetual subservience to archaic models of power and social order should be careful to avoid neglecting the vibrant and assertive nature of *civitas* in Southeast Asia. The problem is that the state has both the desire and the capacity to curb and push back these forces of progressive social and political change – and it can rely on spectacular levels of inequality of wealth and opportunity to constrict the circle of power. Although social media widely broadcasts calls for change and accountability, these demands fall like spent bullets on the tough armour that strong, overly centralised states have adapted to modern democratic norms. And there are critical areas of stress in society that threaten or hold back or undermine this social and economic progress, which generate suffering and provoke violence.

So why have these traditional models of power survived into the modern age? Why is the military holding the reins of power in Thailand, and to a significant extent in Myanmar? Why can't Malaysians use the courts or parliament to censure their leaders? Why do just 25 families in the Philippines own more of the country's wealth than 75 million Filipinos? Going back to the period before independence, one major factor was that indigenous models of power and polity suited the European colonialists, so they were preserved and adapted by colonial administrators. They found the legitimacy of established rulers and strict partition of society such as the distinction between commoners and nobles a useful, efficient means of governing. The success of the Dutch in Indonesia, wrote Pramoedya Ananta Toer, Indonesia's most important novelist, 'was their good working relationship with Java's powerful feudal lords'. The system was lucidly explained in the former Dutch official Eduard Douwes Dekker's famous novel *Max Havelaar*, published in 1860 under the pen name of Multatuli – Latin for 'I have suffered much'. The book describes the forced cultivation system, under which the Dutch compelled Javanese peasants to produce crops using the authority of the local Javanese aristocracy. These petty princes were given the title of 'Resident', and in most cases they reported to a younger, junior Dutch official who was unashamedly called the 'Assistant Resident'. 'All this results in a strange situation where the inferior really commands the superior,' wrote Dekker with a bluntness that shocked readers of the mid-nineteenth century. To force the peasant to grow tobacco, sugar or rice, as the Dutch demanded, 'a very simple policy sufficed. He obeys his chiefs; so it was only necessary to win over those chiefs, promising them part of the proceeds . . . and the scheme succeeded completely.' So did Dekker. His novel was a sensation and forced the Dutch to consider reforms of the cultivation system. What survived, and what made Pramoedya so angry after independence was won, is the persistent sense of obligation in Java and other places to a local chief or feudal lord. Much later in the 1970s, Syed Hussein Alatas, a Malaysian social scientist of Arab descent who was born in Indonesia under Dutch rule, wrote a ground-breaking study debunking colonial notions of the lazy native. He suggested that ingrained notions held by the colonial powers of poor levels of indigenous enterprise and efficiency were later transferred to post-colonial states who considered their own people poor and therefore in need of constant guidance from above.

The myth of the lazy native was rooted also in the fear of the angry, revolting peasant. The solution was simply to replace them. With the introduction of imported Indian and Chinese labour in colonial Burma and Malaya, local forms of discrimination and hierarchy also became a natural asset of effective administration. Being short of manpower, or unable to coax the ruling elite and its clients to be more productive, the colonialists resorted to importing armies of indentured labour. This in turn formed the basis of institutionalised racism and discrimination, which still exists. In colonial Burma as much as half the population of Rangoon was Indian by 1940. In Thailand and other Southeast Asian states from the mid-nineteenth century, the arrival of the steamship enabled tens of thousands of poor Cantonese, Hokkien and Hakka to flee the impoverished coastal margins of China each month and emigrate through the ports of Singapore and Bangkok. Singapore today remains a mainly ethnic Chinese city-state. By the early 1900s, half the city of Bangkok was of Chinese origin. In Malaysia, at independence in 1957, the number of immigrant Indians and Chinese in Malaya amounted to just under half the total population.

The influx of so many non-indigenous people, and the channelling of their labour into certain areas of employment such as estate workers and clerks, is perhaps one of the least-recognised social legacies of European colonial rule in Southeast Asia, giving rise to a form of rigidly defined cosmopolitanism termed pluralism. Pluralism today denotes a healthy form of diversity in which people of different origins, faiths or political views rub shoulders happily. The original definition of pluralism is derived from the work of a British colonial official, John Furnivall, who was stationed in Burma. There he observed members of different ethnic communities artificially thrown together by the colonial economy 'mixing but not combining' in the marketplaces of Rangoon and Jakarta. 'Each group holds by its own religion, its own culture and language, its own ideas and ways,' Furnivall wrote. 'As individuals they meet, but only in the marketplace in buying and selling. There is a plural society, with different sections of the community living side by side, within the same political unit.' The colonial powers used strict lines of racial division to control exploited populations, thus bequeathing the region disintegrated societies at the birth of modern nationhood.

Modern Malaysia and Myanmar remain prisoners of this ugly legacy of pluralism, which helps explain some of the contemporary social pathology and how it is manipulated. The Muslim Rohingya of Rakhine State in Myanmar constituted a sizeable minority of more than a million people, most of them poor fishermen and farmers. The majority population of this, one of the least developed states of Myanmar, which nestles up against the border with Bangladesh, is Buddhist. The Buddhist Rakhine refuse to recognise the Rohingya as indigenous, citing records of imported Bengali labour made by the British in the latter half of the nineteenth century. Even though the government today assures everyone that they are eligible for some form of citizenship, the insistence on a cumbersome process of verification leaves the Rohingya stateless. Deprived of rights and herded into squalid camps or forced to leave on rickety boats, it is not surprising that an armed resistance movement has now evolved among the Rohingya. Violence that erupted in northern Rakhine State in October 2016 led some intelligence agencies to infer that the Rohingya armed resistance had established links with Islamic terrorist organisations in Pakistan. An audacious attack on dozens of police posts in Northern Rakhine State almost a year later on 25 August 2017 by this fledgling Rohingya insurgency, calling itself the Arakan Rohingya Salvation Army, provoked a ferocious counter-attack by the Myanmar Army. By the end of November more than 650,000 Rohingya had fled in terror across the border into Bangladesh, establishing the largest refugee camp in the world. The plight of the Rohingya is a vivid example of how potent the colonial legacy of ethnic division and management remains today.

Different countries have managed this complex social pathology in different ways. In Thailand and Indonesia, there was intermarriage and a degree of cultural assimilation. But in Burma and Malaya, where British rule strongly reinforced the ethnic division of labour, it sowed the hardy, perennial seeds of racial prejudice and political conflict. Tens of thousands of Indians were denied citizenship and forced to leave Burma after independence in 1947; those who remain are subject to discrimination and referred to by the derogatory general term: '*Kalar*'.

In modern Malaysia the Indian community, predominantly of south Indian origin, is poor and politically weak; the ethnic Chinese, who constitute a third of the population, are well off but subject to discrimination. The foundation of Malaysia's discriminative

New Economic Policy, established in the 1970s to provide government financial support to Malays, was that the Chinese owned the lion's share of the country's wealth. Thus under the NEP lucrative contracts were awarded to Malays, all companies were required to appoint Malays to their boards and in senior executive positions. As a result, many Chinese have emigrated and a large number have settled in Singapore, where the Chinese majority prevails. Enduring social and political inequality promotes both exploitation and corruption, as wealthy Chinese businesses bribe the Malay-dominated political establishment to survive.

There is something paradoxical about the political development of Southeast Asia. For in spite of the archaic structures of power and patronage, and the overlay of colonial models of exploitation that reinforced them, the struggle for independence in all the states of Southeast Asia in the first decades of the twentieth century involved evocations of modernity, either in the spirit of Wilsonian principles of freedom and self-determination, or in the mould of the socialist revolutions that swept the West after the First World War. Perhaps the most important of all Southeast Asian writers to capture the first stirrings of modern nationalism was Pramoedya Ananta Toer in his quartet of novels: *This Earth of Mankind*. The four books, two of them narrated orally when Toer was a political prisoner on remote Buru Island in the mid-1960s, trace the political awakening of Minke, a young Javanese of aristocratic lineage. Minke, like the Pramoedya I knew in real life before he died in 2006, was drawn to socialist notions of equality. At the same time he was very much aware of the revival of Asian sensibilities, and the competition for primacy in the realm of political culture.

I first met Pramoedya Ananta Toer when he was restricted to a small house in a Jakarta suburb in the dying days of the Suharto regime that had first jailed him, then sent him into internal exile, and which finally allowed him to live under 'city arrest'. There was an air of disarming humility about the man. He liked to smoke clove cigarettes, as did I. Our first bonding was through the medium of tobacco; we established a relationship by lighting each other's cigarettes. Pram had an infectious laugh and a broad grin. His bony hands would grip your own and, because he was partially deaf, he enhanced his communication with gestures and expressions. His eyes shone brightly. I was luckier than some; the tone of my voice penetrated Pram's damaged eardrums and we could have long conversations. The economy with which he navigated the rich Indonesian language encouraged less fluent speakers like myself. Pram was not your typical Indonesian cultural grand master, or *budayawan*. He did not take airs or make sweeping generalisations about one issue or another. His observations were always couched in pithy epithets and grounded in the gritty perspective of the common man.

For his ability to represent the common Indonesian and give voice to the disappointment and despair of half a century of unrealised national aspiration in one of the largest nations on earth, Pramoedya was for me one of the towering literary figures of our age. Sadly, he died without the world or indeed many of his Indonesian compatriots fully recognising this. One of my favourite short stories by Pramoedya is titled *Gambir*, about two dirt-poor coolies living along the railway tracks outside Jakarta's Gambir station. There's nothing too profound here, no portentous symbolism or larger meaning. Yet Pramoedya artfully reveals the seamy underside of a nation that has never managed to uplift the wellbeing of millions who still live in poverty and despair. His lowly station porters sleep in the open, catching chills, forever dealing with runny noses and stomach ailments. They awake 'scratching the crust from their eyes, coughing, spewing out the phlegm that had risen in their throats again and from time to time scratching themselves from their asses to their necks'.

These *Tales from Djakarta* were written in the 1950s, but the same people can be seen along the streets of the city today. They suffer the same ailments and have little or no recourse to modern health facilities. In 2005 Jakarta tabloids carried the story of Supriono, a poor street sweeper found carrying his daughter's corpse at Gambir station. Like countless others living on the margins, Supriono's only real possession was the plywood trolley he had bought for five dollars, and which he used to collect plastic bottles and cardboard for recycling. When his three-year-old daughter Nur fell ill with diarrhoea, he was at a loss. What could he do? His average daily wage was a little over a dollar; a visit to the local clinic cost him fifty cents. Poor and uneducated, he was unable to understand what was needed for his dehydrated child. Nor could he afford to visit the clinic twice. Nur died as he carried her fever-racked body on his filthy plywood cart.

Desperate to bury her, yet with no money to pay for an ambulance to take her to a nearby cemetery, he decided to wheel her several kilometres in his cart to a city train station, where he could afford to buy a ticket to the nearby town of Bogor. There, he had friends who could help him. It was while he was waiting at the station, carrying his daughter's body enshrouded by a sheet of cloth – and still with less than a dollar to his name – that local vendors grew suspicious and rang the police. The tragedy of Supriono is one played out daily in Jakarta, a city of 12 million, where middle-class Indonesians who parade the tree-lined boulevards in brand-new SUVs were shocked to hear that an estimated 8,000 children in the city were suffering from malnutrition. In fact, there are close to 1.5 million malnourished children across the country, with the rate of infant and maternity mortality the highest in Southeast Asia.

For Pramoedya, the history of Indonesia was one of unremitting disappointment: 'A nation of coolies,' he would say, referring to the present. First enslaved under the Dutch, and then under the feudal Javanese elite who assumed the reins of power after independence, Javanism, he insisted, keeps the country enslaved. Pramoedya was born in Blora, East Java in 1925. His father was a teacher and a nationalist. His mother was the strong Javanese matriarch who imbued in Pram a keen sense of the mystical world and a tender faith in womankind. Unlike many of his contemporaries, he wasn't sent away to Holland for an education. His experiences until manhood were indigenous and rooted in Java. Of all the interpreters of Javanese culture, Pram was the one with his feet planted firmly on the ground. He was something of an unreconstructed leftist and a closet revolutionary, and when in 2003 he appeared at the Hong Kong Literary Festival, he was besieged by old friends from Indonesia's communist era, most of them Indonesian Chinese still in exile. At a lunch hosted by the Asia Society at a five-star hotel, he addressed a room full of bankers and stockbrokers, and railed against the sins of capitalism:

> I don't like the politicians in America. They think they can do what they like with impunity. As an Indonesian, it reminds me of Eisenhower and the 1950s, which was a bad experience for us, because the Americans helped bring down President Sukarno, whom they believed to be a communist. It was a tragedy because since that time we have never been able to find a true leader for our country.

It was a performance of moving sincerity, earthy and anachronistic. Yet he could point to modern Indonesia and all its ills and ask: 'Has anything really changed?'

CHAPTER FIVE

BYGONES BE GONE

'No one can be a true nationalist who is incapable of feeling ashamed if his or her state or government commits crimes including those against their fellow citizens.'

Benedict Anderson

Murder doesn't rate much punishment in a country where the value of a life is determined by the power of who took it away. Throughout my Southeast Asian sojourn, I have been haunted by the casual, unaddressed manner in which powerless people lose their lives. Whether it is the cruel way in which Indonesian soldiers tortured then dispatched people they regarded as separatists in contested places like East Timor, Papua and Aceh; or the secret killing of human rights activists in Thailand; or the disappearance of dozens of citizens demanding redress in Cambodia, Laos and Myanmar. Even more disturbing is the astonishing ability for those in power or with powerful connections to completely evade all forms of justice and punishment for violent crimes involving the loss of life. The number of times I have shaken hands with powerful people who have blood on their hands makes me shudder when I realise how easy it is for them to forget the past, shoving their crimes under a sizeable carpet already lumpy with the shameful acts of those who came before them, and move onwards, as well as upwards, with impunity.

Ours is an age of enforced universal norms and values. Over the last seventy years these values have been reinforced and implemented through international bodies and agencies such as the United

Nations, the International Committee of the Red Cross, and more recently the International Criminal Court. In recent years, there have been remarkable instances where collective humanitarian action and the due process of international law have made a difference to people's lives. Even if indictments produce few convictions, for the people of Bosnia Herzegovina, Kenya and Sudan, there has at least been hope and a modicum of closure. Yet for the four decades I have known Southeast Asia, starting with the mass murder of around two million people by the Khmer Rouge (whose reign of terror in Cambodia ended just as I arrived in the region for the first time in 1979), and continuing today with the failure to deliver justice to the victims of political violence in Cambodia, Indonesia, Myanmar and Thailand, the sum total of efforts to apply these norms and values and administer justice is almost nil.

In this chapter I will focus on one of the least acknowledged but most widespread of the social and political challenges facing modern Southeast Asia. For impunity afflicts the region rather like a chronically infectious disease, one that leaves the host outwardly healthy but which nonetheless inhibits many critical bodily functions and leads to long-term paralysis in the form of unresolved grievance and conflict. When my *Far Eastern Economic Review* colleague Nate Thayer interviewed the notorious Khmer Rouge leader Pol Pot in 1997, a few months before he died, it was hailed as a global news scoop. Frail and broken as he neared the end of his life, the French-educated former revolutionary had no regrets. 'I want to let you know that I came to join the revolution, not to kill the Cambodian people,' he told Thayer in a remote jungle hideout. 'Look at me now. Do you think . . . I am a violent person? No.'

I have long wondered about the motivation for this brazen burying of the truth, suppressing the conscience that every human must confront when it kills another. Passivity because of the acceptance of one's fate ascribed to Buddhist teaching is often cited as a determining factor, but seems insufficient. Blind deference to authority stemming from lingering remnants of the Hindu caste system is another. But this doesn't quite address the wilful manner in which those with the power to crush dissent flaunt their handiwork. When a newly elected Myanmar parliament met in early 2016 to choose a president and two vice presidents, the powerful military proposed a former security chief and chief minister of Yangon, Myint Swe, who was in office at the time of a bloody crackdown on student protesters in 2012. Indonesian President Joko Widodo apparently had no qualms appointing former armed forces chief Wiranto to a senior cabinet position overseeing security, in spite of a UN-backed indictment naming him for crimes against humanity because he was in command when the Indonesian army withdrew from East Timor in 1999 and around 1,400 people were killed. 'That was a long time ago,' said a colleague in Jakarta; 'time to move on.' Wiranto denies the charges and there has never been any sanction against him in Indonesia, where he has twice run for President.

It's also a fact that for all the vaunted institutions of enforcement mentioned earlier, the United Nations and its affiliates have a weak presence in Southeast Asia. Sovereignty in this case acts as an effective repellent. Bangkok hosts the Asia regional headquarters of the United Nations, yet together with Indonesia and Malaysia, Thailand has yet to ratify the 1951 Refugee Convention, now considered customary international law, that governs the humanitarian treatment of refugees. Since 2006, a special court, jointly created by the United Nations, has conducted a trial of the remaining leaders

Iron bed used by the Khmer Rouge as an instrument of torture at Tuol Sleng Prison outside Phnom Penh.

of the Khmer Rouge in Cambodia. The process has cost $293 million and produced only three convictions amid waning Cambodian government support for the process. The United Nations is thin on the ground in Southeast Asia. Its political department has a minimal presence. International agencies charged with implementing international norms of human security, such as the ICRC or Médecins Sans Frontières, have much less extensive operations and more limited mandates than exist, say, in many parts of Africa. Accession to the Rome Statute establishing the International Criminal Court is underrepresented in Asia compared to other regions of the world; Thailand is a signatory that has not yet ratified, while Malaysia recently signalled its accession. In early 2018, the ICC opened a preliminary examination of the War on Drugs in the Philippines.

There is perhaps a much deeper historical reason that explains why Southeast Asians are so good at shoving all the bad memories under the carpet. For those countries emerging from centuries of colonial rule, the use of violence to impose and maintain control had become an ingrained aspect of their lives. The *cultuurstesel* or cultivation system imposed by the Dutch in Indonesia in the mid-nineteenth century forced peasant farmers to grow profitable cash crops instead of rice, inducing famine in many areas and a violent reaction by Dutch-appointed middlemen whenever the farmers revolted. There was next to no avenue of redress. More to the point, the power-holders in the shape of European colonial officials were for the most part immune from prosecution – a privilege that seems to have been passed down to their nationalist successors. Most countries in the region have established human rights commissions, but their mandates are weak and the courts are unwilling to punish power-holders. The Association of Southeast Asian Nations that groups all ten countries of the region in a loosely structured way has an inter-governmental human rights mechanism, but the culture of non-interference is so strong that hardly anything is said about abuses in one country by concerned activists in another. For most of this chapter, I will focus on Indonesia, where the record of impunity is nothing short of spectacular. But high levels of impunity prevail across the region.

Of all Pramoedya Ananta Toer's works, perhaps the least

acknowledged is an essay that he wrote towards the end of his life on the building of the Great Post Road from the western tip of Java to its eastern shore. Over a thousand kilometres long, the road cost the lives of an estimated 12,000 unpaid labourers when it was built in the early nineteenth century. Pramoedya gave me a copy of the essay one day when I visited him two years before he died. 'Read it,' he said. 'It could be the best thing I have ever written.' I was puzzled. Was this a reckless show of humility from the man who penned some of the finest novels of Asian nationalism? On reflection, I suspect not: for Pramoedya, the long-forgotten tragedy of those who died of exhaustion and disease building that road offered an allegory for the long road that Indonesia has travelled from colonial servitude to independence; one that is littered with death and repression. Herman Willem Daendels, the Dutch Governor General who ordered the Great Post Road's construction, may have shamelessly used unpaid forced labour, but Pramoedya's real anger is directed at the leaders of modern Indonesia; their callous indifference to the suffering of the Indonesian people who have been killed in large numbers.

The tally started to build just as independence was won in the late 1940s: 5,000 communists killed around Madiun in central Java in 1948; around 30,000 rebellious Islamic fighters in outlying provinces of Sumatra in the 1950s; then around half a million people in towns and villages, mainly on Java and Bali, in the mid-1960s in a frenzy of anti-communist killings (as already mentioned there are no definitive figures, so half a million is considered about right). The Indonesian Communist Party, then one of the largest in the world, was accused of being behind a coup attempt on the night of 30 September 1965 that resulted in the deaths of seven officers including six army generals. The so-called coup attempt was put down within hours, although it was never proved that a coup was under way, and some suspect the generals were killed as a pretext to seize power and launch an anti-communist putsch. The man who emerged as the chief beneficiary, a quiet smiling general from central Java named Suharto, was in the senior chain of command, but mysteriously not visited at his central Jakarta home when the alleged communist coup plotters rounded up the others in nearby homes in the dead of night. In the ensuing vacuum, Suharto assumed control and went on to effectively seize power from President Sukarno. Once in power, Suharto ordered the army to begin a sweeping operation towards the end of 1965 to suppress the Communist Party.

The killings in Indonesia have continued in the modern period, too: at least 30,000 in counter-insurgency operations in Aceh after 1976 and around 20,000 after the Indonesian occupation of East Timor in 1975. When the Dutch handed West Papua over to Indonesia in 1962 some 30,000 people are alleged to have been killed in the run-up to the UN-sponsored plebiscite on the future of the territory in 1969, in which 1,025 men selected by the Indonesian authorities voted in favour of inclusion in the republic. Since then at least 18,000 people are believed to have been killed at the hands of the security forces, although human rights activists commonly cite much higher figures. Altogether that's at least six hundred thousand people killed across the country since 1949; ten thousand violent deaths a year if notionally annualised. It was out of shame and embarrassment that Pramoedya liked to call Indonesia 'a child among nations'. Pramoedya died embittered in 2006, unconvinced there was any end in sight where this culture of killing was concerned.

With each passing year, the memories of violence dim as old photographs lose their colour. It has now been fifty long years since that September night in Jakarta when seven Indonesian army officers were slaughtered by rebel troops, unleashing an orgy of organised killing across much of Java and Bali. The victims of the mass killings were Indonesians from towns and villages across Java and Bali, killed cruelly and without mercy, cudgelled or strangled in the middle of the night, on the merest hint of their communist sympathy. Most would have joined some Communist Party-organised activities – after all, with a membership of three million, it was one of the largest political parties in the country and had the tacit backing of President Sukarno, the nation's founder. It was believed that intellectuals were prone to communist sympathies, which meant that many of the victims were educated. In some areas people faced death merely because they wore spectacles.

For three long decades, the victims suffered in silence. They were even confronted with a parade of official lies that added sulphur to their wounds. Every year, to mark the events of 30 September, President Suharto's New Order government showed a slickly produced dramatic reconstruction of the events of that fateful night which portrayed the murdered generals as heroes, and the communist plotters as ruthless killers, staying silent on the mass killings that followed.

There was hope for a reckoning of the past after 1998, when Indonesia threw off the authoritarian yoke and finally embraced the democratic system envisaged by the country's founding fathers. But liberal democracy has proven a weak tool for either justice or reconciliation in Indonesia. The media's ability to chronicle the country's tragic past has not resulted in a collective commitment to establishing the truth or holding those responsible accountable. Instead, the victims have been tortured further – promised some form of recognition in the form of a national apology, only to be told that the killings were justified by aggressive Islamic hardliners and a military establishment that continues to stand by its anti-communist beliefs three decades after communism collapsed.

When he was president, Susilo Bambang Yudhoyono (who was directly elected in 2004 and served until the expiry of his second term in 2014) endorsed a National Human Rights Commission report into the killings. The voluminous report recommended action to provide redress to the victims and Yudhoyono contemplated a national apology, but met with fierce resistance from within the ranks of the military and Islamic organisations, whose members carried out many of the killings. In fact, Yudhoyono's own father-in-law, Sarwo Edhie, was the Special Forces general ordered in late 1965 to initiate the crackdown on communists and their sympathisers. Before the end of his presidential term, Yudhoyono mulled a proposal to make Sarwo Edhie a national hero.

It's not that the victims are forgotten. The problem is that almost no one is prepared to this day to push for accountability. The victims are expected to move on, let bygones be bygones. And as we saw in Joshua Oppenheimer's powerful documentary *The Act of Killing*, those who carried out the mass killings in the mid-1960s were happy to demonstrate their prowess at killing. Jusuf Kalla, who was elected vice president of Indonesia for a second time in 2014, is quoted in the film as saying that 'we need gangsters to get things done'. A special edition of the weekly news magazine *Tempo*, published in reaction to Oppenheimer's startling film, opined: 'Executioners emerged from nowhere, swinging their sickles, whether out of personal revenge, religion or a sense of duty to the state. They killed anyone labelled or suspected as a PKI member, disposing the bodies into ravines, rivers and caves. Did the executioners ever feel remorse or guilt over their horrifying actions?'

As someone who has studied Indonesia and lived and worked in the country for the past thirty years, it's a question that has haunted me and imposed a heavy qualification on my otherwise deep affection for the country. Something in the genetic memory of my mixed Levantine ancestry understands the notion of moving on in situations of chronic communal tension – albeit accompanied by the shadow of eternal grievance and hatred. My Greek relatives in Athens would speak in hushed tones about the legacy of the Greek Civil War, during which neighbours fell on one another across towns and villages to settle old scores; and because they were raised in Palestine, I grew up with the vivid images of the never-ending murderous struggle between Israelis and Palestinians. My Indonesian friends have taught me that their country was forged in the cause of freedom and backed by universal principles of equality and justice. They find it hard to explain the stench of senseless death that lurks around every historical turn.

I had the opportunity to explore this question of unresolved grievance when then-President Susilo Bambang Yudhoyono mooted the idea in 2012 of a national apology for the 1965 mass killings. This followed the publication of an 850-page report by the National Human Rights Commission that unsurprisingly determined that the systematic persecution of suspected communists was a gross human rights violation and recommended a formal investigation with a view to prosecuting those who could be held responsible. The head of the investigative team who compiled the report pointedly said: 'Many of the victims had nothing to do with the Communist Party or its subordinates. The military officials made it look like those people were linked to the party.' The report made clear that after the killings ended in 1966 the persecution continued, as

anyone suspected of having a communist affiliation or association
was barred from official employment. Those who had been imprisoned and survived carried special indications on their identity cards
that made it next to impossible to seek employment until well into
the 1980s:

> The events of 1965–66 constitute a humanitarian tragedy that is a
> dark chapter in the history of the Indonesian nation. These events
> occurred as a result of a state policy to annihilate the members
> and followers of the Indonesian Communist Party . . . [This]
> state policy was carried out using excessive and inhumane vio-
> lence . . . leading to death and injury . . . constituting for the
> victims and their families violations of human rights . . . among
> others: murder, extermination, enslavement, forced removal,
> deprivation of liberty/arbitrary imprisonment, torture, rape, per-
> secution and forced disappearance. In addition, victims and their
> families have suffered psychologically, and subsequently they have
> continued to suffer civil, political, economic, social and cultural
> discrimination.

The Human Rights Commission report was the first by any official
body to recognise the scale of the tragedy and point to the culpability of state officials. It included the testimony of almost four
hundred victims and surviving relatives, who had hitherto been
voiceless. Even with the lifting of curbs on free speech after the end
of the authoritarian era in 1998, there was hardly a sound from those
who suffered, lost family members, or were prevented from getting
jobs. There is the odd reference in a memoir, such as a well-known
Balinese doctor, Djelantik, who gives an account of living in Bali,
where an estimated 40,000 people were killed. 'Even the mere fact
that out of kindness one might have provided lamps for a festival, or
a rally of a local branch of the Communist Party, was enough to be
suspected as a member – or at least a follower – of the Party and so
run the risk of being killed,' he wrote. Djelantik also observed what
others saw in Java, which is the mute submission to their fate many
of the victims displayed. After being taken away by the killing squad,
his own nephew, an official with the pro-communist information

*Survivor of the 1965 anti-communist killings in Indonesia
retelling her story in 2015.*

ministry, calmly surrendered his wristwatch and wedding ring before
being beheaded. 'The Balinese accepted these horrible killings as
acts of purification,' writes Djelantik, who was known for his direct
no-nonsense manner of speaking in a circumspect society:

> In some instances – in Sukawati and other villages – the Commu-
> nists clad themselves in white and marched to the police to give
> themselves over to be killed on the spot. Killers and killed alike
> believed these happenings were manifestations of transcendental
> forces.

Given this heavy burden of impunity, I felt it was strangely futile to
be invited to a closed-door discussion at the presidential palace to
explore the idea of a national apology. As the impartial outsider, I
was asked to prepare some opening remarks on the process. I spoke
in general terms about truth and justice and their healing properties. Seated around the table were representatives of both sides
of the argument. There was advocacy for the victims from Galuh
Wandita, a well-known Indonesian expert in transitional justice;
there was also retired Lt. Gen. Agus Wijoyo the son of one of the

six generals murdered, allegedly by communists, on 30 September 1965. The discussion soon grew heated. Galuh spoke with emotional insistence about the need for justice, and the longing for some kind of memorial so that the lives of those lost so senselessly could be remembered. But Agus Wijoyo was offended by the assumption that victimhood was one-sided. 'What about those six generals?' he asked. 'Were they not also victims?' Perhaps the clinching argument against moving forward with the apology came from Hari Tjan, a Catholic Indonesian-Chinese and leading member of the generation of students who had helped overthrow the pro-communist Sukarno order and install Suharto as president in 1968: 'What we are forgetting is that the Communists struggled for land reform,' he said in a soft voice trembling with restrained emotion. 'Have we ever made land reforms?' There was silence. 'So why open this whole can of worms again?' he said. It was as if the lights went out in the room.

Three months after the National Human Rights Commission report was issued, the attorney general said the evidence gathered 'was insufficient to justify an official legal investigation'. When President Yudhoyono's coordinating minister for political, legal and security affairs, Djoko Suyanto, rejected the Human Rights Commission report, saying the killings were justified to save the country from communism and that no official apology was necessary, the matter appeared to be closed. 'We must look at what happened comprehensively. The communists planned mutiny against the state. Immediate action was needed to protect the country against such a threat. Don't force the government to apologise,' he was quoted as saying by the *Jakarta Post,* adding: 'This country would not be what it is today if it didn't happen.'

Nevertheless, there was renewed hope that Joko Widodo, popularly elected to the presidency in 2014 and with no links to the old conservative establishment, would finally address the issue. Contemplating an apology for human rights abuses was one of the many vague promises he had made as he rose to power. He even went out of his way to meet some of the victims of 1965. But as the fiftieth anniversary approached, his officials announced that he had more pressing issues of social and economic development to attend to. In reality it seemed as if this was one of the many promises that the

newly elected president was advised to shelve by his coterie of conservative advisers, among them prominent Catholic and Chinese
activists who had led the anti-communist campaigns of the 1960s,
and military men who helped him get elected. The fact is that the
army remains a strong pillar of the establishment and seems unwilling to make amends for its bloody past. Indeed, there is residual
anger in military circles about the alleged communist involvement
in the deaths of the generals. Neither do Islamic organisations implicated in carrying out the killings want their role highlighted by
any move to apologise for the past. News of Jokowi's decision not
to issue an apology came after a meeting with Muhammadiya, the
country's second-largest Muslim organisation.

Behind the excuses, the disappointment and the failure to address
what the rest of the world considers a forgotten genocide, lies a
fundamental fear of the future. Fear of social change in a society
plagued by inequality perhaps explains why anti-communist protests erupt each time political leaders contemplate addressing the
mass killings. The poverty rate may have halved in the last fifteen
years, but income distribution has become much more unequal;
about 40 per cent of the country's 250 million people live on less
than $2 per day.

Threats to social cohesion could also be a factor preventing
accountability. Javanese society in 1965 was composed of a more
balanced mixture of Christian and Muslim communities; the Communist Party made gains in the Christian community (much to
the horror of the Vatican), and anti-communist sentiment found
root among Muslims. It is no secret that much of the actual killing
was carried out by Muslim youth gangs and militia, encouraged by
the army. Afterwards many Christians converted to Islam to escape
suspicion and further harassment. The legacy of accelerated Islamisation since then has weakened the traditional cultural mechanisms
for maintaining harmony between faiths and, as a result, religious
conflict is on the rise in Indonesia.

To be sure, opening up these murderous moments in history
could lead to destabilising surges of retribution in delicately balanced plural societies. Many of the most enthusiastic killers in
1965, especially in East Java, were members of a paramilitary wing

associated with Indonesia's largest Muslim organisation, Nahdlatul Ulama. And in Cambodia, in a situation where you either complied with the Khmer Rouge or were bludgeoned with a backhoe, how far do you go to root out those who committed atrocities? Now that two-thirds of Cambodians were born after the end of the Khmer Rouge era, it is easy to bury history – and transfer the blame to some external enemy, such as Vietnam, which actually helped end the reign of terror. Thailand's approach was to fully rehabilitate those who rebelled against the state and to expunge the memory of insurgency. In the 1980s, all those who fled to the jungle and joined the communist insurgency were given amnesty.

Whether it be Indonesians who are killed, or those from other places in Southeast Asia, there seems to be a stunning absence of compassion for those murdered by powerful people. This enduring propensity for impunity is one of the more insidious drivers of perpetual conflict alongside an incapacity for reconciliation. Grievances fester and intensify for decades, even centuries. While the past half-century has seen genuine efforts to reconcile and make amends for a violent past in places like South Africa and Chile, little effort has been made in Southeast Asia to address injustice or establish the truth of why people's rights were violated, their property destroyed, their livelihoods curtailed, their lives lost. Very few have been jailed for perpetuating violence in the name of the state.

One problem is that history is a relative concept in a region that prefers to interpret its past through comforting or heroic myth and legend, rather than by recording actual events, and where survival is very often the priority of those who endure harsh conditions, retribution an unforeseen luxury. There's also a sense of shame associated with the past. All that is broken must remain in the past, argues Tash Aw, a Malaysian Chinese writer with an understanding of Eastern and Western sensibilities. 'Now that we are rich, we do not talk about the past; to study history is backward-looking, and we are concerned only with the future.' Indeed, it is often said that Southeast Asians have short memories; how else would Indonesians have coped with the mass killings of the 1960s, many of the victims bludgeoned to death and beheaded, their bodies tossed over cliffs into the sea or into rivers that ran red for weeks? How have Cambodians lived with memories of a spectacular genocide that cost two million lives in the mid-1970s? In April 1975, the Khmer Rouge marched into the Cambodian capital Phnom Penh and initiated a ruthless, barbaric re-ordering of society that emptied the cities and killed anyone with the faintest trace of education. A United Nations-backed tribunal has since handed down full-life sentences to only one of the surviving Khmer Rouge leaders. Many lower-ranking officers, perhaps 'simply doing their jobs' – as Hannah Arendt observed about the banality of evil – have escaped indictment, though there are some notable exceptions. The whole trial process received lukewarm support from a Cambodian government reluctant to see the trial of former Khmer Rouge officials who switched sides towards the end. Prime Minister Hun Sen fought for the Khmer Rouge before defecting to Vietnam.

Yet let me be clear: it would be wrong to assume that Southeast Asians are somehow immune to feelings of loss, to victimhood. How does any human overcome the loss of immediate family members through acts of violent depravity, sometimes committed before right in front of them? The natural impulse is to seek redress, justice, even compensation, with the truth as a salve, establishing why and for what end, helping those victims and their families try to make some sense of the brutality.

Reckonings, though rare, do occur: in two recent cases, courts in the United Kingdom and the Netherlands have either ruled or nodded in favour of the victims of colonial-era killings. In 1948 British soldiers killed twenty-four unarmed rubber planters in the village of Batang Kali during a counter-communist operation in then-colonial Malaya. Despite many investigations, no charges were ever levelled at the British army until subsequent appeals to higher courts in the United Kingdom, where representatives of the victims secured official admission of blame, although the United Kingdom Supreme Court later ruled that the British Government was not obliged to hold a public inquiry. In 2011 a Dutch court ruled that relatives of the 431 men summarily executed by men under the command of the infamous Captain Raymond Westerling in Rawagede, south Sulawesi, were eligible for compensation.

In as much as these verdicts could be seen as too little too late, the fact that these processes of 'transitional justice' seldom unfold in the region says a lot about the depth of buried grievance and mistrust in these divided societies. Decades after the Cold War ended, anti-communist sentiment remains an official Indonesian government position. The Communist Party is banned in Indonesia and students are still taught an official, glossed-over account of what happened in 1965, focusing on the slaying of six generals, allegedly by pro-communist conspirators. In 2015, activities to mark the fiftieth anniversary of the Indonesian killings were either banned or forced offshore. In 2015, an informal people's tribunal was established in The Hague, organised by civil society activists. In 2016 the judges hearing witnesses at the tribunal ruled informally that the Indonesian government was culpable of crimes against humanity and that Australia, the United Kingdom and the United States were complicit in this crime. Even though the judges' ruling is not legally binding, the Tribunal organisers hope it will lend momentum for the case to be taken up at the United Nations Human Rights Council in Geneva.

If we assume, which I think we must, that outward passivity is not an indication of either forgetting or forgiving these atrocities and crimes, we can also assume that the conflicts at the root of these atrocities persist among succeeding generations and get recycled in new and often deadly forms. When analysts asked why Indonesia was so badly affected by the wave of Islamic extremism unleashed by 9/11, it turned out that many of the eager recruits joining the ranks of Jemaah Islamiyya – Al Qaeda's Indonesian affiliate – harboured grievances over the violent treatment of their families who were connected with the Darul Islam revolt, a bid led by fanatical clerics to turn Indonesia into an Islamic state spanning the 1940s to the 1960s. Thousands of the movement's supporters were either killed or jailed as the military battled the rebels in outlying island provinces of Sumatra, Sulawesi and parts of west Java. Darul Islam's leader, Sekarmardji Kartosoewirjo, was executed by firing squad on a remote island in 1962.

We see the same repetitive transmission of unaddressed grievance down through generations fuelling violence in other parts of the region, notably in Thailand. The roots of a decade of often violent political turmoil and conflict in Thailand since 2005 are ascribed to contemporary confrontation between a selfish conservative establishment who wish to preserve their wealth and privilege, and a more electorally enfranchised peasant populace in the north and northeast of the country who are demanding a greater share of the wealth. There are historical reasons for the geographical cleavage, but the intellectual ideas underpinning this challenge to the conservative elite are driven by a small group of former leftist student leaders who still harbour grievances stemming from the harshly violent manner in which their uprising was suppressed in the mid-1970s.

Following a wave of student protests in the mid-1970s there was a violent military-led crackdown on students in Bangkok accused of communist or left-wing sympathies. In the 1976 massacre at Thammasat University that saw police and soldiers firing on protesters and standing by as a militant right-wing mob lynched defenceless students, the atrocities were filmed and witnessed by foreign and local reporters. The footage makes for shocking viewing, both for the brutality of the killings and the casual manner in which the authorities participated. Those who survived fled upcountry to the jungle and joined the communist insurgency, which at that time was backed by China. After their surrender and rehabilitation in the 1980s, some of these students, most of them as it happens of ethnic Chinese ancestry, re-emerged, rehabilitated as university academics. Some joined political parties. Thaksin Shinawatra, who had met many of the insurgents as a police officer attached to a rehabilitation unit in the Ministry of the Interior, took on a small group of them as his advisers when he entered politics in the mid-1990s, including Phumtham Wechayachai, who became his political party's secretary general. Influenced by idealistic socialist notions, but perhaps more importantly driven by grievances against the entrenched conservative establishment they held responsible for killing their friends and relatives, they helped the aspiring politician shape populist policies and win two successive elections in 2001 and 2005. As hothead radical student leaders in the 1970s they had called for equality; now they had positions of power they were more able to bring it about. A petition box was introduced at the prime minister's office; cabinet meetings were held in upcountry rural areas where the Thaksin and his ministers would ostensibly 'listen' to the people and then hand out grants and small loans. They also unveiled, amongst other things, a revolutionary health-care programme entitling everyone in Thailand to medical treatment for around one dollar. It was as if the old Communist Party of Thailand's notions of a more equal society had become reality.

Not surprisingly these and other populist policies were taken as threats by the ultra-conservative royalist establishment who feared being usurped, knowing the motives of the characters behind these schemes. The mere symbolism of a petition box, which in ancient times was a prerogative of Siamese kings, was sufficient to arouse suspicion. By 2005 conservative forces had mobilised disruptive street protests against Thaksin and his left-leaning lieutenants, effectively paralysing government and ultimately precipitating the 2006 military coup. There was no jungle insurgency to flee to this time, so the populists stood their ground, erecting barricades in the heart of Bangkok and crippling the city's retail and business district. On 13 May 2010, after negotiations to end the standoff failed, armoured vehicles and armed soldiers breached the barricades, leaving ninety dead. In emotional speeches and writings, these activists expressed resentment of domination by a royalist clique of military and bureaucratic officials bent on subverting popular sovereignty. In response, the authorities wielded a draconian *lèse majesté* law, Article 112, which has since been used liberally to send critics to jail.

One of the more outspoken representatives of the left-wing group of former students is Thongchai Winichakul, who until recently taught history at the University of Wisconsin. Thongchai has written eloquently on the roots of Thai nationalism. In 1996 he and I watched the grainy black-and-white film footage of the 1976 campus assault. He wept. As well as being moved, I was conscious of the fact that these were exactly the years I spent as an undergraduate, safe and sound in London. Many years later, choosing his words carefully, Thongchai described what he calls hyper-monarchy in Thailand as an invented culture:

As I was growing up in a hyper-royalist environment, the craze for the monarchy began to pick up increasingly, and after 14

October 1973 it got increasingly extravagant until it reached the momentum of the last fifteen to twenty years. In reality, it is just people who protect the monarchy for their own political and economic end. They also promote customs and traditions which are considered protective of the monarchy while enforcing Article 112 to prevent criticisms and negative remarks against the monarchy.

At the heart of this polarising conflict afflicting Thailand for the past decade, and which has resulted in 200 deaths since 2010, is a deeply felt grievance of inequality and injustice rooted in the lost decades of the 1970s and 1980s, a grievance that has never been addressed.

For all the contortions one can make to justify forgetting the past, what remains is the harsh injustice of impunity. The world watched in horror in 1999 as Indonesian troops aided and abetted angry mobs of Timorese running amok in the streets of East Timor after the results of a referendum showed the overwhelming majority of Timorese favoured independence. The resulting violence cost around 1,400 lives by UN estimates, and was only stopped after Indonesia agreed to withdraw troops and allow an international peacekeeping force to step in. Army chief General Wiranto, now a minister in the Indonesian cabinet, denies ordering the scorched-earth policy after the referendum. He was a key suspect in the consequent demands for accountability by the United Nations Security Council and was indicted for crimes against humanity. A joint Indonesian–East Timor truth and reconciliation commission established in 2002 concluded that Indonesia was to blame for human rights abuses and then President Susilo Bambang Yudhoyono issued an official apology in 2008, but this has not led to any prosecutions of military personnel. Yet even more remarkable was the way Indonesians sprang to the defence of their armed forces. A year later I was speaking with Indonesia's arguably most liberal, most open-minded and compassionate president, Abdurrahman Wahid, whose Democracy Forum helped pave the way for the opposition to autocracy and a new era of reform and democracy. He assumed the presidency in 1999 after a bout of political manoeuvring in the national assembly that saw his nomination and election by a majority of national assembly members. I asked him about Wiranto, given the international outcry. 'People have the wrong impression of General Wiranto,' he said. 'This comes from generalisation – we generalised our view of the military; we thought of them as bloodthirsty and coup-prone. In fact, no: they are loyal and important to the country in providing manpower.' He went on to say that he was doing his best to head off the possibility of an international tribunal to call into account Wiranto and his fellow officers.

Understanding the cultural drivers of such ingrained forgetfulness has always been an enduring quest for me in Southeast Asia. One of the most inspiring Indonesian intellectuals I ever met was Soedjatmoko Mangoendiningrat, a former diplomat who retired and was appointed rector of the United Nations University in Tokyo before he died in 1989. Shortly before his death I asked him about the passive stance his fellow Javanese adopted towards injustice and repression. 'The Javanese elite is not really concerned about what was imposed on them, so long as they can preserve the cultural context,' he replied in a steady tone that betrayed no trace of emotion. Soedjatmoko possessed the typical qualities of passive equanimity considered a virtue in high Javanese culture. The only way for them to survive, he told me, 'is by not questioning the structure of power, but learning to operate within it. It is a profoundly cultural adjustment to subjugation and repression.'

But culture is a highly subjective lens through which to view suffering. Soedjatmoko's daughter, Galuh Wandita, has become Indonesia's foremost expert in transitional justice. Galuh is passionate about those who suffered in the past, something she witnessed first-hand during Indonesia's occupation of East Timor. In 2015 she arranged for some of the elderly victims of the 1965 killings to participate in a writer's festival in Bali, where the government had banned all discussion of the killings. It was moving to see the composure in these frail but dignified women who lost their siblings and parents in those dark months half a century ago. Even more moving for me was the sight of a young woman in her thirties listening to a reading, who declared herself a victim. She wasn't even born when the killings happened, she said, but had lost relatives and wanted to know why they had died. The pain she suffered from not knowing had affected her mental state. 'Why can't I know why they died, what for?' she sobbed.

Opening up these old wounds, many Indonesians argue, will only highlight modern inequalities and reinforce social divisions that already frequently result in conflict. So why rock the boat? The old photographs may fade and the images of death and immense suffering on such a massive scale all but physically disappear, but the collective social trauma lives on in the Indonesian psyche. It appears in the creative works of modern writers; it has been vividly expressed by some of the actors themselves – both killers and their victims – in the films of Joshua Oppenheimer. What photographs hide is how people feel. Deep down many Indonesians feel ashamed about a period in their history they can't erase. This dark spot on the past clouds their vision of the future.

Perhaps the harsh reality is that in a political context in which power is to be preserved at all costs, recalling the past and offering victims redress is not worth the risk of losing prestige and position. Why open avenues for challenging the established status quo? In Thailand, no member of the security forces who has been involved in well-documented human rights abuses and instances of unwarranted violence against civilians has ever been prosecuted. There have been investigations, but for the most part they've been half-hearted exercises involving idealistic lawyers and civil society activists who get no cooperation from the security forces. Culpability, if any is found, often rests with subordinates rather than travelling up the chain of command. The results get buried or are glossed over for political considerations. An official investigation into the role of the army in the shooting of students during protests after the 1991 military coup in Thailand was said to have been lost. When I asked the lawyer who conducted the investigation if he had a copy, he said that he had lost his too. Impunity extends to ordinary soldiers and covers well-connected family members of the elite. In 2013 a squad of Special Forces soldiers walked into a prison in central Java and executed four men who had been detained on suspicion of murdering one of their colleagues. The soldiers were arrested and received short jail terms. A decade earlier the youngest son of former President Suharto was convicted of ordering the murder of a judge who had convicted him of corruption. He went to prison for just four years. Death loses all meaning in a country where people have died for no good reason in large numbers since the dawn of the nation and for generations before that. In this sense, Pramoedya was right about his people. But what could be taken for a callous disregard for life is more accurately the product of unreconciled history.

CHAPTER SIX

ORDERLY OPENING

'For civil society to thrive, there must be a strong and vibrant economy, which in turn is predicated on a stable social and political order.'

Anwar Ibrahim

One of the least celebrated waypoints of the modern era globally was the wave of political change that began in the mid-1970s. Triggered by the 'Carnation Revolution' overthrow of military rule in Portugal in 1974, this so-called Third Wave of Democratisation, as described by the American political scientist Samuel Huntingdon, reverberated most loudly across Latin America and saw powerful military regimes fall in Chile and Argentina. The impact was soon felt in Southeast Asia, where students across Indonesia, Malaysia, Thailand and the Philippines began agitating against tyranny and corruption. These expressions of popular anger were for the most part effectively repressed, often with violence. In Thailand, as already described, troops fired on students inside their campus in October 1976 and allowed right-wing mobs to lynch student leaders, hanging them from trees and then burning their corpses. In Indonesia all campus freedoms were curtailed – a process bizarrely characterised by the government as 'normalisation'. In the Philippines, government goons hunted down communist sympathisers and summarily executed them. Fearing for their lives, thousands of students, cowed and repressed, fled the university campuses of Bangkok and Manila for the jungle, where they joined armed communist insurgencies, at that time backed by China.

The spectre of communist uprising instilled palpable fear in the West, reinforced by the communist victory in Vietnam, that Southeast Asia was sliding towards the communist bloc. It was around this time, in 1975, that the United States and Australia turned a blind eye to Indonesia's invasion of East Timor, presumably because it was feared that a left-wing regime would assume power on the island after its colonial ruler, Portugal, left. These left-wing student movements had a measurable impact on the modern-era struggles for freedom in Southeast Asia that erupted in the 1980s. But the specific way in which these movements for change altered the political landscape, laying the foundations of rapid economic growth and development, says much about the inertia of traditional power dynamics and the limits of revolutionary politics.

The first moves towards political change happened in the Philippines, where Ferdinand Marcos was elected for a second term as president in 1969. Marcos wielded power artfully at first; harnessing grand development plans to friendly oligarchs, who in turn helped him line his own pockets. But by the early 1970s, the resulting rampant corruption and cronyism highlighted increased social and economic disparities and generated popular anger and resentment. Faced with rising rural discontent that fuelled a burgeoning communist insurgency, Marcos declared martial law in 1972. The consequent suppression of dissent and resistance involved widespread detention and assassinations by squads of thugs in a practice that became known as 'salvaging'. The US and other Western powers chose to ignore these practices because Marcos was said to be killing alleged communists. By the early 1980s, Marcos had long exceeded his legal term in office, assumed full dictatorial powers and abolished the elected Congress. Most of his opponents were either in jail or in exile. One of them, Senator Benigno 'Ninoy' Aquino, decided to return to Manila in 1983, despite the death sentence that hung over him. 'I have carefully weighed the virtues and faults of the Filipino and I have come to the conclusion that he is worth dying for,' Aquino famously told an audience in New York in 1980.

That he did. Aquino's assassination as he stepped off a plane on his return to Manila from exile in the United States galvanised

popular resistance to Marcos and finally forced the US to pay
attention. The Americans persuaded Marcos to call a snap election
held in February 1986, which was contested by Aquino's widow,
Corazon Aquino. Marcos swiftly claimed victory. But for the first
time anywhere in Southeast Asia, where elections were regarded as
rubber-stamp exercises, official tallies of the vote were disputed by
a civil society-led poll-watch organisation that credibly indicated
a narrow victory for Aquino – by almost a million votes. Marcos's
intransigence initially prompted disaffected elements in the military
to launch a coup, which failed. If it had succeeded this might have
merely inaugurated a new cycle of authoritarian repression. Instead,
probably unsure of how much support they had in the ranks, key
military opponents to Marcos, Juan Ponce Enrile and Fidel Ramos,
turned to the powerful Roman Catholic Church, which in turn
called for mass protests using a popular radio station. With hundreds
of thousands of Filipinos thronging Manila's main artery, a grimy
concrete highway known as EDSA, and ringing the military base
where the renegade officers rubbed shoulders with the lower ranks
and defiantly opposed their commander in chief, there was a sense of
inevitability about Marcos's fall. From my studio at the BBC World
Service in London, I felt the excitement of liberation transmitted
down scratchy phone lines as I spoke to breathless commentators
and some of the emotionally charged players. The end for Marcos
came late on 25 February when a US military helicopter flew him,
his wife Imelda and what was left of their retinue to a US military
airfield in the Philippines where he boarded a plane for Hawaii.

To the outside world, events in Manila were portrayed as a victory
of people's power. The scenes of mass protest had a galvanising effect
on struggles for freedom as far away as South Africa. What made
the impact even more immediate was coverage of events by CNN.
Using relatively new satellite technology, CNN provided live feeds
and constant updates of events as they unfolded. The effect was
cathartic. The world welcomed the people's power revolution – its
trademark yellow ribbons offering a clear distinction from communist affiliation, consciously or otherwise. America's distancing from
Marcos and eventual embrace of people's power served as a useful
corrective to a long record of support for authoritarian regimes in

Asia and elsewhere. Within a matter of weeks, the new Philippines president, the assassinated Ninoy Aquino's widow Corazon, was addressing both houses of Congress in Washington DC. A decade after its defeat in Vietnam, the US was able to hold up a triumphal example of democracy, which for so long its policy-makers had worked hard to stall, fearing that the eventual winners would be communists. This was a pivotal moment for Southeast Asia. However, its effects were not evenly distributed – and they soon wore off.

Much like the Arab Spring that lifted hopes of freedom in the Arab World in 2011, the impact of people's power elsewhere in Southeast Asia in the 1980s was uneven and left a trail of broken, disappointed movements for change suffering even more political hardship. Young Burmese who went up against military rule in the late 1980s were much less fortunate than their Philippine contemporaries. Thousands of them were shot down, imprisoned and tortured as they protested three years after people's power swept the Philippines. Myanmar's military rulers used poorly grasped socialist principles to impose rigid nationalisation on the country, with bizarre economic decisions based on the views of economists trained in the pre-war era and soothsayers. In 1985, just as the economic boom was getting under way in neighbouring countries, the Myanmar currency was demonetised to make way for banknotes denominated in the favourite numbers of strongman ruler General Ne Win.

Three years later, on what should have been the propitious date of 8 August 1988 (eight is considered a lucky number in much of East and Southeast Asia), thousands of students and Buddhist monks rallied in the streets for change in a conscious mimicry of the people's power uprising that had swept Marcos from power in Manila two years earlier. However, unlike their Philippine counterparts, the Burmese military did not side with the people; troops responded with brute force, cutting down the protesters in the street using automatic weapons and machine guns, murdering thousands. Despite the carnage, the military prevailed, but perhaps recognising the shortcomings of the discredited and unpopular Burmese way to socialism championed by General Ne Win, renamed itself more menacingly the State Law and Order Restoration Council (SLORC). Surprisingly, the new military regime declared that it would not cling to power and honoured a promise to hold multi-party elections in 1990. The army must have believed the people genuinely liked them, because it allowed a relatively free poll to take place, which gave an overwhelming majority to the newly minted National League for Democracy led by Aung San Suu Kyi, the daughter of slain nationalist leader General Aung San. Suu Kyi emerged from obscurity, married to a British historian and scholar, Michael Aris, and living in England, to take up the struggle for democracy. Initially, it looked as if SLORC would honour the outcome and yield to the people's desire, but two months later the results were annulled, and a new era of military dictatorship dawned. Aung San Suu Kyi was placed under house arrest and those who managed to escape fled to the border with Thailand, where they established camps or new lives, their voices unable to reach their target audience at home.

There were stirrings in Indonesia and Malaysia too. I watched Indonesian students march through the streets of Jogjakarta in 1989 calling for change. They wore jeans and T-shirts and smoked incessantly; they sat in small groups by the roadside belting out revolutionary songs all night long. They cracked jokes about Suharto and then laughed nervously, fearing that they might be overheard. Avoiding direct criticism of the government, they focused instead on land disputes and people's welfare issues. All the same, conscious of what had just happened in the Philippines, President Suharto trod carefully. The army, already beginning to feel alienated and shut out of power, was inclined to go easy on the students, which forced Suharto to acknowledge that a little more openness was needed.

In Malaysia, the sweeping powers the government wielded under the colonial era Internal Security Act already constrained student activism, which had been fomenting since the mid-1970s. So when in 1987 a number of social and ethnic issues prompted stirrings of protest, the government was quick to act. On the night of 27 October 106 activists, students, politicians and intellectuals were rounded up and detained under the ISA. Singapore launched a similar operation on a smaller scale in the same year, allegedly uncovering a 'Marxist conspiracy'. In Indonesia, Malaysia, and Singapore, nothing like the same level of protest that first swept the region at the start of the third wave of democratisation in the mid-1970s was reached, neither was there any appreciable impact on the political system. In both Singapore and Malaysia, in fact, it marked the start of a firmer, more authoritarian style of rule.

The fall of the Berlin Wall and the end of the Cold War at the close of the 1980s, heralding the triumph of free market values and the political freedoms needed to ensure the smooth operation of capitalism, boosted hopes for the blossoming of democracy in Southeast Asia. There was a strong belief in academic and global policy circles that democracy as a system of governance would prevail and that the authoritarian systems that lingered in Asia would soon disappear. Writing in 1991, Clark Neher argued that the transformation of the bipolar world of contest between the United States and the Soviet Union opened a vista of change, with democratisation the welcome by-product of a world in which 'economic as opposed to security considerations' would dominate. Soon, however, expectations that Southeast Asia would catch the tail end of the third wave of democratisation began to dim. Having effectively crushed incipient people's power movements demanding a say in government, strong leaders in Southeast Asia moved to consolidate their power.

They did so using a judicious mix of carrot and stick. The 1990s saw the start of an extraordinary boom in economic growth in Southeast Asia, with capital and investment from buoyant liberated Western economies pouring in to capitalise on economic reforms. Indonesia introduced sweeping financial and economic reforms in the late 1980s that attracted swarms of foreign investors and millions in capital. At the same time, President Suharto in Indonesia addressed his growing number of critics by declaring a carefully calibrated measure of opening, which as I chronicled in my study of Suharto and his politics in the 1990s, meant that a limited amount of polite criticism was permitted, leaving the mass media a bit less bridled. There was, however, no indication of any intention to fundamentally reform the system, and Suharto himself gave no hint of being ready to give up power. Moreover, the measured liberalisation of markets and the banking system allowed the lion's share of investment and profit to flow to his family and cronies.

Vietnam normalised relations with the United States in the mid-1990s, two decades after the America's ignominious defeat and departure from Indochina. As the trade barriers fell, Vietnam was regarded as a new frontier of economic growth and investment – despite the persistence of communist rule. A foreign investment law in 1987 heralded a flood of foreign direct investment. Vietnam amended its communist constitution to recognise the private sector in 1992; a stock market started trading at the turn of the twenty-first century. Vietnam's pragmatic leaders managed to turn the staid communist state, that had until the mid-1980s relied on Soviet technical expertise, into one of the most sought-after tiger economies a decade later. Vietnam's workforce was disciplined and productive, and with some of the million exiles who fled the country after the war starting to return with education, skills and capital, there were many who expected Vietnam to emerge as a dragon among the region's tiger economies. There was no hint of political change, however, only a carefully calibrated opening to the outside world. Even war-ravaged Cambodia was showing signs of new life, as the United Nations helped to rebuild the country after 1992, harnessing around 20,000 personnel at a cost of $1.5 billion to put in place the elements of a parliamentary democracy.

This was an orderly opening that, in spite of its profound economic impact, brought superficial changes to the social and political status quo in the region. Reforms, such as they were, facilitated the movement of capital rather than a drastic change of political scenery. Vietnam continued to be ruled by a closed Communist Party clique; Suharto remained the authoritarian president of Indonesia. At the time, optimists saw this economics-first approach as an ideal form of non-disruptive transition – helping to build a base of prosperity upon which a more educated middle class could then begin the process of orderly reform. Yet as much as the emerging middle class was alert to the need for social progress and democratic change, significant increases in levels of income and consumption also reinforced its stake in the status quo and therefore put a premium on stability, which in turn hindered meaningful reform and change.

As levels of investment increased, so concerns about constraints on political freedom diminished. More confident leaders such as Lee Kuan Yew in Singapore and Mahathir Mohamad in Malaysia used their articulate English-language skills to advocate a style of leadership patterned on what they termed 'Asian values', insisting that Western models of democracy were inappropriate; that citizens were willing to trade untrammelled freedom for a protective, paternalistic style of government. Lee Kuan Yew opined that 'every country must evolve its own style of representative government', by which he meant that Western models of democracy needed modifying. Mahathir was at the time more strident, lashing out at the West for bridling his vain efforts to forge an exclusively Asian trading bloc, wondering if it was because 'our faces are brown'. With hindsight, the problem with so gradual a pace of political change is that it stored up tensions that have played out violently over the past decade. But the period is worth recalling, given that much of the social and economic fabric of the region today was laid down in the decade from the late 1980s to the dawn of the new century.

The Bangkok and Kuala Lumpur I lived in during the 1990s were considered the epitome of Southeast Asia's go-go economies – moderately free markets overseen by what looked like liberal, reform-minded states. It was in fact an alluring state of semi-democracy, with pernicious authoritarian characteristics. As Malaysia's economy grew and investors poured in, the government jailed critics and gagged the press. If the foreign media, which I represented, was even mildly critical, government toadies retorted that Westerners were 'jealous of Malaysia's success'. Our articles were subject to censorship and each week I waited nervously to see if the magazine I wrote for would be allowed into the country. I remember Prime Minister Mahathir Mohamad being asked at one of the myriad gala investment seminars in Kuala Lumpur why he felt he could thumb his nose at the West when so much of the country's economy now depended on foreign capital and investment. 'I can say what I want and still you come invest in my country,' he retorted, glowering at the besuited bevy of bankers seated below.

The economic growth was real enough. In the period 1985–95, according to the World Bank, Thailand was the world's fastest-growing economy, growing an average of 8.4 per cent annually (today Thailand struggles to make 2 per cent). Much of this, as Thai economist Pasuk Pongpaichit points out, was on the back of almost $50 billion in Japanese foreign investment that fled the rising yen. Then there was a ready supply of disciplined and low-cost labour – not just from Thailand but also from neighbouring Myanmar – plus a strong base of entrepreneurial talent and capital in the form of the sizeable and wealthy Sino-Thai business community.

The wealth and dynamism was palpable. Living in Bangkok at the height of the boom in the mid-1990s, I sat sweating on buses inching through monstrous traffic jams, and observed the new rich watching videos comfortably in the back of their brand-new Mercedes or BMW sedans. I met business tycoons like Dhanin Chearavanont, the soft-spoken CEO of Charoen Pokphand Group, Thailand's largest conglomerate. Dhanin grew hi-tech companies and a diversified international portfolio of investments in twenty countries on the back of an agricultural commodity firm. His father had arrived dirt-poor from China in the 1920s, like millions of other poor Chinese fleeing the end of empire, and built an agricultural seed business based in Bangkok's Chinatown. By the mid-1990s, Charoen Pokphand was one of Southeast Asia's largest private companies with pioneering investments in China, around Southeast Asia and in the United States. CP earned annual revenues in excess of $45 billion in 2016 and Dhanin and his three brothers are the richest men in Thailand, worth almost $20 billion. When I first met Dhanin in 1994 he was just making the leap from agribusiness into telecoms, and I travelled with him to Shanghai for the opening of a joint-venture bank. As we cruised the city's famous Bund, he boasted of being the first foreign investor in China after Deng Xiaoping had opened the economy in the late 1970s. By the 1990s, he was the largest single foreign investor in China. The media marvelled at how Dhanin, best known as an agribusiness magnate in Thailand, had bought a small motorcycle company in China, acquired new technology from Japan and cornered 15 per cent of the Chinese motorcycle market within a decade. Over modest Chinese meals around large round tables, always featuring his food products, I met some of his senior managers who had been hired specifically out of business-savvy Shanghai. The CP man who ran the successful 7-Eleven franchise in Thailand – which has the third-largest number of stores after the United States and Japan – was one such character: among his many accomplishments he was a champion player of the ancient board game 'Go'.

The 1990s saw the triumph of Southeast Asian overseas Chinese conglomerates on the global corporate stage; they borrowed and spent profligately and acquired assets across the world. A study commissioned by the Australian Department of Foreign Affairs and Trade calculated in 1995 that the 30 million or so ethnic Chinese of the region generated an estimated GDP of $450 billion, which at the time was on a par with China's GDP of around $500 billion. This spectacular effervescence of corporate energy dazzled the global financial world, drawing investment bankers and stockbrokers to the region in droves. They stepped off planes in dark, wilting suits and peppered journalists like me over expensive hotel buffet lunches for insights they could use to justify the millions they were pouring into unknown companies run by inscrutable family dynasties. They only wanted to hear the good news; their eyes glazed over their cappuccinos when I started listing all the risks of over-extended credit, monopolistic practices, and dangerously wide income gaps. When the Indonesian stock market first opened to foreign capital in 1988, millions of dollars were sunk into shares in a little-known Jakarta hotel company. It was the only stock that could be traded on the just-liberalised market. Still, there were profits to be made for investors in search of alternatives to the depressed markets and rock-bottom interest rates in Europe and the United States.

A thriving cottage industry sprang up in books with breathless titles such as *Asia Rising* and *The Bamboo Network – How Expatriate Chinese Entrepreneurs Are Creating a New Economic Superpower in Asia*. There was an implicit element of fear, much like the scare about a possible Japanese takeover of corporate America a few years earlier. It didn't stop the money flowing, however. Yet, unlike the Japanese, the overseas Chinese of Southeast Asia pursued a cautious, always prudent approach to growth and development. They put a premium on preserving ownership and harvesting profit from consumers and producers at the expense of pioneering industrial development, which ended up selling the region short when the financial crisis hit in 1997. As the new century dawned, China and South Korea had pulled far ahead of Southeast Asia in technological and industrial prowess and potency.

For those riding the boom, it seemed to matter little that nothing much had changed politically. Certainly, for the families and cronies of those in power, say in Indonesia and Malaysia, there was no real desire for political reform. They justified their special privileges as a means of enabling the *bumiputera* (or *pribumi* in Indonesia) – sons of the soil – to catch up with the overseas Chinese. By the early 1990s, the region was awash with capital, which fuelled corporate ambition and greed: in 1993 Setiawan Djody, a flamboyant *pribumi* Indonesian businessman, bought the struggling Italian car manufacturer Lambhorgini together with Malaysian *bumiputera* partners. He dreamed of manufacturing an affordable luxury sedan for Asia's new rich. In the late 1980s I was invited to his luxurious home in Jakarta to hear a jamming session for a rock band, for which he played lead guitar. Djody's flamboyance and candid admission that he relied on close ties to Suharto's family to get ahead in business belied the fact that he started life as a musician and is listed in *Rolling Stone* as one of Asia's leading guitarists. The live performance of his expensively arranged *Kantata Takwa* that I watched in Jakarta's expansive Gelora stadium conveyed an impressive sense of creative verve and, yes: freedom. But life caught up with Djody; a decade later in his sixties he had to undergo a liver transplant, and has since returned to the performing stage. As for Lamborghini, it was sold to Volkswagen in 1998.

There were dozens of stories like this emerging from booming Southeast Asia: cronies and well-connected officials investing in businesses that transformed themselves into glitzy corporate empires – many of which crashed in the eventual financial crisis of 1997. Nonetheless, the wealth created in the period was staggering; its impact can be seen on the steel-and-glass skylines of all the Southeast Asian capitals – and also in the appalling gap between rich and poor that still generates so much suffering. In 1992, Thailand's Gini coefficient, a measure of income distribution in which the higher figure denotes greater inequality, was at 0.536, one of the highest in the world.

As the money flowed and a better-educated, wealthier middle class blossomed, the region's politics seemed ripe for change. People's power was already a dim and perhaps discomforting memory in the minds of the legions of foreign investors who had placed bets on long-term stability not upheaval. All the same, exposure to foreign capital and the opening of these economies was inevitably accompanied by demands for transparency and accountability. In this way, the booming stock markets and shiny new office buildings were seen as precursors of democracy – even if their impact was felt mainly at elite levels and in urban areas.

There was no mistaking the mood for change. I spoke with politicians regarded then as progressive – such as Abhisit Vejjajiva from the Democrat Party in Bangkok, and Anwar Ibrahim, by then finance minister in Malaysia – and listened to their claims of a new liberal wave in Asian politics.

Abhisit, the Eton- and Oxford-educated son of a doctor, was one of the youngest politicians I had ever met. He was thirty at the time, slightly built and possessed of a lithe sensitivity normally associated with artists. His dark, intelligent eyes and ready smile were a huge hit with Bangkok voters – especially the housewives. He was already battle-scarred from his attempt to reform Thailand's over-centralised and woefully inadequate education system. He failed after the bureaucracy warned teachers that, under the independent school boards Abhisit proposed, they would not get paid. Abhisit, who went by his English nickname Mark, was determined to harness his Western education and upbringing to developing effective parliamentary democracy based on transparent rules and procedures. He sparred with MPs using a mixture of Oxford Union debating skill and Thai high-society polish; in English, he was combative and never liked losing an argument. To the Thai media he came across as haughty and a little arrogant, yet I noticed he never failed to defer to authority. His family traced their ancestry to Sino-Vietnamese immigrants who served at court; his doctor father attended the aristocracy. Like many members of the elite who were fortunate to be sent overseas, Abhisit presented a Janus face: on one side the polished Westerner with fresh ideas; on the other a loyal member of the establishment with one foot in the feudal past. Both faces served him well initially, but the more it became clear that his loyalties lay with the elite and the establishment status quo, the more his good looks wore off on an underclass demanding empowerment.

Anwar Ibrahim on the stump in 1992.

In Malaysia, I covered Anwar Ibrahim's meteoric rise to political power in the early 1990s. Anwar made his name as head of the Muslim student youth movement, where he had honed skills as an impetuous activist. He was a beneficiary of Malaysia's New Economic Policy, established in 1971, which sought to elevate the native Malays out of extreme poverty and enfranchise them through a mix of privileged access to education and wealth. Anwar's father, a humble hospital porter, rose to become a member of parliament and senior health official. The young Anwar attended Malay College in Kuala Kangsar, modelled on Britain's elite public schools. At the University of Malaya he became active in student politics, speaking out against poverty and injustice, and was jailed for almost two years in the mid-1970s. A natural politician with a remarkable talent for oratory, Anwar joined the ruling United Malays National Organisation in the early 1980s. Anwar came to mainstream politics with fresh ideas about empowering civil society and harnessing better-educated youth to the framing of national policies. He commanded the loyalty of many bright young educated Malaysians.

When I first met him in 1991, Anwar was already finance minister and was considered to be heading to the very top, a man in a hurry. With his elegant goatee, fashionable angular spectacles and a penchant for expensively tailored suits, he cut a thoroughly modern figure. But Anwar has always been mercurial, prone to speaking to the gallery. At one political rally I attended in the early 1990s I was struck by a speech he made in a rural Malay village that was critical of the non-Malays. After finishing his speech, Anwar was surprised to see me, together with a Malaysian colleague, Kalimullah Hassan, also then working for the foreign media. He took us aside and with one of his conspiratorial smiles appealed to us not to report what he said.

For all their flaws, both Abhisit and Anwar in their own ways and particular contexts represented a fresh stab at promoting democratic politics. They were not trying to incite people's power, but worked inside the system; they engaged in a discourse about ideas, attracting talented young people to support their efforts. Theirs was a progressive, but also orderly opening to the world. Neither of them were revolutionaries; they both had one foot planted firmly in the establishment camp. Yet they gave many people hope and drew support from both conformists with a modern outlook and from the disgruntled. They were lionised in international circles because of their ability to communicate and synthesise liberal Western values with the Asian context. Chameleon-like Anwar would engage foreign visitors with the latest ideas on international relations gleaned from *Foreign Affairs* magazine. Abhisit came across as a member of parliament from the UK Home Counties – except that he was a fanatical supporter of Newcastle United, the city of his birth. Sadly, the trajectory of their political careers says a lot about how ineffective their orderly, less disruptive approach was and how little the politics of Southeast Asia has progressed over the past thirty years. In Thailand, Abhisit headed an unelected government and presided over an army crackdown against protesters that cost almost a hundred lives in 2010. In Malaysia, Anwar was jailed for alleged corruption, released and then jailed again for sodomy after almost winning a general election in 2013. What went wrong?

While the 1986 People's Power revolution in the Philippines only initiated a strictly controlled pace of change in the rest of Southeast Asia, the collapse of the Thai baht a decade later triggered a more cataclysmic effect. The origin of the crisis was a market-led vote of no confidence in the Thai currency, which was seen as ripe for speculative trading because of high levels of foreign debt taken on by companies during the economic boom of the 1990s. This came as a surprise, because the massive inflow of capital was accompanied by what seemed to be prudent fiscal policies – inflation was low (between 3 and 5 per cent), the currency pegged to a stable basket of currencies, and the government boasted modest fiscal surpluses. The high savings rate and 8 per cent GDP growth made Thailand look like a typical Asian tiger economy. The glitz and glamour, however, proved to be unsustainable. With growth and easy capital flows, the banking sector ballooned and became harder to scrutinise. Banks and finance companies borrowed profligately from abroad. The stock market was a high-rolling casino – notably in the property sector. It was a bonanza for speculators. Market liberalisation exposed assets to speculative trading on the hunt for quick returns. High interest rates and hot money flows inflated the price of assets, which were poorly conceived, underfunded ventures and oversized undersold properties. It all came crashing down on 2 July 1997 when the Thai government decided it could no longer sustain the peg to the US dollar and floated the currency. Overnight, the Thai baht lost half its value against the dollar, as did the Philippine peso. The Indonesian rupiah dived from around 3,000 to the dollar to 14,000.

Social unrest and instability followed on the heels of the crisis, In Indonesia, the International Monetary Fund stepped in with bailouts that were tied to strict financial reforms. Bad banks were closed; interest rates were hiked; wasteful subsidies phased out. The IMF tried to zero in on the monopolies controlled by Suharto's family and cronies, but in trying to cure the disease, almost killed the patient. As a result, the IMF struggled to find a vein. A run on the banks and drastic subsidy cuts hurt ordinary Indonesians. Overnight, the emerging urban middle class found their savings wiped out, their spending power decimated. The very poor could no longer eke out a meagre existence based on a sachet economy of small packets of noodles, soap and other essentials sold in roadside stalls; the better off had to bring their kids home from suddenly unaffordable schools and universities overseas. Severe economic hardship and social embarrassment boiled over into violent anger when Suharto, having secured automatic re-election in 1998, appointed a cabinet of outright cronies and corruptors, including members of his own family.

When economic crisis hit in 1997, people felt that their strong leaders no longer fulfilled the social contract promising prosperity in return for limited freedom. Suharto's dramatic fall in 1998 created a watershed moment for Indonesia. Like so many dictators the world over, he had failed to recognise that his time was up, and desperately tried to remain in power using a mixture of mailed fist and velvet glove. In the end, it was treachery that ended the thirty-two years of his rule, as members of a newly appointed cabinet turned against him and declared support for the students waving flags from the humped roof of the national assembly.

The dramatic transition played out on the streets of Jakarta over a few months, starting in May 1998. Faced with a mounting debt crisis that sent the Indonesian currency into a tailspin and consumer prices skyrocketing, Suharto's normally well-tuned instincts failed him, perhaps because of advancing age and the effects of a mild stroke. With opposition building up in the form of student protests, he opted to worsen the hardship faced by consumers by increasing the price of gasoline, under pressure from the International Monetary Fund to lift subsidies. Then, having lit the touchpaper, Suharto elected to travel overseas to attend an international meeting in Cairo. Both were miscalculations. No sooner had he left the country than tensions boiled over in the streets of Jakarta; shops were burned and looted and their owners, many of them ethnic Chinese, fell victim to lynch mobs. The urban dispossessed roamed the city smashing shop windows, looting department stores and ransacking banks. Along the toll roads Suharto's family had built, gangs of looters stopped expensive-looking cars and dragged out their occupants, beating them if they looked Chinese. The army hung back, uncertain what to do and perhaps unwilling to be held responsible for a bloodbath. I flew in from Hong Kong to join my colleague John McBeth, the Jakarta bureau chief for the *Far Eastern Economic Review*. Our coverage of the fall of Suharto was exhaustive. Much of it revolved around action playing out on the streets of the city's central business district, the epicentre of the country's economic boom, now brought to a shuddering bloody halt.

Every city has a heart; Jakarta's is a concrete flyover called Semanggi – Indonesian for cloverleaf. This multi-lane intersection funnels traffic in all directions, but this mundane function belies its place in the nation's history. For it is here at Semanggi that the Indonesian people confronted the army and stopped autocracy in its tracks in 1998, calling to mind the EDSA highway in Manila that marks the focal point of Philippine popular uprisings a decade earlier. It was late afternoon in mid-November 1998 and the students were protesting new emergency powers for the army, their anger directed at a political elite that had failed in the months since the end of the Suharto dictatorship to realise that democracy was at hand. Calls for reform, which had helped oust President Suharto in May, had turned into furious demands for revolution. I was walking along Sudirman, the city's main north–south artery, towards Semanggi when the troops opened fire on the students.

Ahead of me, not quite in the shadow of the concrete overpass, stood a phalanx of troops, their body armour shining like beetles in the sunlight. Just in front of them, untidy rows of students waving fists and banners stood their ground. I could barely make out their chants, something like 'revolution or death'. Alongside me were office workers, shop assistants and residents from nearby neighbourhoods; everyone was curious to see the outcome of this confrontation. Suddenly shots rang out, sounding like a sudden whack of a firecracker. The students first heaved, then scattered. Then there was more firing. As people around me hit the ground, I took cover behind a granite pillar that was part of what seemed an incongruously modern office tower, given that Indonesia had just taken a massive step back in time.

Today there is no memorial or sign to mark the spot where an estimated sixteen students died; what remain are the memories of people who live in the area. Ahmad sells *laksa*, a pungent curry-noodle soup, in the city's Bendungan Hilir market, only a short distance from the site of the protest. He and his friends at an open-air coffee stall recall the day the soldiers charged: 'They were supposed to be using plastic bullets, but I saw the holes they made in people,' said Ahmad. He described how the students fled into the market area, where they found shelter among the people as soldiers roamed the era hunting down and beating the demonstrators. Those were chaotic times in this city of 10 million people. Students roamed the streets in rowdy bands, wearing headbands and coloured jackets denoting their university or faculty; they streamed into Jakarta atop cavalcades of commandeered city buses; there always seemed to be a march or convoy streaming across Semanggi in one direction or other. The word 'Demo' soon passed into popular parlance. Parliament sits nearby: a vast building resembling a spaceship. Sukarno had it built in 1965 to house a body of non-aligned nations intended to compete with the United Nations. Around 80,000 students occupied its dusty halls ahead of Suharto's resignation in May 1998, littering the place with Styrofoam lunch boxes and plastic water bottles – all donated by rich business groups evidently betting on a change of order. Just a stone's throw away is the dusty Atma Jaya University campus, where the troops lobbed tear gas and shot at students on the night of 13 November. There was more to come the following year, when students again massed around the intersection's sharp-angled arches to oppose the nomination of B. J. Habibie as president. Troops again fired on them. Ten students died. These incidents became known as 'Semanggi One' and 'Semanggi Two'.

There have been attempts to bring the army to justice. In 2001 the country's human rights commission set up an inquiry, and a dozen army and police officers were cited for abuses in the two Semanggi incidents and the Triskati shootings of 12 May, which left four students dead. The military refused to acknowledge any violation of human rights, arguing that its soldiers acted to prevent the spread of mass unrest; parliament agreed, and the case was dropped.

Semanggi today is busy as ever, pumping the city's traffic around and jamming up every morning and evening, when the police try frantically to keep it moving with maniacal arm-waving and whistle-blowing. Nowadays I pass under or over Semanggi in an air-conditioned vehicle, the memories of that time still vivid: the spot where a soldier levelled his gun at me as I hurried to join the students at Atma Jaya; where I saw the limp, lifeless body of a

Indonesian student protestors riding to a rally in May 1998.

student lying in a dark pool of blood. It was here, just along this characterless, purely functional stretch of tarmac, that autocracy died and democracy was born, and that makes me feel a surge of pride. Ahmad, the curry-noodle seller, says things are better these days: 'The soldiers are gone.' But then he smiles and adds: 'Only the police bother us now.'

I wrote extensively about Suharto and the means by which he clung to power in *Indonesian Politics under Suharto*, first published in 1991 and reprinted as a third edition after the events of 1998. On reflection, we all had inflated expectations of a swift transition to democracy, whereas the reality has been a slow, gradual canter down the winding path of reform, with many a stumble and setback along the way. There was also plenty of violence. The immediate aftermath of Suharto's fall in May 1998 was a wave of disappointment provoking more violent protest among student leaders and civil society groups. They correctly saw that the post-Suharto dispensation was essentially in the hands of his former lieutenants, who in turn were in no hurry to liberalise the system from which they had benefited and enriched themselves. The army retained its prominent role in politics for another five years. Disaffected conservatives stirred up trouble on the periphery and at least 5,000 people died in a religious war between Christians and Muslims in the eastern islands of Maluku that lasted from 1999 to 2001. Ethnic and religious unrest also erupted in parts of Kalimantan.

Today, while Indonesia and the Philippines have made palpable progress, democratic transition is still hobbled by the tenacious persistence of traditional forms of paternalistic leadership that has shown a creative ability to adapt and subvert trends towards untrammelled freedom and equality. Freedoms granted are easily withdrawn as governments use arcane laws and naked violence to impose order in the name of stability. Human Rights Watch estimates that more than twelve thousand people allegedly linked to drug selling and abuse have lost their lives to masked goons in the slums of Philippine cities since Rodrigo Duterte was elected president in 2016. Many see a ghastly parallel with Marcos era 'salvaging', with Duterte telling the world to mind its own business. Elsewhere, divisions in society have become more pronounced in the context of more open, ostensibly democratic government. In some cases this has led to violent conflict. Indonesia has held three successive presidential elections that have seen smooth transitions, yet religious intolerance, often resulting in violence, plagues the nation and is increasing – a subject I shall turn to in more detail in later chapters. Indonesian political leaders use the rhetoric of pluralism but stand aside as bureaucrats and extremists unite to tear down Christian churches or threaten to lynch anyone who is accused of insulting Islam. Thailand, once the poster-child of liberal democratic change everyone else in the region looked up to, is perhaps the best example of this divisive trend today. The legacy of almost two decades of open contest between politicians in a notionally democratic context has been the polarisation in society between haves and have-nots (or elite groups that champion their cause); a rural-based electorate that started to feel enfranchised and counted as citizens for the first time, and a privileged urban establishment that felt threatened as a result.

Very often assumptions are made about government actions and social responses in Southeast Asia based on long-held social and political theories fashioned in eighteenth- or nineteenth-century Europe. The advance of political pluralism is regarded as a basis for the emergence of an inclusive, harmonious society. Yet in the modern state of Malaysia, where religious diversity is defended under the law and a constitution framed with pluralism as its basis, Christians are barred from using 'Allah', the Arabic word for god, and Muslims can be arrested for eating bacon or not fasting during the holy month of Ramadhan; in Indonesia, where democracy has made the most gains, lawmakers are debating the revival of a law against insulting the president; and in the Philippines, which was the first country to abjure autocracy in the mid-1980s, those guilty of crimes continue to evade jail or conviction.

Nowadays when I travel along Bangkok and Jakarta's congested streets, the wealth and dynamism is palpable as ever, but two decades on there has been little or no trickle-down. The elite travel in luxurious air-conditioned cars, but around them ordinary people struggle to escape the drudgery of debt and dependency. Around 7 million people live in poverty in Thailand, with almost a third of that total now concentrated in and around Bangkok. And while officially only 4 per cent of Jakarta's 10 million population live in poverty, the city's governor recently declared he thought the figure to be closer to 40 per cent. Pressures to modernise the region's cities and create the kinds of infrastructure and living spaces that will attract investment is forcing tin-shack dwellers out of their homes; there have been around 10,000 forced evictions in Jakarta since 2015. These hardships, fuelled by astonishing levels of inequality, matter because they are the conductor rail of a strong current of discontent that holds back Southeast Asia and threatens instability despite the increasing share of global wealth its economies contribute to. In 2012 the Brookings Institute predicted that by 2030 Asia would be home to 60 per cent of the world's middle class. Yet, with the exception of India, most of these bourgeois aspirants are still governed by authoritarian or barely democratic governments supported by a narrow base of oligarchic interests. This is not a sustainable paradox. In the following chapter I will examine more closely the contemporary state of flux in the politics of Southeast Asia, around which much conflict revolves around the tenacity of selfish elites and the struggle to eradicate corruption and establish just and transparent forms of governance.

CHAPTER SEVEN

DELUSIONS OF DEMOCRACY

'One-man-one-vote is a most difficult form of government. Results can be erratic.'

Lee Kuan Yew, 19 December 1984

It was after dinner, shortly before ten in the evening on 19 September 2006, when the news flashed on the TV screen in my Bangkok hotel room. Tanks in the streets of Bangkok, the BBC reported, a military coup under way. As a seasoned observer of the country, I was often asked about the chances of another military coup in seemingly democratic Thailand. It was easy to cast doubt on the possibility; after all, the last coup had been fifteen years earlier, and since then successive elections had returned and overturned civilian-led governments without army interference. The underlying political logic of the age of orderly opening prevailed. I should have known better.

Military coups reset the direction of politics without the need for messy and unpredictable democratic process. Thailand has a long history of them, the majority brief and bloodless, the usual routine being for the army to step in, hang around until a new, pliable government can be formed and then leave, having first arranged an automatic pardon for itself. There are even special tanks, ageing American-made M41s, which are rolled out on the streets at coup time. The scene was so harmless on that balmy September evening that foreign tourists wandered between them, snapping selfies. Bloodless as it was, the coup resolved nothing in 2006; a new constitution designed to limit the power of politicians was hastily drawn up and put to a referendum. It passed with a small majority. Eight years later, after months of paralysing, bloody standoff between polarised political forces, the Thai army stepped in for the eighteenth time in eighty-two years on 22 May 2014. Again, a bridling constitution was drawn up and put to a referendum. Again, voter turnout was low, but the charter passed – this time with a marginally bigger majority of 61 per cent. The army had banned campaigning and did little to make sure that voters read the voluminous draft constitution, which provides for an unelected upper house and paves the way for the appointment of an unelected prime minister.

However much we would like to applaud the progress of demo-cratic forms of governance and popular sovereignty, the gun is never far removed from the political arena in Southeast Asia. For a part of the world that has made so much social and material progress, that regularly tops charts of economic growth and investment, why do so many countries of the region plumb the bottom of international indices measuring freedom and good government? Why does the region continue to struggle with democratic transition? Admittedly, set against the rise of populist demagogues demanding law and order at the expense of freedom and rights elsewhere in the world, Aung San Suu Kyi in Myanmar and Joko Widodo in Indonesia could be seen as exemplary models of leadership in emerging democracies. Yet as they consolidate power, both leaders have revealed a troubling insensitivity to human rights concerns and a tendency to accom-modate vested interests. The Indonesian president has for example rejected all appeals to grant clemency to convicted drug offenders sentenced to death. Aung San Suu Kyi's refusal to sympathise pub-licly with the plight of the Rohingya Muslim minority in Myanmar's Rakhine State has prompted the withdrawal of many of the honours with which she was showered for her endurance over fifteen years of house arrest. Both leaders have bowed to the concerns of the powerful military establishment with alacrity. An era of hard power constraining rights and restricting political space prevails.

If the 1990s was a decade of reform and political transformation in Southeast Asia, then the first two decades of the twenty-first century have seen disappointing dividends. There were high expectations of stability and prosperity as countries that emerged from the 1997

Asian Financial Crisis settled their political problems and enjoyed a rapid recovery of growth and investment. The military withdrew from politics in Indonesia and Thailand, and came under increasing pressure to yield to civilian-led government in Myanmar. By the beginning of the twenty-first century, more or less freely elected governments in Indonesia, Malaysia, Thailand and the Philippines learned to respond to people's needs and started to address the root causes of inequality and rampant corruption.

Sadly, much of this constructive change has turned out to be ephemeral. For in most countries of the region, pernicious intra-elite struggle generates political polarisation, corruption pervades and economic disparity is soaring to alarming levels – which in turn has fuelled violence. The failure of elected governments to address the alarming growth in inequality has inclined voters towards populist leaders who promise firm action at the expense of freedom and human rights. Meanwhile, the military is back in power in Thailand, continues to hold political trump cards under a democratically elected civilian government in Myanmar and is clawing back a role in internal security in Indonesia. Thirty years after the people's power revolution that overthrew President Ferdinand Marcos of the Philippines, launching a wave of protest and reform across Southeast Asia, a roughneck city mayor promising mass killings of criminals and, if necessary, the abolition of Congress won a landslide victory in presidential elections and Marcos's son Bong Bong came within a hair's breadth of the vice presidency.

The first two decades of the twenty-first century coincided with my final years as a journalist, serving for a period as managing editor and then editor of the *Far Eastern Economic Review*. Based in Hong Kong with a picture-postcard view of the magnificent harbour, I was no longer a reporter in the field. However, my position as editor led me through corridors of power around the region where I found myself sharing croissants with an Indonesian president, lunching with a Malaysian prime minister and engaging in a bitter legal wrestling match with a Thai prime minister. By 2004, with the magazine shut down by its short-sighted American owners, and embarked on a new role as a mediator, I started engaging my long-standing political contacts from inside the fence and was confronted by the grim realities – and paradoxical limitations – of unconstrained power.

The main question I asked myself repeatedly during this period was why has democracy and all its socially beneficial trappings proved so hard to establish in Southeast Asia? Was it really because social change lagged far behind the pace of political transformation? This didn't seem right, because Southeast Asians are better educated, better informed and better off than they had been when I first arrived in the late 1970s. Unlike chronically conflict-affected parts of Africa and the Middle East, Southeast Asia has enjoyed continuous economic growth and development over the past three decades. Myanmar may be one of the poorest countries of Southeast Asia, but it boasts an official literacy rate of close to 93 per cent. Indonesia, Thailand and the Philippines score in the nineties as well. Yet for all the indicators of palpable progress, there are significant time warps. Often, the higher up the social and political hierarchy you go, the more backward the thinking. Across the region, people in power seem to view progressive political change as a threat.

In Thailand, for example, the conservative establishment – defined as a sclerotic bureaucratic and military elite that associates itself with the monarchy – was happy with unstable coalition governments throughout the 1990s where no single elected leader could boast a clear majority and challenge the status quo. But when Thaksin Shinawatra, an enterprising businessman turned politician, forged a single-party government in 2001 and started to deliver on promises made to a strong popular base, rather than embrace this clear manifestation of popular sovereignty the reflexive instinct was to undermine it. In Malaysia, the Malay majority is perennially concerned about the protection of its economic privileges, and so when an urban-based multi-ethnic opposition emerged to challenge its monopoly on power in the late 1990s, no effort was spared to tarnish its leadership using criminal law and the power of the courts. Malaysia stands out as the country that in recent years has most effectively blocked expressions of popular sovereignty using criminal prosecutions and arcane laws of internal security. A new internal security law passed in August 2016 makes it legal for anyone to be detained without charge on the word of a police inspector and for the government to declare martial law in any area and suspend all civil rights, ostensibly as a means of combatting terrorism. The prime minister has also established a special paramilitary force to enforce the new security law. From his jail cell on the outskirts of Kuala Lumpur in 2016, Anwar Ibrahim lamented what he called a 'catastrophic slide to authoritarian kleptocracy by a country that was set to be a shining example of pluralistic democracy in a multi-religious Muslim majority country'.

Derived from this reinforcement of hard power are the weak institutional roots of democratic reform. Political elites in Southeast Asia are in a constant state of flux, always bargaining for better position and for prolonged extension in positions of power; they operate for the most part in fluid, capricious political environments characterised by weak institutions that allow a good deal of room for manoeuvring. Political reform and other progressive forms of change, if they occur, tend to be pushed through by force of personality rather than being cemented by lasting institutional change. Malaysian Prime Minister Abdullah Badawi, who succeeded strongman Prime Minister Mahathir Mohamad in 2003, opted not to use the courts to deal with critics. He released Anwar Ibrahim and allowed the opposition party he led to flourish. Malaysians felt the yoke of authoritarianism momentarily lifted. But as a result, the ruling UMNO party started losing popularity and in fact the government lost its commanding two-thirds majority in the 2007 elections. Not long afterwards, in 2009, Badawi was pushed out of power and ever since the courts have been used to crush the opposition. Charged and found guilty of sodomy, Anwar went back to jail in 2015.

Another example of this lack of institutional rigour can be seen in the Philippines, where the popularly elected president's single six-year term allows for an initial wave of creative change and reform, followed by a period of inertia as the oligarchic status quo fights back, leading to a long, slow, destructive descent towards transition as potential contenders for the presidency in the next period vie to undo the incumbent's legacy. No sooner than a successor is elected, his or her predecessor ends up being confronted by the colourfully named charge of plunder, and sent to jail.

As a result of this singular lack of institutional coherence, compared with other parts of the world that have endured years of political upheaval and popular struggle, Southeast Asia has made the least progress. The lost decades of violent coups and counter-coups in Latin America ended in the 1980s and have, with some notable exceptions, left a sustained legacy of reasonably stable democratic rule. For all the horrors of tribal- or religious-based civil wars that marked West Africa, the bloodletting has given way to fragile but respectable democratic government in countries like Nigeria, Ghana, and even Rwanda. But unlike Latin America with its remote and self-contained economy, or West Africa, which doesn't produce much of vital importance to the global supply chain, Southeast Asia matters. The region accounts for sizeable chunks of global investment and manufacturing capacity; it straddles vital lines of trade and communication. What then makes Southeast Asia one of the least politically progressive and most perennially unstable regions of the world?

I lived in Thailand during what could now be called the high period of parliamentary democracy in the 1990s, when weak coalition governments came and went through a revolving door of free and, on the whole, fair elections, lending the impression that popular

Thaksin Shinawatra, Prime Minister of Thailand 2001–2005, in his office in 2002.

sovereignty determined who governed. When Thaksin Shinawatra, the former policeman turned telecoms entrepreneur, won a clear majority in parliament, forming the first single-party government in living memory, after his re-election in 2005, many believed that Thailand's democracy had come of age. Here was someone who spoke for the majority, and who promised cheap loans and healthcare for all. In countries like Thailand where there is no government-funded safety net, Thaksin's decision to offer subsidised health care for less than a dollar per consultation was revolutionary.

Thaksin made an impression in the wider neighbourhood with his brand of populism that was dubbed 'Thaksinomics'. Amiable and animated, the son of a local politician of Hakka Chinese descent who owned a bus company in Chiang Mai, the fresh-faced and always smiling Thaksin impressed colleagues when he served as deputy foreign minister. He was particularly well received in Singapore, where Lee Kuan Yew, a Hakka Chinese himself, took a distinct shine to him. When I met Lee's successor, Prime Minister Goh Chok Tong, in 2000, he went so far as to suggest that Thaksin could be a new leader for the region: 'Thaksin, I think, would be a useful leader for ASEAN,' he said. 'I encourage him and of course on his own he's an activist.'

Precisely because Thaksin was an impatient activist, this was not to be. There was a build-up of resentment in the conservative establishment, which felt threatened. 'Critics condemned our policy and called it, with contempt, a populist policy,' Thaksin told a gathering of business executives in Manila in 2003: 'I must confess I was bemused. A populist policy, so called because it must be a policy so liked by the people. The people like it because they find it beneficial. So if they like the policy and benefit from it, what's wrong?'

The conservatives were uncomfortable with the potential for Thaksin's charisma to eclipse that of the king. I was made aware of this on a visit to his party headquarters ahead of the second election that he won in 2005, where I spied a blown-up black-and-white picture of Thaksin bending down to receive a woven ring of flowers from an elderly peasant woman. The picture was a virtual copy of one of the most famous images of King Bhumibol. A Thai journalist friend with me at the time visibly blanched and predicted trouble

ahead. Then there was Thaksin's abuse of power, the business favours to his family, the charges of tax avoidance that he alleges were
rigged but for which he was repeatedly indicted and convicted in
courts. All this has culminated in a lost decade of perpetual protest,
disrupted democracy, and the imposition of military rule. Like Italy's Berlusconi, Thaksin equated his wealth and success in business
with a mandate to rule as he pleased. As early as 2002, during his
first term as prime minister, Thaksin bridled at any suggestion he
could do wrong. On his regular radio talk show, he railed against
rumour-mongers and worried about gossiping taxi drivers; he made
no bones about his admiration of the soft authoritarian styles of
prime ministers Mahathir Mohamad in Malaysia and Lee Kuan Yew
in Singapore. Shortly after banning my friends Rodney Tasker and
Shawn Crispin, both correspondents of the *Far Eastern Economic
Review*, he told me in an interview: 'Strong leadership is important.
I realise that is both good and bad for democracy but I need to
punch things, otherwise nothing will change. You have to be strong.'

Almost a decade later I met Thaksin again, in rather different
circumstances. He was relaxing in his luxurious European refuge in
Montenegro soon after his Red Shirt army of provincial peasants occupied central Bangkok in May 2010. Over chilled glasses of white
wine and canapés he told me he found it hard to believe what had
happened to him. He placed the blame on conservative elements
around the ailing monarch, King Bhumibol Adulyadej. Working
since 2010 to help open the space for dialogue and mediate between
the two contrasting visions of Thai society – one conservative and
unchanging, the other neo-socialist and disruptive – has given me
a ringside view of the selfish, narrow interests that manipulate the
struggle for power and claim to speak for the majority.

In May 2010, I sat down in a refrigerated sea container planted
in the centre of Bangkok just a few steps away from the entrance to
a five-star hotel where I frequently met friends and contacts in the
café, or at the bar. This was the improvised conference room arranged
for negotiations between the Red Shirt leaders, whose tens of thousands of followers had been protesting against the military-backed
government, and the army, who were threatening to storm the Red
Shirts' camp. Protected by bamboo and rubber-tyre barricades, the

makeshift camp sprawled like the Hollywood set of a medieval battle scene across a series of city-centre intersections. Shots had already been fired. One of the Red Shirt leaders, a former army officer, had been gunned down in broad daylight, shot in the head by a sniper as he spoke to a foreign journalist. Wandering through the protest site, I was amazed by the passion and commitment of the crowd, who were kept entertained by a constant stream of speakers on a protest stage. They were fed and watered by well-organised and well-funded protest machinery, for which Thaksin and his backers presumably paid handsomely. Rumours swirled about armed elements poised for insurrection and breathless commentators spoke of civil war.

Helped by one of the Red Shirt sympathisers, whose father, an ex-policeman, was handling their security, I tried to draft the text of a ceasefire agreement. But we never reached a deal. I noticed that all the men in the leadership group that sat around the table with me were intimidated by the fierce and dogmatic mother-leader of the Red Shirts, Thida Thavornseth, a former student activist from the mid-1970s who had fled to the jungle and joined the underground Communist Party. As a guerrilla, she made a name for herself as a cadre proficient in handling weapons and grenades. Storming into our shipping-container conference room, she banged the table and

Bangkok burning in May 2010.

demanded: 'You want to give up now? What are we all fighting for?'

A few days later, army armoured vehicles ploughed through Red Shirt lines. I checked into a nearby hotel where the staff had put up huge wooden planks to protect the windows; the acrid smell of burning rubber tyres wafted in regardless. This was Bangkok in the second decade of the twenty-first century. All my optimism disappeared as I watched video footage of protesters huddling incongruously behind glitzy advertising boards being shot at and from the terrace of the hotel I saw dark smoke rising from the plush city centre, the region's shopping paradise transformed by a vortex of senseless violence.

The trend hasn't been unidirectional. Southeast Asia's diversity is also reflected in the differential pace of political progress and regression, which often is bewilderingly out of synch. Just as Thailand was sliding into the archaic ooze of repressive military rule a decade into the twenty-first century, Myanmar was awkwardly emerging from it. After a long-drawn-out deliberation of a new constitution that in the end preserved the privilege and power of the military, strictly managed elections were held in 2010 and a hybrid civilian government emerged. Most of its leading figures were military men who traded their dark green uniforms for *longyis*, the woven Burmese sarong worn by men. They spoke softly in halting English about a commitment to reform 'step by step'.

The democratic opposition represented by Aung San Suu Kyi's National League for Democracy boycotted the 2010 elections, which were characterised as unfair. But the party was persuaded to run in the 2012 by-elections, which it won convincingly. With the doggedly determined Suu Kyi now in parliament, the military continued with its hesitant 'step-by-step' approach. They focused on reforms to open the creaking, formerly socialist economy in an effort to attract much-needed foreign capital, but kept the military's role in politics firmly enshrined. In terms of cementing democracy in place, these were baby steps – and on occasion backward steps. The media was granted freedom but then hit with new laws and regulations aimed at curbing those freedoms; a few political prisoners were released only to have their place taken by fresh detainees.

In downtown Yangon, shortly after the polls closed at 4 p.m. on election day 2015, the streets were empty save for the pigeons huddled in the mouldy eaves of old colonial buildings. One of these buildings had been turned into an election-commission counting centre where the first ballots were taken out of a plastic box and stacked in solemn silence. Not a word was spoken as all eyes focused on the small brown envelopes. Slowly and with reverence election officials opened each ballot and passed it down a line towards a row of plastic trays, not unlike those used in kitchens. The scene was repeated up and down the country, amid a subdued air of apprehension. People could scarcely believe they were being given a chance to choose who governed them. And when the first results were announced it was clear that Myanmar had voted for a complete change. Aung San Suu Kyi's iconic resistance to army rule had made her an international symbol of freedom, but support for her wasn't the primary motivation of many of the voters I spoke to that day; they had turned out because they wanted to bring about an end to military rule. Some of those I met outside Suu Kyi's party headquarters had returned to the country from overseas to vote. Only when the provisional result was announced quite late in the day did the crowd – the majority of them wearing red T-shirts or headbands, the colour of the NLD – allow themselves to cheer. And then the heavens opened, and it poured with rain.

The free world cheers when competitive popular elections determine changes of leadership, as they have in Myanmar. As an observer in that election, I marvelled at the discipline and patience of the Burmese as they queued to vote in the early hours of 8 November. Even compared with countries such as Indonesia, Malaysia and, until recently, Thailand, where I have covered regularly held elections, the voting went smoothly and was astonishingly free. It was hard not to share a sense of joy and optimism for a bright future, although memories of Bangkok in 2006 loomed as ominously as the clouds that stormy afternoon.

While it was encouraging to see many young Burmese return from exile and begin to contribute to the rebuilding of their country after decades of darkness and isolation, it was nonetheless frustrating that the military showed no sign of relinquishing its grip on

Voters queuing up in Yangoon,
Myanmar on election day in 2015.

power. The delusion was partially displaced by the outcome of the November 2015 election, which many seasoned observers expected the powerful military to find some way of subverting. Even if they tried, by harnessing hard-line Buddhist nationalists to scare people away from the NLD, the result was unambiguous. The government's military-backed party was routed at the polls. The people's desire, as they say in Burmese, was made crystal clear. By March 2016, the NLD was in power, even if the presidency eluded Aung San Suu Kyi because of the constitutional bar. Instead, she was appointed state counsellor and foreign minister, positions from which she wielded effective executive power, for when I quizzed some of her ministers about challenging issues in mid-2016, they all referred to decisions of the state counsellor as paramount. Meanwhile, the army insisted on the sanctity of the constitution and the sitting army commander, General Min Aung Hlaing, vowed to stay in place till 2020. Whatever Suu Kyi's ministers said, it was clear that the army retained its paramount position.

Myanmar's epic struggle for freedom, so brightly illustrated by Aung San Suu Kyi's heroic endurance, obscures the enduring constriction of democracy that afflicts the most modern and advanced parts of Southeast Asia. Singapore is indisputably the region's most advanced economy; it has the highest income per capita, the best health indicators, and the biggest concentration of smart phones on the planet. Yet the economically successful city-state has defied all the predictions about long-term viability without broadening popular participation in government. Strict controls on media expression and public dissent remain in place. When Amos Yee, a teenage blogger, decided not to join the vast majority of his countrymen and women and post disparaging images and comments about Lee Kuan Yew upon his death in 2015, he was charged in court with obscenity and harassment and sentenced to four weeks in jail. Higher standards of living and education in Singapore have meant that the better-off dissenters can afford to leave. Indeed, in 2016 Amos Yee sought and was eventually granted asylum in the United States; many more simply opt to remain silent. Perhaps that's because, unlike Malaysia, strong, one-party rule has neither led to economic profligacy and corruption nor violent social conflict. Singapore has defied all predictions of regression and ruin, often made at considerable cost to foreign media organisations sued in its courts for defamation (including *The Far Eastern Economic Review* on multiple occasions).

Yet Singapore, my home for the past decade, has also changed far more than its smugly confident mandarins like to admit. Immigration has soared as professional and unskilled workers have flocked to enjoy the benefits of its high-wage, low-tax economy. Construction sites of high-end condominiums, mainly bought these days by rich Mainland Chinese and overseas Indians, teem with Mainland Chinese or Bangladeshi workers who are conveyed to and from crowded dormitories in the back of open trucks. Young graduates from the Philippines or Myanmar, who often speak better English and certainly smile a lot more, now staff mobile phone service centres, which once provided work for newly graduated Singaporeans.

This significant influx of outsiders has made itself felt politically. In 2011 the ruling People's Action Party (PAP), which has never been out of power, won only 60 per cent of the vote, its poorest performance since independence. The weak and poorly organised opposition won six seats in parliament, the highest number since independence. Cherian George, a Singapore media expert and scholar, wrote of the election: 'Decades of depoliticisation, in which normal politics has been replaced by technocratic administration, seem to have given way to an openly contentious culture.' Why did this happen? Immigration: Singaporeans began to rebel against the pressure of competition for jobs, higher basic prices and over-crowded social services. This was democratic pressure of sorts, but no revolution. Five years later, the PAP recovered much of this lost electoral ground and said it had listened to the voters.

When Singapore's founding father Lee Kuan Yew died in early 2015 at the age of ninety-one, those who predicted chaos and up-heaval were proven wrong. And yet the signs of strain are there: in the muted but growing popular concerns about how savings are invested by what daring bloggers call the 'gahmen'; in the first signs of social unrest over immigration resulting in a brief bus drivers' strike; and in the volatility of the sizeable immigrant workforce, as demonstrated by a night of violence in the city's Little India area in 2013. Like all successful city-states, Singapore is exceptional, but for a country of such wealth and prodigious investment in education it lacks soul. It won't acquire one without more freedom of expression, which involves a trade-off against security. In 2016 several migrant workers from Bangladesh were detained and deported on suspicion of involvement in Islamic extremist activities.

I first visited Singapore in 1979 and have vivid memories of the crumbling stuccoed shop-houses and bumboats that littered the backdrop to Peter Bogdanovich's classic film of Paul Theroux's novel *Saint Jack*, filmed only a year earlier. I remember worrying that my hair was too long – even though the rules that once outlawed long hair had already been scrapped. Changi Airport was not yet open. The newly opened OCBC building was the tallest in Southeast Asia and reminded me of a giant electric shaver. A little over a decade later, I moved to Kuala Lumpur as the economic boom got under way and it seemed to me so much more vibrant and jovially cos-mopolitan. Today the electric-razor building is obscured by a forest of steel and glass, immigration has transformed the city, and com-pared with contemporary KL, Singapore manages to be – as Prime

Minister Lee Hsien Loong rightly stressed in his fiftieth-anniversary National Day speech in 2015 – a genuinely multiracial society. I'll drink to that, even if I firmly believe Singapore could be so much more without controls over expression and a trammelled media. Asia needs a free city, where anything goes, and this is particularly true now, with Hong Kong gradually surrendering its freedoms to Mainland China censors.

For those arguing that the glass is half-full of democratic dividends in Southeast Asia, the past two decades of democratic transition in Indonesia seem at first blush hard to argue with. Yet the long and winding process, although still on track, highlights some of the ways in which Southeast Asia's enduring and prevailing characteristics of culture and society throw obstacles in the way of achieving effective popular sovereignty.

The 1997 Asian Financial Crisis lit the touchpaper of social unrest that enabled Indonesia to throw off the authoritarian yoke in 1998. The country has managed to stay on the democratic path since then. I have travelled across Indonesia's most populous island of Java for each of the presidential campaigns since 2004; I have seen the determination of Indonesians to freely elect their leader, and to vote for change, as in Myanmar, when change is what they want. In the 2014 presidential election, the popular mood was in favour of Joko Widodo, a reed-thin small businessman turned city mayor who instead of following the conventions of elite-driven patronage and dispensing jobs without caring how they were done, made a name for himself dropping in on government offices unannounced to make sure officials were doing their job. At the main market in the Central Javanese city of Solo, where Joko Widodo became famous as mayor, I met traders who knew him personally because of the sheer number of visits he made, wandering the pungent rows of wilting fruit and vegetables, stopping to check on prices or stand-ards of hygiene. This was the essence of what government should be, I was told; and with the help of their votes, Joko Widodo would take his brand of clean, accountable government and apply it to the whole country. It was hard to find anyone who disagreed with this kind of change.

Yet I consistently found these same people profoundly disinterested in some of the basic elements of a functioning democracy, such as who represents them in the national parliament. Popular sovereignty in their minds is exercised once every five years to elect the president of the republic. Not one of those I met during the 2004, 2009 and 2014 campaigns cared about their local member of the legislature, because it was assumed these politicians were all selected and then elected on the basis of money and patronage, and that once they got to Jakarta and sat in the parliament, their votes were bought and sold. Democracy has travelled a long hard road in Indonesia; founded on modern principles of liberty and democracy, the fledgling nation took half a century or more to realise them. Although there has been no turning back since 1998, when the authoritarian government of President Suharto was overthrown, many ordinary Indonesians are cynical about whether the journey has been beneficial. They see political parties dominated by figures from the pre-democracy era: their platforms devoid of meaningful policies; a parliament that doesn't deliver legislation beneficial to the people; and an executive office and cabinet so indecisive that it neglects constitutional obligations. Yet there is no doubting the enthusiasm for democracy.

Hugging the north coast of Java, which lies parallel to the equator, runs one of the oldest roads in Indonesia. The Dutch built the Post Road in the nineteenth century to carry mail and goods between the colonial capital of Batavia and the eastern port city of Surabaya. As already noted, tens of thousands of workers lost their lives during its construction – countless numbers of them from disease and maltreatment. Two centuries later, the road remains the principal transport route across this crowded island of a hundred million people. Laden with lorries and buses careening perilously along its two lanes, the road links the capitals of Java's pre-colonial sultanates and the graves of prominent early Muslim converts from the fifteenth century, collectively known as 'the nine saints'.

Travelling along this road over a four-day period at the start of the official presidential election campaign in the first week of June 2014, I joined my close friend and former colleague, John McBeth, to speak to people living across an area of central and east Java that is a highly contested battleground for votes. We began our journey in Jogjakarta on the south coast, making our way north through Solo and Purwodadi, hitting the coast at Demak, famous for being home to the oldest mosque in Indonesia. We had taken the same journey ahead of the two previous direct elections for the presidency, in 2004 and 2009, albeit along a somewhat different route. We met farmers, factory workers, and fishermen. As on our previous journeys, we were told how important the vote for the president is. We saw the first signs that Indonesians were doing more than just voting this time – they were actively participating in political campaigns.

A few kilometres beyond the old port of Rembang, in the small town of Lasem where stout fishing boats some fifty metres long are still built by hand out of local teak, a group of volunteers had strung up a length of white cloth across a bridge in what appeared to be a new and progressive approach to politics. The volunteers were all supporters of Joko Widodo. Joko served two terms as mayor of Solo and then went on to be elected governor of Jakarta in 2012, where his popularity grew and he gained national stature. In the space of barely two years he went from city official to the man many believed would be Indonesia's next president. They were right, but it was a close-run fight, with popular activism making the difference.

The white cloth was being prepared so that locals pledging their support to Joko could sign it. 'They are all volunteers. No one is paying them,' a party representative told me. He was eager to dispel scepticism in a country where most organised activity is driven by patronage of one form or another. 'What's more,' he added, 'many of them are contributing money to his campaign.'

As normal as such contributions are in an established democracy, for Indonesia they represent a significant change in voter behaviour, fifteen years into a democratic transition that began with the fall of the authoritarian and military-backed regime of President Suharto. In previous years, political parties have tried to elicit funds from people using marketing gimmicks. This time, up and down the country, even the poorest donated to Joko's campaign funds, often as little as a dollar or two, and often through local banks. Handoko, a tour guide from Jogjakarta who was our driver for the trip, proudly declared that he had contributed 75,000 rupiah – about

$10, or perhaps 10 per cent of his disposable monthly income, using a local bank transfer. Media reports suggested as much as $3 million was raised this way. In Lasem I was told that that the contributions collected in cash would be forwarded to Joko's campaign in the presence of local reporters.

Political scientists argue that democracy only really serves the people if the people participate. In many parts of Southeast Asia, however, politics has tended to be more about elite power games and vote buying. Indonesians traditionally have low expectations about their participation in the electoral process, expecting their votes to be sold to the highest bidder. Despite the popular enthusiasm for Joko Widodo, I found evidence of this: a group of fishermen we met in the small port of Lukung were adamant that they needed to be paid at least 50,000 rupiah (about $5) to vote on election day – mainly to compensate them for a day's lost income. Things started to change when Indonesians were given a chance to cast a direct vote for the president. In 2004 and 2009 I met Indonesians who refused to be told who to vote for, or be paid to vote for. They took their responsibility seriously. The difference this time was that voters were so excited by one of the candidates that they actively participated and made commitments ahead of casting their vote.

Joko Widodo had a ten-point lead over his closest rival, former Army Special Forces Commander Prabowo Subianto, when we travelled around Java a month before the election. But towards the end of the race, Joko's lead narrowed. He and his running mate, Jusuf Kalla, a former Toyota car salesman who served as vice president to incumbent President Susilo Bambang Yudhoyono from 2004–9, presented themselves as coming from the people to serve the people, while Prabowo and his running mate, Hatta Rajasa, another former Yudhoyono minister, projected themselves as strong and visionary leaders. The optics to the folks in Lasem – and in almost every other stop along the old Post Road – were clear: Jokowi, as he is popularly known, had the people's interests at heart; Prabowo represented the old elite with its top-down 'we know what's best' approach.

For this reason, it seemed to matter little what Joko's stated policies were. In Kudus, another town along our route, we encountered a group of men sitting around a small space on the edge of the market watching a cockfight. Nurul, a security guard from the nearby Djarum cigarette factory, the main employer in the town, looked on as the scrawny birds flew at each other in a blur of feathers, blood and talons. 'All we care about is that Jokowi is one of us. He is clean and free of corruption,' said Nurul, tugging on a clove-scented *kretek* cigarette and keeping his eyes on the cockfight. Ironically, for men who admire the fighting qualities of their roosters, none of them professed attachment to the macho image projected by Prabowo. Although less vociferous and often shy about identifying them-selves, Prabowo supporters all cited the former general's forceful, decisive personality and his experience as a commander. At a small shipyard in Sarang on the road towards Lamongan, we met Musli, a shipbuilder, among the teak and ironwood timbers he used to create the sturdy, broad-beamed fishing boats that ply these waters. Musli told us he would vote for Prabowo 'because he is from the military and is firm and decisive'. Jokowi may be clean and honest, he added, but he is just 'an ordinary man'. Even Jokowi supporters from his hometown were willing to admit Prabowo's strengths. 'He is definitely a man of the world and has experience as a statesman,' said Karno, a food vendor in Solo's downtown Klewer Market.

This then was the dilemma for the 180 million Indonesian voters who went to the polls in July 2014. Jokowi was likable, humble and honest, but Prabowo looked more like a leader. 'Indonesia can't afford to have a civilian leader,' insisted a rice famer with a weather-beaten face from Lamongan, a region traumatised in recent years by the fact that it is home to one of the men convicted of bombing a Bali nightclub in 2002. Liberal commentators inside and outside Indo-nesia were alarmed at how popular the so-called representative of the dark forces of military rule was with voters and blamed smear campaigns that projected Jokowi, a Javanese Muslim, as somehow Chinese and Christian. At the same time, most of the voters we spoke to had low expectations and, despite their enthusiastic donations, were remarkably unexcited about the contest. Perhaps this reflected the fact that Indonesians felt more secure and worried less about political transition than they did a decade ago. But it also reflects an enduring reality, which is that national politics, however much it excites people in the capital Jakarta and dominates the media, remains rather irrelevant to the lives of ordinary Indonesians. What then to make of the popular activism and participation in Jokowi's campaign? At the end of our journey in the eastern industrial city of Surabaya, we met Huljono, a grey-haired party activist wearing a stained black beret, outside the headquarters of the National Democrat Party, which threw support behind Jokowi. Huljono pointed to a large billboard carrying a picture of Prabowo and his running mate, Hatta Rajasa, on the street corner. 'That wasn't there two days ago,' he said. 'There was a billboard for Jokowi on the same spot. That's the power of money politics.'

A key aspect of the campaign both at the elite level and along the rural Java byways is that Jokowi represented a new face of Indonesian politics: clean, transparent and honest, working for the people. Corruption was clearly a touchstone of the campaign. Jokowi engendered trust and a degree of excitement rarely seen at lower levels of Indonesian society. The worry many have is that the old dynamics of Indonesian politics, the harnessing of bureaucratic and political machinery, as well as primordial ties to ethnic and religious affiliations to build a strong base of support for the status quo, may well prevail. Sadly, the way Jokowi's administration has played out thus far appears to justify their fears. By early 2016 Jokowi was forced to trade economic reforms badly needed to open the country to more foreign investment for the effective dismantling of a national counter-corruption commission that had sent dozens of officials and politicians to jail. Reshuffling his cabinet later in the year, many technocrats were traded for political allies who had helped finance his campaign. Jokowi allies and apologists argued that this was simply the reality of political power play in a system that has one foot planted firmly in the old-fashioned culture of patronage; they insisted that the President was playing a long game of transformation that required short-term trade offs.

One of the attributes missed about the man was perhaps his innate conservatism; he came of age in a period of strong orientation towards the military, whose territorial commanders were viewed as protectors of stability and useful business partners. The military ensured that regulations were not overly burdensome for small businessmen like Joko. Should it be so surprising then that he

has surrounded himself with former military officers of a distinct-
ly backward-leaning persuasion? Armed forces commander Gatot
Nurmantyo shocked many when he declared in 2013 that democracy might not be the best system for Indonesia. 'The many are not
always right,' he said. As a result, the scales started to fall from the
eyes of those who heralded Jokowi as the leading edge of a new wave
of reform. 'The notion that Jokowi is a truly reform-minded president, who is working to change the political "rules of the game",
is therefore no longer sustainable,' wrote Tom Power, an Australian
observer. 'Though his appointments may not reflect party loyalties,
they are every bit as particularistic and politicised as those made by
his predecessors in Indonesia's highest office.'

Nonetheless, Jokowi introduced a wild card. Unacquainted with
Jakarta society, without a single friend or even a home in the city
that had elected him governor in 2012, Jokowi assumed the presidency with the same goofy grin that had won him the hearts of
ordinary people as mayor in Solo. There was a very high expectation that Jokowi would break the mould, forever shattering the
monopoly of elite interests. How misplaced this was: the fresh-faced
new president was swiftly contained. His administration was soon
captured by conservative elements from the military, the Islamic establishment and the nationalist political party under whose banner
he ran. As a result, some of his bold promises, such as opening up
far-flung Papua to scrutiny by the foreign media, ended up being
countermanded. And the most powerful member of the president's
team, another former Army Special Forces commander, Luhut Pan-
jaitan, gave a public lecture in Singapore less than a year after his
friend Jokowi was elected, and made no bones about the key role
the army still played in securing Indonesia's stability. 'I'm not used
to wearing a suit and tie,' quipped Luhut, who retired from the
army in the 1990s.

The army took advantage of this opportunity and started pushing for a bigger role in domestic security affairs, arguing that the
national police, who had stepped in to play the role in the immediate post-reform era, were not up to the job. Former Armed Forces
Commander Wiranto, who served under Suharto, argued that the
biggest threats to Indonesian security were 'armed separatist groups,

radicals and terrorists, theft of natural resources, narcotics, human trafficking and transnational crime'. By mid-2016, Wiranto was appointed the new coordinating minister for politics and security. Indonesians are innately worried about security because of social and economic fragility. Faced with a choice between divisive and corrupt civilian politicians or strong military leaders who ensure that pluralism is respected and government delivers, Indonesians are not averse to a firm hand on the tiller – as long as it is cloaked in the trappings of democracy and not run by a thief.

The democratic process appears more stable, and therefore more mature in the Philippines, a country where the political system most closely resembles that of the United States, the former colonial power until the 1930s. But while the Philippine bicameral Congress, the institutional trappings of its presidency, and the colourful expression of political activity down to the community level all point to a truly democratic spirit, appearances are misleading. For at the root of the country's stability is the effective entrenchment of elite interests and the close hold they have on party politics.

The families that control Philippine politics may become rivals at the polls, but they don't differ all that much on core issues of preserving their wealth and privilege. Two-thirds of the Philippine Congress is comprised of members of some 170 political families in a country of almost one hundred million people who have enjoyed universal suffrage of open democratic elections since 1986. President Macapagal Arroyo, elected in 2001, was the daughter of a president; she in turn was succeeded by President Benigno Aquino, whose mother was the late President Corazon Aquino. His father, Benigno Jr, was a senator whose slaying at Manila airport in 1985 precipitated a popular protest movement that led to the ousting of President Ferdinand Marcos. As traumatic as the Marcos period was, Imelda Marcos – the flamboyant and profligate former first lady famous for her 3,000-strong shoe collection – saw no shame in seeking re-election in Congress and is a member of the House of Representatives for the family's home province of Ilocos Norte. Her son, Ferdinand Jr (who goes by the nickname Bong Bong), was elected to Congress as a senator, and almost clinched the vice presidency in 2016. Guarding the home flank, his sister, Imee, is provincial governor of Ilocos Norte.

The unchanging nature of this Philippine political culture traces its roots to indigenous tribal clan structures enmeshed with the feudal imposition by the Catholic friars who were the predominant influence on Philippine society for the five centuries of colonial Spanish rule. The renowned Filipino nationalist José Rizal wrote his famous novel *Noli Me Tangere* in the late nineteenth century to highlight the injustice and inequity of Spanish rule. The book helped launch the independence movement and resulted in Rizal's execution in 1896. Sadly, reading Rizal's novel today leaves you wondering what has changed. The oppression of the Spanish aristocracy and Catholic friars has been replaced by the impositions of modern hacienda owners and political clans. As in Spanish times, the rich get richer, while the poor stay poor. 'It's the oligarchs on top, the limited few, the elitists who can buy whoever is in power, whoever wins. We are in a feudal state.' This is how President Rodrigo Duterte, former mayor of the city of Davao, described the system he assailed when he came from behind a pack of establishment figures to win a landslide victory in the Philippine elections in May 2016.

What stands out so starkly in the contemporary Philippines, for all its democratic pageantry, is the spectacular gap in wealth between the minority of elites and the majority of the population. Since 2010, for example, the wealth of the ten richest Filipinos has tripled from around $14 billion in 2010 to around $45 billion in 2015. In that time, twelve Filipino billionaires have joined those listed annually in *Forbes*, among them Henry Sy, owner of the Shoemart retail empire, who with an estimated net worth of $20 billion rose to seventy-third-wealthiest in the world in 2015. During the same period, the real value of the average daily basic wage increased by less than a dollar. The increase in average daily basic pay for all industries was only 8.8 per cent. In 2012, the combined net worth of the twenty-five richest Filipinos was equivalent to the combined income of the 70 million poorest Filipinos. Little wonder then that the Philippines is home to one of the last communist insurgencies in the world – a violent conflict that kills several hundred people a year. Intriguingly, one of the first things Duterte did was to pardon jailed communists and bring a handful of communist sympathisers into his government.

The advance of democracy in Southeast Asia promised equality and transparency with the push to eradicate corruption and level the playing field. But competition for power that seeks to subvert or overturn democratic outcomes has instead generated conflict and bureaucratic paralysis in the larger mainland states of Southeast Asia. It has generated social tension and periodic instability in the more successfully democratic island states. Despite Indonesian President Jokowi's obvious popularity, conservative interests that he has struggled to contain hobbled his first two years in power. This has set back the corruption-fighting, economy-boosting agenda he was elected for and forced him to accommodate less progressive interests. This was amply illustrated when in November 2016 a ragged coalition of hard-line Islamic forces occupied the heart of Jakarta demanding the resignation and prosecution of Jokowi's close colleague Basuki Tjahaja Purnama, a Christian Indonesian Chinese who was elected governor of the city. Ahok, as he is popularly known, was accused of insulting Islam. Rather than confront the rabble, Jokowi adopted an accommodating low-key approach that prevented serious violence, but made things harder for the governor – and perhaps for other non-Muslims to hold high office. Jokowi's delicate juggling act – accommodating conservative interests, the forces of religious and racial pressure and elite concerns – has helped sustain stability and investor confidence. Yet while no one predicts at this point that either Jokowi or the system of regular direct elections for leadership of the world's fourth-largest country is in danger of being overturned, there are growing concerns about the extent to which Indonesia's social fabric is being stretched by the unruly forces of race and religion, a topic I will explore in a later chapter.

Tensions of this nature look set to become the norm for the next decade or so, as democratic elections start to rearrange the furniture in the halls of power and adjust to the changing dynamics of society. The scenes of mass, often violent protest in Bangkok, Kuala Lumpur and Phnom Penh over the past five years have alarmed those who consider the ballot box the bedrock of democracy. Protesters in these capitals were demanding that the winners of successive democratic elections leave power and, in the case of Thailand, surrender sovereignty to an unelected people's council. Despite encouraging signs of popular activism and involvement in politics, democracy is facing a serious challenge in the region: as popular sovereignty gains traction and ordinary voters start to have a say in who governs, so the traditional order – established factions and circles – will fracture. Faced with unpredictable outcomes at the ballot box, which threaten their interests, conservative forces are resisting electoral change and challenging the legal basis of the democratic process – often by harnessing popular protest and threatening violence, as is the case in Thailand and more recently Indonesia. When Cambodian Prime Minister Hun Sen arrested Kem Sokha, leader of the opposition, and banned his Cambodian National Rescue Party in late 2017, the government insisted that it was applying the 'rule of law'. And when the establishment wins, the opposition cries foul and seeks to overturn the result, again using the power of the mob. As a result, after a long period of struggle to establish democratic representation as the basis of government in the region, the electoral process is turning into a flashpoint for violence and conflict. Real democracy remains a delusion.

In May 2014 on a Friday night in Bangkok, a city of eight million, you could hear the dogs barking. Normally the city pulsates with life, especially on a Friday night with the sound of honking cars, raucous drinking parties and discordant nightclub bands puncturing the hot, still air. But because the army had just seized power for the second time in a decade, a curfew was in place. It's at times like this that the reporter writes: 'An uneasy calm has descended.' The cliché was misleading in the case of Thailand. For unlike the coup in 2006, I hadn't seen a single soldier, and heard some cynics express disappointment that it had been a tank-less coup. The coup itself consisted of a few truckloads of soldiers surrounding an army club, where all the political leaders had been invited to discuss a way out of the impasse. The situation was anything but calm, for beneath the imposed tranquillity lurked anxieties about where the country was headed, and there was no evidence that the new national stewards in their neatly pressed green uniforms had a coherent plan.

After six months of perpetual protest and paralysis, Thailand was back where it was almost a decade ago. Sure, the army's intervention brought a halt to the nightly skirmishing that killed dozens of people and injured over seven hundred. And certainly, many Thais were grudgingly grateful for that. The rhetorical hyperbole and insults that flowed from protest stages on either side of the divide were heard no more on the airwaves, because all independent radio and TV programmes were shut down. A taxi driver hummed along to the patriotic song playing on his radio. It was a tune he'd last heard as a child. 'They can't keep this up for much longer,' he said. 'Politics is politics, and we the people decide who governs at the ballot box.'

This seemed a far-off possibility at this point. The people were told that the army had stepped in to restore harmony and 'happiness to the people', that those who had been detained were 'happy and grateful'; using deliciously Orwellian phraseology, the army said their 'attitudes were being adjusted'. The world protested and demanded the immediate restoration of democracy. But Thais tend to be astonishingly impervious to outside influence and pressure. They are taught in school how this stance has preserved their independence over centuries. Perhaps it has. But today's world presents no palpable threat to sovereignty and offers opportunities to prosper. Nearly 10 per cent of the Thai economy is built on the 30 million foreigners who flock annually to their temples and beaches. Why turn your back? Albania wasn't much fun under Enver Hoxha, North Korea is building a ski resort no one will visit. Who visits the beaches of Mogadishu after decades of civil war? Is this the path Thailand has chosen? Almost certainly not, but then the country was deadlocked, paralysed by a social, economic and to some extent cultural divide that has left the Lao-speaking north and northeast of the country at odds with the centre, while the Malay-speaking deep south remains mired in a violent struggle for autonomy. The soldiers in charge don't really have a plan other than to smother this polarised nation with meaningless nationalist nonsense and keep the lid on dissent.

Logically, there is a peaceful way out of this mess through dialogue and the techniques of mediation. But as my friend and former

Thai Foreign Minister Surin Pitsuwan observed, Thai politics is also a helpless prisoner of contingency. There is an air of improvisation about the way government and politics is conducted in Thailand. Instead of addressing a problem by establishing a collective consultative mechanism or committee, the Thai preference is to manipulate individuals using calculations of degrees of leverage and obligation. This prevents the design of coherent resolution strategies and leaves plenty of room for ambiguity. So there I was, back where I started in 2006: another coup, another anachronistic step backwards. The army imposed a strong repressive ban on politics and popular protest. Politicians were prevented from gathering or meeting, their funds withheld. On day two after the coup a small number of students gathered in central Bangkok and unfurled banners denouncing the coup. There were scuffles and one or two arrests. The same thing happened a year later, on the anniversary of the coup. I was reminded of my Indonesian friend Sarwono Kusumaatmadja's image of political paralysis from the Suharto era in Indonesia: Salvador Dali's melting clock. Two years later, it was clear at the time of writing that the military was entrenched, ruled unopposed, and was preparing for a long period in power. One of those at the sharp end of military repression in this period was Chaturon Chaisaeng, one of Thailand's intellectually most creative politicians.

Emotionally drained and exhausted, Chaturon sat slumped in his chair over a mug of peppermint tea. 'We failed,' he told me. 'We can now look forward to ten years of military rule.' I was speaking to the former education minister and a deputy leader of Thaksin Shinawatra's Pheu Thai Party a few weeks after the 7 August 2016 referendum in which a majority of Thais had voted for a conservative constitution that few had read and which paved the way for an unelected leadership of the country. 'The people want security; they seem to be happy,' he said, his voice tinged with irony. 'How could we fail to see this? We obviously didn't know what our own people were thinking.' It was a bitter realisation for Chaturon, a political warhorse and veteran of left-wing student militancy in the mid-1970s. Could it be true that democracy is not in fact what the people want?

The reality is that what many people yearn for in these societies is security. Of course people would like the freedom to choose how they are governed and by whom, but as we also see today in many more developed parts of the world, democracy becomes a secondary consideration when livelihoods are threatened. For the rest of this book, I will examine some of the underlying factors of insecurity that have held up political progress and help explain why there are other priorities in the minds of many people of the region. This situation of chronic insecurity primarily benefits the power-holders. Regressive governments in Southeast Asia can rely on societies that remain divided by class, race and religion. Conflicts at the margins justify martial law and the harnessing of crude nationalism and jingoism to keep the international community at bay. Malaysians anxious about the abuse of power are told that behind the exposure of scandal the West is plotting to undermine the primacy of Muslim Malays; Thais looking for support in their struggle against military rule are told that outsiders harbour malicious intent. The answer is for people in these countries to seize the initiative and forge popular movements that unite weak progressive civil society groups and en-lightened political actors. There is hope, but the price will be high, as those wielding hard power will not go without a fight.

CHAPTER EIGHT

GREED, GRAFT AND GORE

'Don't think I steal the people's property, I am the prime minister
for the people.'

Najib Tun Razak, Prime Minister of Malaysia

Bad politics and poor governance hold up Southeast Asia's progress,
but driving all this like a reliable combustion engine is a pernicious
culture of graft and greed. Southeast Asian countries regularly figure
high up global tables measuring corruption and a lack of transparency. In 2015 Cambodia ranked 150th out of 168 countries in terms
of the perception of corruption index, according to Transparency
International (TI), an international watchdog. Thailand sat at 76,
Indonesia at 88 and Vietnam at 112. Singapore was ranked 8 and,
oddly, given the country's current predicament, Malaysia ranked
just below 50 on the index in 2015. Such high levels of corruption
are alarming in a part of the world increasingly at the centre of
global finance and investment.

The comforting expectation in the 1990s was that increasing
growth and investment would be accompanied by a commensur-
ate sense of responsibility towards safeguarding the dividends. The
expectation of probity increased after Southeast Asia's economies
lost almost $10 billion in GDP during the Asian Financial Crisis of
1997. The IMF was forced to intervene with a $40 billion package
to stabilise Asian currencies and there was the unforgettable image
of IMF Managing Director Michel Camdessus standing with his
arms folded like a colonial supervisor over Indonesia's President

Suharto as he signed far-reaching financial reforms into law. But while the legacy of the crisis was somewhat better management of reserves, as the economist Joseph Stiglitz pointed out, the collusion between hedge fund managers and well-heeled members of the elite with their secret bank accounts continued as normal. In the years after the crisis, wherever I travelled in Southeast Asia I saw precious little evidence that any real lessons had been learned: capital flowed unhindered, and for the most part unquestioned, so that the rich got richer.

Rapacious corruption threatens not just the quality of the business environment and social stability, but also impinges on regional security. Corruption scandals affecting governments and their leaders expose them to international prosecution, and upset bilateral relationships that help balance the contest between larger powers such as China and the US, and ultimately the contest for strategic supremacy in Asia. Corruption also impedes political reform and encourages kleptocratic leaders to maintain repressive measures to protect their hold on power. Corruption is more than a troubling affliction; it is crippling Southeast Asia's progress.

Modern Southeast Asians have grown up in a world plagued by corruption at all levels of society. The venerable *Far Eastern Economic Review* reported in the mid-1970s that 'tea money' – under-the-table payment for goods and services – was a 'way of life' in the region. Sadly, it appears that, despite the passage of time, decades of reform, more transparent, representative government in some countries, and the wonders of modern media technology, little or no progress has been made – except perhaps to highlight the problems more acutely. In addition to the spectacular scandals littering the last thirty years, the burden of petty corruption and daily rent-seeking behaviour continues to afflict ordinary citizens.

As anyone stopped for speeding in Malaysia or Thailand, or applying for a driving licence or building permit in Indonesia or the Philippines will know, such basic law enforcement and civic services involve the greasing of palms, the surrender of unaccounted cash. There are regular procedures for doing these things, but these formal avenues are almost never used. A policeman in Jakarta once pulled me over, insisting that I was speeding. He offered me the chance of visiting the police station to pay the fine, and described in laborious detail how much time this would take, the forms that would need filling and so on. Then he offered me a way out: pay him a substantially lower fine. He even offered me a receipt! I have had similar experiences in Malaysia and Thailand. The roots of corruption lie in the weakness of institutions: police who turn a blind eye to crime for money; regulatory authorities who take bribes to ignore rules; administrators and government officials who demand extra payment to carry out their duties. Perhaps it should come as no surprise, given how poorly financed government is in Southeast Asia, with the exception of Singapore.

Let's start with Indonesia, where low-ranking civil-servant monthly salaries are around $300 on average. There might be additional allowances for travel and attending meetings, but these vary. One of my close friends, who secured a job at the president's office after 2004, wasn't paid for over a year and even then took part of his salary home in the form of a bag of rice. By contrast, a junior secretary in the private sector can expect to earn double this amount. The Indonesian armed forces, with 400,000 personnel financed by a budget of $8 billion, covers only half its real costs. Military expenditure in Indonesia – one of the lowest in the region – comes in at less than 3 per cent of GDP, but that is because many of the costs are covered by off-budget business enterprises. Regional and territorial commands are expected to 'forage' to cover their costs of operation. As a result, Indonesians expect officials to be corrupt. The few who aren't quickly become heroes and often succeed in winning elected office, like the current President Joko Widodo and the man who succeeded him as Governor of Jakarta, Basuki Tjahaja Purnama, also known as Ahok.

In Thailand, corruption is as much a slogan as it is a reality. In 2015 the country's anti-corruption commission established a museum of corruption, complete with dioramas and recreations of famous scandals. Every new government, whether military or civilian, makes solemn promises to eradicate corruption. In 2016 there were even moves to make corruption a capital offence. To underline the gravity of the problem, or perhaps the lack of a word that captures it in Thai, politicians have coined a term that is in fact a bastardised form

of the English word '*caw-rap-shan*'. Yet civil servants in Thailand
are better paid than their Indonesian counterparts, and the Thai
bureaucracy has its tradition of prudence and probity rooted in the
first modern reforms under royal tutelage at the turn of the twentieth century. I have had plenty of experiences with Thai officials who
have carried out their duties fairly, transparently and with a show
of moral idealism. One day I found myself stuck at a border post
between Thailand and Laos without a proper stamp in my passport.
Embarrassed and concerned, I made vague noises in Thai about
speeding up the process. But the jovial immigration official would
hear nothing of it: sitting in his exhausted swivel chair beneath the
ubiquitous portraits of the king and queen, with a flourish of official
stamps and flutter of official papers, he made an elaborate display of
sticking to procedure to sort out the problem. Buddhist teachings,
insofar as they weigh on personal behaviour in the Thai context,
regard greed as a key factor contributing to stress and bad karma. So
at the very least, corruption is something to be hidden, conducted
out of sight. Yet the modern Buddhist church in Thailand has also
been associated with embezzlement in the pursuit of power. In 2013
a video surfaced of a popular monk clutching a Louis Vuitton bag
and lounging in the seat of a private jet. Police brought charges of
fraud and money laundering against him and sought his arrest, but
he fled to the United States.

Yet the cultural driver underpinning corruption – specifically
the primacy of patronage – has yet to find its replacement. Under
the patronage system, those with seniority (*run phi*) use money to
ensure their underlings (*luk nong*) are looked after and therefore
remain obliged to them in some way. The culture of patronage is so
ingrained that to gain entrance to the police academy in Thailand,
applicants must pay hefty up-front sums on the understanding that
these can be recovered later on the back of illicit earnings.

In the wider region, more modern states have managed to contain corruption levels. For example, both Singapore and Hong
Kong long ago created strong independent bodies to manage, if not
eradicate, corruption, which had been (and remains) endemic to
the underground activities of Chinese clan associations, or Triads.
In Singapore, astonishingly high civil-servant salaries are justified

as a prophylactic against corruption: the prime minister earns $1.7 million, the highest salary of any leader in the world. But Singapore has a population of less than 5 million, and a somewhat high tax base. In Indonesia and Thailand the tax base is so narrow it is almost indiscernible. Indonesia, a country of 260 million, has only 30 million registered taxpayers. In 2014 only around one million of them paid what they owed. The government hopes a tax amnesty will encourage Indonesians to bring back as much as $200 billion estimated to be stashed away, much of it in Singapore's banks. So why does the rest of the region remain so afflicted, even with the realisation that rampant corruption holds up political and economic progress and is a driver of conflict?

One reason can be traced to the social pathology of Southeast Asia, where power is concentrated in the hands of the few. Their self-serving interests are fuelled by an entrenched mechanism of elite survival: bribery, which becomes a social separator. Those who can afford the bribe will secure the best access to services or resources. Doing away with bribery and corruption would bring about a levelling of society, which would undermine and erode existing hierarchies and mean that scarce resources need to be shared more widely. Moreover, paying extra for services ensures that the rules serve those who pay. A cushion of graft therefore sustains the selfishness of elite behaviour. In this way, as the Thai columnist Kong Rithdee aptly describes, parents bribe to get their children into top schools; the rich bribe to have ledgers adjusted, to avoid paying tax; and government officials bribe to have their wives and children allocated the best jobs. 'The system allows officials to pocket differences and shape our thinking that anything can be fixed if you know the right person.' Throughout my career in Southeast Asia people thought I was mad to consider applying for visas or work permits without going through a 'fixer', who would know the right person and the exact sum of money that must be paid informally to obtain the service required. Across much of Southeast Asia people don't pay income tax; instead they pay petty bribes. A bit like taxation: the richer you are the bigger the bribe.

As well as sustaining high levels of wealth for the elite, corruption is a handy political tool for those who wish to control the elite.

Authoritarian leaders such as Suharto of Indonesia used massive levels of corruption to fuel the patronage system that sustained his three decades in power. Loyalty was secured and sustained by granting licences for businesses or monopolies on the import or export of goods. The practice started with the nationalisation of Dutch-owned assets in the 1950s; most of these were parcelled out to members of the military and political elite, upon which the country's first indigenous fortunes were built. Suharto distinguished himself by narrowing the economic base considerably. The president's three eldest children had the most lucrative monopolies, controlling the import of essential primary resources for industries such as plastics and petrochemicals. When foreign investors put pressure on the government to open up areas of manufacturing, the president's family simply adjusted their approach and secured controlling stakes, thus supplanting the need to monopolise imports they once controlled: upstream or downstream. By the time of his fall in 1998, Transparency International declared Suharto to be the most corrupt leader in modern history, estimating that he embezzled as much as $30 billion over his thirty-two-year rule.

Widespread corruption acts like a huge brake on social and political progress in Indonesia. A major struggle over the past two decades of democratic transition has been the reform of the police force and the judiciary, the proper guardians of law and order in a modern democracy. Both these institutions are popularly perceived to have failed to live up to their modern roles. According to a Gallup survey, in 2010 only 40 per cent of urban Indonesians had confidence in the courts. The same survey reported that 90 per cent of all Indonesians felt corruption was widespread throughout the government. The tide began to turn when an anti-corruption commission was established in 2002 with strong powers to investigate and even arrest suspects. In its first dozen years of operation the commission achieved a remarkable 100 per cent conviction rate. Indonesia's jails started to fill up with disgraced officials, including ministers caught stealing from the public. Jakarta's dilapidated Cipinang prison, once home to hollow-eyed political dissidents and rebels, filled up with overweight members of the elite relying on daily food deliveries made by their domestic servants or family members. Even then, the degree of punishment was subject to corruption: some of the better-resourced prisoners found it possible to visit shopping malls on the weekend and sleep at home, so long as they returned to prison on Monday.

Key to the commission's success was its ability to investigate suspects without going through the notoriously corrupt police force. Alas, it was too good to be true: commission officials grumbled about the lack of cooperation from the government and police; the public, eager to report malfeasance, created a backlog of over 16,000 cases. By 2009 the commission found itself in a bitter fight with the police after it started investigating one of their senior detectives. One senior police officer described Anti-Corruption Commissioners as 'geckos trying to fight a crocodile'. More recently, political horse-trading saw the popular and successful commission emasculated. In President Joko Widodo's first year, his administration found it necessary to trade off the progressive dismantling of the anti-corruption commission to allow itself political space to operate.

Corruption is often a built-in cost of doing business in Southeast Asia. In the state sector this means that prices for all kinds of goods and services are inflated to supplement poor salaries. A survey conducted in Malaysia in 2014 found an astonishing 64 per cent of people surveyed saying that business could not be done without paying bribes. In the private sector this is usually the cost of keeping predatory official oversight and interference at bay, or avoiding tax. The popular perception of the ethnic Chinese, who dominate the business landscape across Southeast Asia, is that they are the most prone to corruption. This isn't entirely fair. The accusation has its roots in the insecurity of overseas Chinese entrepreneurs, who relied as outsiders on the forbearance of officials upon whom they depended for essential licences and permits. This dependence in turn bred practices of paying under the table to ensure the necessary permissions flowed uninterrupted, often at the behest of the officials themselves, who saw an opportunity to make extra income by preying on the Chinese.

There is a common and unvoiced acceptance that paying to speed up the delivery of services and goods has helped the economies of Southeast Asia, made them more efficient and often cuts through bureaucratic red tape. As a result, kickbacks and bribes litter the corporate scenery to such an extent that it goes almost unnoticed. The case of Malaysia is a stand-out example of how business and politics have become inextricably intertwined, laying the basis for massive levels of collusion and corruption at the highest level of corporate and political affairs to the present day.

Malaysia won independence from Britain in 1957, inheriting a Westminster-style parliament, courts that used British Common Law and a constitution that enshrined racial and religious freedoms for a society in which Malay Muslims and non-Muslim Chinese and Indians lived side by side in sizeable numbers. For the first twenty years, the country made admirable strides towards equality and prosperity under the rule of law. Remarkably, policies that aimed to redistribute wealth to the poorer Malay community eliminated extreme poverty and helped train a skilled workforce that led one of the region's earliest tech booms in the island state of Penang. According to World Bank figures, total income grew an average of 6–7 per cent a year from 1970 to 2000, and levels of poverty were reduced from half the total population in 1970 to less than 4 per cent in 2008. When I lived in Malaysia in the early 1990s it was one of the most developed Southeast Asian countries, where English was widely spoken and, although strict measures were in place to prevent racial unrest, there was a lively and open debate in the political arena. This was surprising because, despite a lively culture of political contest, the government has only ever been ruled by an exclusively Malay and Muslim party called the United Malays National Organisation (UMNO), which has retained a commanding two-thirds majority in the parliament until very recently in a ruling coalition with submissive minor ethnic-based parties.

The original source of the corruption problem was, as Malaysian academic Terence Gomez points out, the very high level of foreign ownership that Malaysia inherited at independence. Large, mostly British conglomerates owned the lion's share of assets in natural resource production. On top of this, the next level of corporate ownership sat with the Chinese, while the majority Malay population, which now possessed all the political power, had next to nothing. As in Indonesia, nationalisation was the order of the day. But instead of distributing the wealth equitably across Malaysia's diverse population, the New Economic Policy initiated in 1970 envisaged the creation of a viable Malay business community based on 30 per cent ownership of the corporate sector by 1990. This in turn generated a profusion of public-sector enterprises aimed at acquiring corporate assets and placing them under Malay ownership. It also encouraged UMNO to acquire assets and establish a formidable corporate empire of its own.

Throughout the 1980s a shrewd and inscrutable character who served as both party treasurer and finance minister directed UMNO's business interests. Daim Zainuddin hailed from the same home town in the northern Malay state of Kedah as his boss, Prime Minister Mahathir Mohamad. A British-trained lawyer, Daim gave up his legal career to go into business. He started out humbly enough in the salt business and then moved into property development, which in turn drew him into politics. The diminutive and always modestly dressed Daim was notoriously hard to pin down. He avoided the limelight, disguising his immense wealth with outward humility – often wearing a faded old batik shirt and well-worn sandals. When I would visit his office in a nondescript low-rise building off the federal highway in Kuala Lumpur in the 1990s, he was always dressed casually and sitting in front of a bank of screens watching the markets. He was at the height of his power, but when interviewed he mumbled and rarely gave a straight answer, leaving you to interpret the twinkle in his eye and twitch of his moustache. Yet Daim was the principal mastermind behind UMNO's corporate empire, using a coterie of loyal corporate executives to build a tangled web of holdings in key areas of the economy through complex share swaps and reverse takeovers.

By the early 1990s, some estimates put the value of UMNO's corporate assets well in excess of $1 billion. As in Suharto's Indonesia, many of these UMNO-linked companies amounted to monopolies, notably in the area of corporate finance. The idea was that you could appoint cronies to head such enterprises and find smart young people to run them. The proceeds of these deals and revenues earned were used quite simply to underwrite elections. In addition to enriching UMNO barons and ensuring their loyalty, the money was used to influence wavering voters or to mobilise canvassers, who would literally bring people to the polls. The money also funded local economic initiatives, lending the impression that government cared for them.

Fearful of censorship and prosecution under strict laws of sedition backed by courts inclined to deliver judgements favourable to government, the local media were deterred from reporting these lucrative corporate manoeuvres and the harnessing of assets to politics. But determined regional reporters like *Asian Wall Street Journal's* Barry Wain and Raphael Pura did their best to reveal the tangled web of deals of huge conglomerates including Renong and United Engineers of Malaysia (UEM), two of the largest UMNO cash cows. Wain and Pura uncovered the vulnerability of the UMNO-linked companies, due to their financing and debt gearing, and that the Malaysian economy was essentially becoming hostage to the interests of its political elite who wanted to ensure an unending mandate, no matter how regularly elections were held. Barry Wain said of Daim: 'By his actions, Daim made it clear that he was not going to let conventional notions of conflict of interest interfere with the way that he ran his private business empire, the economy, or UMNO's financial affairs. They became deeply entangled.' Daim himself has always denied being responsible for any corporate malfeasance and was never accused of any crime. Many years later, I encountered Daim, then in his seventies, at an airline check-in desk in Rangoon. He was wearing a threadbare batik shirt and his trademark sandals, and had on a red baseball cap almost obscuring his mobile, mischievous face. We chatted and with his usual insouciance he shrugged off the legacy of his years in office and at the helm of UMNO's business empire. Today he is better known for his patronage of the arts.

Daim Zainuddin's legacy is a corporate landscape in which politics and business are so closely associated they cannot be distinguished. This situation set the stage for one of Southeast Asia's most spectacular corruption scandals, one that has transfixed Malaysians and set new standards in terms of the amounts of money involved and the trail of greed and destruction left in its wake.

*

Not since Ferdinand Marcos was deposed in the Philippines in 1986 has so much attention been focused on the source of a leader's wealth. Marcos, whose annual salary did not exceed $15,000 a year as president, was accused of stealing as much as $10 billion, enough to pay off half his impoverished country's national debt. Much of the money was stashed in offshore bank accounts. Thirty years later, only a fraction of this ill-gotten wealth has been recovered by a government body set up to track down the stolen money in the 1980s. It was perhaps one of the most spectacular political heists in the world.

In 2015 reports started to surface that implicated Prime Minister Najib Tun Razak of Malaysia in an alleged audacious plot to siphon public money from a government-supervised investment fund. The central allegation, which Najib denies, is the transfer of almost a billion dollars from the fund into Najib's own bank account. Government investigations have insisted these sums of money are all legitimate donations. Officially the Malaysian prime minister earns around $6,000 a month. For those who hoped that a culture of transparency and open government had somehow suffused the region after two financial crises and decades of pressure for reform and democratic change, this was perhaps one of the most dispiriting moments.

Suspicions were first raised in 2013 about the financial health of a state investment vehicle called 1 Malaysia Development Berhad (1MDB), which Prime Minister Najib managed in his capacity as finance minister. The fund's aim was to fan out and establish global partnerships, thereby attracting more foreign direct investment. Some of these deals were very big. In 2009 1MDB announced a $1.5 billion joint venture with Petro Saudi International and, a year later, a cooperation agreement with an Abu Dhabi-based energy venture. There were similar deals with Chinese and Qatari state enterprises, and a string of bond issues that elevated 1MDB's borrowings to $11 billion. With news that payments on these bonds were likely to default early in 2015, the opposition raised questions about the apparent lack of transparency. Despite the large sums allegedly raised overseas, the government was suspected of injecting funds into 1MDB to keep it afloat. Where had all the money gone?

These concerns were underlined by a succession of statements from 1MDB that indicated trouble with bond issues, statutory audits and requests for more time to explain transactions. In the end, the government itself grew suspicious and a request for a bailout was denied – unusually for a state-owned vehicle.

Then, out of nowhere, a small flyspeck of a blog based in the United Kingdom, and run by the sister-in-law of former British Prime Minister Gordon Brown, started publishing detailed stories that peered closely at the inner workings of 1MDB. The blog apparently had access to key documents allegedly related to the deals, scanned copies of which were published by the blog. The blog reported that the relevant files were handed to a Malaysian media outlet by a disgruntled former Petro Saudi partner, Xavier Justo, who was later arrested and jailed in Thailand for allegedly bribing the company he once worked for. The blog, which was called *Sarawak Report*, together with *The Sunday Times*, revealed in early 2015 that a young British public-school-educated Chinese businessman, Low Taek Jho, with close ties to Najib Tun Razak's stepson, Riza Aziz, had allegedly helped siphon off nearly $700 million from the 1MDB joint venture with Petro Saudi, which somehow ended up in one of Najib's personal accounts:

> a total of $681,999,976 was separately wire-transferred from the Singapore branch of the Swiss Falcon private bank owned by the Abu Dhabi fund Aabar into the prime minister's private AmBank account in Kuala Lumpur, on March 2013, just in advance of the calling of the General Election.

Najib denied any wrongdoing, claimed the money was a 'donation' from a member of the Saudi royal family to help win the 2013 general election, and that the bulk of the money was later returned. Emerging from a meeting with his Malaysian counterpart in early 2016, the Saudi Foreign Minister indicated that the funds were indeed a donation, as far as he knew. 1MDB insists that it never paid any money to Najib personally; however, the revelations kept coming. In March 2016 the *Asian Wall Street Journal* reported that overseas investigators believed that in excess of $1 billion flowed into

Najib's personal accounts, much of it originating from 1MDB. *The Economist* reported that the payments were routed through a company linked to – or made to look as if it was linked to – a venture involving 1MDB and Middle Eastern interests.

The allegations were made even more sensitive by initial moves by Malaysian authorities to investigate at the highest levels. Before Najib removed him, Attorney General Abdul Gani Patail had allegedly drawn up charges against the prime minister, though this was vigorously denied by his successor, who conducted another investigation and cleared the prime minister of any alleged wrongdoing. Neither Najib nor the Malaysian government has yet brought a law suit against the *Asian Wall Street Journal* or any other overseas publication to challenge the increasingly detailed and apparently well-sourced revelations, However, *The Edge*, a Malaysian business weekly had its publication licence suspended briefly and several politicians and activists in Malaysia who have voiced concerns about the scandal have been charged with sedition.

Despite consistent government denials the scope of the scandal grew as authorities in Switzerland, Singapore and the United States began looking into the trail of alleged financial malfeasance spawned by 1MDB. Several senior foreign bankers in the region lost their jobs, or resigned. At least one Swiss bank and Goldman Sachs were named as the possible targets of investigation. In July 2016 the United States Department of Justice filed lawsuits alleging that $3.5 billion had been stolen from 1MDB and moved to seize assets associated with Low Thaek Jho (since nicknamed 'Jho Low'), and Najib's stepson, Riza Aziz – both men were named in the suit. A spokesman for Riza Aziz told the *Wall Street Journal* that there was nothing inappropriate about his business dealings. Low Thaek Jho has not spoken to the media about the allegations but members of his family are fighting the bid to seize assets in his name. In a public statement US Attorney General Loretta Lynch said public officials had used the 1MDB fund as a 'personal bank account', but would not name any of the officials. She did refer to someone defined as 'Malaysian Official One'. Subsequently, in an interview with the BBC, a Malaysian Minister in the Prime Minister's Department acknowledged that Najib was 'Malaysian Official 1', insisting that the Prime Minister had done nothing wrong.

Yet in Malaysia the government's response was to protect 1MDB and sack those politicians and officials who had been critical of the government's handling of the case. Heads rolled, including one minister, a chief minister of a state, and a deputy prime minister who was also deputy president of the ruling UMNO party. Members of a so-called independent investigative panel were promoted without warning to junior cabinet positions. If there were voices within UMNO uncomfortable with this, they remained for the most part silent. Seasoned observers assumed that time-honoured methods of patronage involving hefty cash payments would be enough to keep the party rank and file quiet. Beneath the surface, however, Malaysians of all stripes seethed with anger, dismayed at the inability of any legal or political institution to address what seemed to the ordinary punter a clear case of outright corruption. When hundreds of thousands took to the streets of Kuala Lumpur to protest in mid-2015, the authorities threatened them with arrest using a newly refurbished sedition act that makes almost anything said against the government liable to prosecution. 'Injustice is happening all over the country; the government is going mad,' thundered commentator Azmi Sharom at the opening of the Georgetown literary festival I attended in the opposition-controlled state of Penang. At the same event in late 2015, renowned Malaysian cartoonist Zulkifli Anwar Ulhaque, popularly known as Zunar, proudly exhibited dozens of his drawings highlighting the corruption case using comical images of the Prime Minister and his wife usually clutching bags of money. He stood before a rapturous crowd in a dilapidated shophouse-turned-makeshift gallery, and provocatively waved two of his banned books featuring many cartoons on the theme of corruption. 'You can ban my books and cartoons,' he had told the police, 'but you can't ban my mind.' Subsequently, Zunar was briefly arrested and charged with sedition.

Quite apart from the remarkable scale of the alleged web of corruption around 1MDB, the case illustrates how destabilising this magnitude of official graft and collusion can be, not just for a government but also a country as socially fragile as Malaysia. For despite the outward trappings of modern democratic government that Malaysia inherited at independence, the harsh reality is that modern Malaysia remains a sum of its racially divided parts. So when exposure of a corruption scandal threatened Najib's leadership, the government's reaction was to trot out the spectre of a loss of Malay domination – in other words, play the race card.

Officially, the Malay and native-born '*bumiputera*' population, a term that means 'sons of the soil', accounts for over 60 per cent of the Federation of Malaysia's 28 million people. The Chinese account today for around 25 per cent, and Indians number under 8 per cent. Over the years, the proportion of Malays has increased, and is projected to exceed 70 per cent in the next decade. Meanwhile, the number of Chinese as a proportion has declined from close to 40 per cent at independence. Malaysia's ethnic alchemy underpins all government policies and drives all political calculations; despite official integrative visions of 'One Malaysia', there is in reality virtual ethnic and religious segregation. Each ethnic group has its own political party – UMNO is exclusively Malay and Muslim, for example. There is a Malaysian Chinese Association and a Malaysian Indian Congress, both of which sit in the ruling coalition. Efforts by the opposition to pull together a multiracial coalition have fallen victim to internal inter-racial suspicion and bickering. Racial and religious boundaries are strictly observed, and even if no longer official, there are quotas for the number of Malays a company is supposed to hire or promote to management.

Thus, in response to the 1MDB revelations, the government resorted to generating fear in the Malay community, suggesting that the opposition was using the scandal to threaten Malay privileges and the status of Islam. Uncritical receptivity to fears about the threat to Islam reinforces divisions in Malaysian society — to the point where calls for Muslims to be provided with separate shopping trolleys in supermarkets to avoid being tainted by non-halal food drowns out other concerns, such as corruption in high places. In a sign of how far Najib, once hailed as a force for liberal reform and champion of moderate Islam, was prepared to go to defend himself against his accusers, the government department responsible for scripting the Friday prayer sermons across all mosques in Malaysia wrote one in March 2016 that insisted: 'The decree to be loyal to the country's leaders does not come from the leaders themselves, but from God. Therefore, if the citizens are disloyal towards the leaders, that means they have been disloyal to God.' This mixing of the religious and the secular carries dangerous overtones in a country where the boundaries of faith and ethnicity coincide. A Malay academic, and quasi-government spokesperson, opined that reports of corruption in 1MDB should be disregarded, because they came from 'kafir' or non-Muslims. This sent a clear message projected to the Muslim Malay majority that Najib's name was being tarnished by the Malaysian Chinese. A ruling party official even claimed that the US government, having spent the past few years killing Muslims in Iraq, was now turning its sights on Muslim Malays.

Najib Tun Razak came to power in 2009 on a wave of promises to reform the country's unfair policies of ethnic favouritism and archaic internal security laws. The British-public-school educated son of Malaysia's second prime minister, Tun Abdul Razak, has served in government for three decades and I knew him well enough as an effective minister and politician in the 1990s when he served as minister of defence and then education. Charming and amiable, Najib was in many ways a smoother-edged version of the kind of leadership that Mahathir Mohamad represented, with his provocative oratory betraying deeply felt prejudices and obsession with domination. Najib is at heart no Malay ultra-nationalist or Islamic firebrand; his English accent is so plummy even his Malay sounds as if it is being spoken with a silver-spooned disdain for the masses. But he lacked courage. I remember a campaign trip I made with him to Sabah in east Malaysia, where UMNO was under some pressure from the opposition back in the mid-1990s. We travelled from Kuala Lumpur in a Malaysian military transport aircraft, and then transferred to a helicopter to join a political rally. As the helicopter approached what seemed like a jungle clearing, Najib looked nervous. 'Where is everyone?' he asked an aide. I could see a small group of people below, but no banners of welcome.

'Come on,' I said, 'you're a politician. Surely you aren't worried about a bit of heckling?' Najib looked at me with fear in his somewhat bulbous eyes and then ordered the helicopter to return to base.

Najib came to power promising reform, both of the arcane

security laws that impede free speech, and the affirmative policies that privilege Malay ownership and marginalise non-Malay and Muslims citizens. He also promised to put Islam in Malaysia firmly on the path towards tolerance and moderation. He even established a Global Movement of Moderates, which won plaudits in the West and was embraced as a regional initiative by ASEAN leaders. But the 1MDB scandal has forced him to reverse course in order to shore up his power base and block opposition efforts to sanction him. Since 2014, Najib has reinstated a more repressive internal security act, using the arcane laws of sedition to silence his critics. Far from advocating moderation, he has curried favour with Islamic hardliners in order to split the opposition and shore up his Malay Muslim base of support. A proposed law to implement harsh Islamic Hudud criminal law, which prescribes caning, amputation and other draconian penalties, was languishing at the state assembly level, but after the 1MDB scandal broke suddenly found a path to the floor of the federal parliament. And there is no sign of any reform of the New Economic Policy, which he dare not tinker with for fear of upsetting party loyalists.

Najib may win the next elections, due before May 2018, but if the ruling party, UMNO, doesn't regain its commanding two-thirds majority, he could fall victim to the 1MDB scandal, which threatens to expose not only the lengths to which he and his immediate family have gone to amass their fortunes, but also the violence they are said to be prepared to tolerate to protect themselves. For accompanying the staggering corruption reports are sordid and murky stories of intimidation and murder: a beautiful Mongolian model, Shaariibuugiin Altantuya, kidnapped and disposed of using C4 explosives after being linked to one of Najib's close aides (the aide was later acquitted, but two of Najib's bodyguards were found guilty of the murder); Hussein Najadi, the Bahraini-born founder of AmBank, where Najib held his accounts, who was mysteriously murdered in a car park one evening in 2013; and the deputy public prosecutor involved in the investigation of 1MDB, Kevin Morais, whose chopped-up torso was found stuffed in an oil drum. Seven people, including a senior army doctor, have been charged with his murder. None of these cases involve Najib or his family but some feel they are too close to him for comfort. A number of potential whistle-blowers have been shamelessly bought off or intimidated. One of them – the widow of a private investigator – was bribed with so paltry a sum that it seemed like a joke; another, one of Najib's security detail found guilty of the Mongolian model's murder, later acquitted and then re-sentenced to death, skipped bail and now sits in an Australian detention centre under the thumb of UMNO lawyers who have allegedly paid handsomely for his silence.

Malaysia is the ultimate victim: the value of its currency has plummeted alongside its reputation as a middle-income tiger economy managing overseas aid and investment in Africa. Little wonder that many Malaysians – those who can afford to – are choosing to emigrate, or invest abroad. The real-estate agency Knight Frank estimates that in 2014 Malaysians invested close to $5 billion in property overseas. In early 2016 the Malaysian government revealed that 50,000 people had renounced their citizenship since 2010. 'Malaysia's current political leadership no longer articulates a vision that serves Malaysia's people. Malaysia's leadership is no longer one admired by and hopeful for others around the world,' lamented Danny Quah, a former government economic adviser, now working as an academic overseas. By the end of 2017, Najib Tun Razak remained very much in power, having avoided any form of domestic censure at the political level; the only victims so far were among those seeking to reveal wrong-doing in high places, including a prominent member of the opposition in parliament, Rafizi Ramli, who was sentenced to eighteen months in prison for releasing a copy of the classified government audit of 1MDB.

There's an even bigger consequence, however, which affects the wider region. In early 2016 it was announced that a Chinese state-owned enterprise had paid $2.3 billion dollars for the power-generation assets of 1MDB, giving China a major foothold in Malaysia's energy sector, and significantly helping to liquidate some of the estimated $9 billion dollars in debt accrued by 1MDB. The government insisted the deal was commercially sound. Earlier, another Chinese company had invested $1.7 billion in a 1MDB-owned property development. Both deals made China by far the largest investor by value in Malaysia in 2016 and set the stage for securing a stake in the construction of high-speed railways worth billions of dollars. Less well articulated was the leverage this now offered China over Malaysia on a raft of strategic issues affecting the wider region. When China objected to an ASEAN statement critical of China regarding the South China Sea at a foreign ministers meeting in Yunnan in mid-2016, Malaysia raised no objections, even though, as a claimant state, Malaysia has plenty of issues with China. When a potentially explosive international court of arbitration ruling was issued in The Hague that undermined China's claims in the South China Sea, Malaysia could be counted on to stay silent and, its foreign minister stayed away from a critical ASEAN meeting where the issue was raised for undisclosed reasons. In November 2016 Najib visited China and used the visit to warn the Western colonial powers not to lecture countries they once exploited on how to run their own internal affairs. He returned with $34 billion in trade and investment deals and four Chinese warships for the navy. Just a year earlier, Prime Minister Najib was pictured golfing with US President Obama in Hawaii and Malaysia was a leading proponent of the Trans-Pacific Partnership that Washington pinned hopes on as a bulwark against Chinese economic power in the Asia-Pacific. Arguably, the Malaysian government was susceptible to China's inducements because its leadership was in a bind, exposed to a corruption scandal on a massive scale and instead of sweeping it under the carpet, the US authorities subsequently chose to magnify and highlight it in an investigation led by the Department of Justice.

For embattled leaders and governments under scrutiny in the West for corruption, China is a friend. It was a lesson heeded by Cambodia's Prime Minister Hun Sen, whose 2011 declaration that his annual salary totalled $13,800 a year was called into question by NGO Global Witness. In summer 2016 Global Witness reported that Hun Sen's fortune stands at somewhere between $500 million and $1 billion, with members of his extended family acquiring vast swathes of the corporate and public enterprise landscape. 'Companies associated to the Hun family,' the report states, 'span the majority of Cambodia's most lucrative business sectors, including trade, finance, energy and tourism. They also operate within a number of sectors notorious for corruption including gambling, construction, agriculture and mining.' There was no official response from Hun

Sen himself, but his daughter Hun Mana posted a message on Facebook accusing Global Witness of tarnishing her father's reputation with 'lies and deceits to confuse the public' ahead of elections.

China initially sidled up to the royalists who held power in the mid-1990s in Phnom Penh – King Sihanouk was close to China and maintained a home in Beijing until his death. But Sihanouk and his son, Prince Norodom Ranariddh, were great balancers in the tradition of Southeast Asia's traditional royal rulers and sought to establish ties with Taiwan. Therefore, from the late 1990s, Beijing curried favour with Hun Sen, who finally threw off the royalist alliance in which he had served as second prime minister until 1998. By 2006, with Hun Sen well established, China had pledged $600 million in grants and loans, helped restore Angkor Wat, built bridges across the Mekong and offered millions in military assistance. By 2012 the total level of Chinese investment in Cambodia was close to $10 billion.

Cambodian Commerce Minister Sun Chanthol told the *Washington Post* that none of this came with strings. 'It is because we need infrastructure fast and quick, nothing more than that. Are there any conditions put on Cambodia by China? I can tell you, absolutely nothing. No conditions at all.' Yet faced with dwindling trust and support from the West, which recoiled from his approach to government, Hun Sen became a grateful and palpable ally. So when China came knocking in 2012 to head off an ASEAN consensus critical of China's behaviour in the South China Sea, Hun Sen, as host of an ASEAN ministerial meeting in Cambodia, could be relied on to prevent that from happening.

The extent of corruption and the levels it has reached across all levels of government in many countries of Southeast Asia is both a source of concern to the citizenry of the region and a major strategic headache. The persistence of graft and greed in leadership circles is also a considerable obstacle to progressive political reform and change. We see this most clearly in the case of Malaysia and Cambodia. There has been some effort to address the issue, though with mixed results. Thailand's military rulers have used fighting corruption as one of the key planks of their bid to win support for prolonged military rule, although the longer they stay in power the more prone to corruption they become. Populist reformers such as Joko Widodo of Indonesia and more recently Rodrigo Duterte in the Philippines have made fighting corruption a centrepiece of their campaigns. The day he was inaugurated president in July 2016, Duterte made a point of issuing his first executive order at the ceremony. 'I order all department secretaries and heads of agencies to refrain from changing and bending the rules of government contracts, transactions and projects already approved and awaiting implementation,' he thundered in his opening speech. These were fine words. Putting them into practice will be extremely challenging.

PART 2

CONFLICT

CHAPTER NINE

SMALL WARS AND CONTESTED IDENTITIES

'This country, the Republic of Indonesia, does not belong to any group, nor to any religion, nor to any ethnic group, nor to any group with customs and traditions, but the property of all of us from Sabang to Merauke!'

Sukarno, Founding President of Indonesia

'We are not terrorists. We just want to be free.'

Benny Wenda, Papuan leader

I have a picture on my office wall of a man probably about twenty years old, wearing army fatigues and a slouch cap, smiling at the camera with an ageing sub-machine gun slung in front of him. I took the photograph in 1982 on a surreptitious trip across the Myanmar–Thailand border, to visit one of the many camps run by ethnic armed groups fighting the Burmese army. The young man was on guard in a remote camp belonging to the Pa O National Army, located just a few kilometres into the Burmese side of the border. The Pa O people are Myanmar's seventh-largest ethnic group who inhabit the eastern littoral of modern Myanmar along the border with Thailand, known as the Shan State. The camp was set in the deep red earth of the cleared hillside, on a slope fringed with tall dipterocarp trees. A flimsy bamboo picket fence marked the perimeter, which was guarded from a central sand-bagged bunker equipped with a Second World War Bren gun and a rusty alarm clock – for sounding the watches, I was told. The young smiling soldier in my photo

Young soldier in the Pa O National Army,
circa *1982.*

fingers his weapon nervously – an image that captures the essence
of insurgency in Southeast Asia, where the young find themselves
shackled to hard-to-win struggles in remote places, living with the
only aspect of dignity they have left: their identity.

Southeast Asia has a spectacular record of internal conflict – harbouring some of the world's longest civil wars in forgotten corners
of territory. These small wars might not impinge on the daily life of
citizens in the more developed capitals. Nor do they affect foreign
visitors and tourists, except once in a while. But they do cost tens of
thousands of lives. They undermine prosperity and interrupt lives,
and so more hidden costs are incurred and progress denied. In recent
years, evidence has come to light that in some areas these conflicts are
fuelling international terrorism in the way that chronic tribal conflict
in Afghanistan and Pakistan has so spectacularly done. The northern
quadrant of Myanmar's Rakhine State is as far away as you can get in
Southeast Asia. The principal towns of Maundgaw and Bhutidaung
nestle close to the border with Bangladesh and are mostly populated
by the stateless Rohingya people. When a group of several hundred
Rohingya carried out attacks on police officers and army outposts

in early October 2016, intelligence reports emanating from India and Bangladesh indicated they were aided by the Lashkar-e-Taiba, a Pakistani Islamic extremist group that has carried out attacks in India – which the Rohingya group denies. Left unattended, festering ethno-nationalist struggles for autonomy or independence in some of the marginal Muslim areas of Southeast Asia have already attracted the attention of the Islamic State (IS) in Syria and Iraq. In 2015, an armed group in the southern Philippines notorious for kidnapping foreigners for ransom released a professionally made video declaring allegiance to IS. They beheaded two Western hostages and filmed the atrocity. In 2017, a group of IS-linked militants occupied the sizeable city of Marawi in Muslim Mindanao; it took the Philippine army five months to retake the city at cost of more than a thousand lives. While the war that rages in Syria and Iraq and the internal strife afflicting much of North Africa and Western Africa is the backdrop against which fears of a new wave of extremist violence play out internationally, Southeast Asia's unresolved conflicts offer a conducive environment for more barbaric forms of terrorism to take hold. That these conflicts remain unresolved sixty years after most of them erupted is mainly the fault of governments that have for generations ignored them, taken advantage of them, and fended off all efforts from the outside to help bring them to an end.

The Asia Foundation calculates that sub-national conflicts across Asia have cost an estimated 1.6 million lives since 1947. Between 1999 and 2008 more people died in sub-national conflict in Asia than in all other conflicts elsewhere in the world. This is remarkable because in recent years the proportion of battle deaths overall has declined drastically in East Asia. According to the East Asia Peace programme, a research body at Uppsala University in Sweden, East Asia accounted for 80 per cent of the global total of battle deaths from 1947 to 1979, but in the period since then the proportion is less than 4 per cent. Although sub-national conflicts in Asia affect a small minority of the overall demographic total (around 7 per cent) this amounts to around 130 million people. In some cases the level of violence is high: a dozen years of fighting in southern Thailand has killed 6,500 people and injured 40,000, in an area populated by three million people.

The insurgents in Southern Thailand have at times taken their campaign of violence beyond the three contested provinces and targeted areas popular with foreign tourists. However, the majority of sub-national conflicts in Southeast Asia are situated on the margins – the uplands of Myanmar, the deep south of Thailand, the southernmost island of Mindanao in the Philippines, the far eastern province of Papua in Indonesia, and in small pockets of the highlands of Vietnam and Laos, all distant from the buzzing metropolises, traffic jams and shiny shopping malls, and usually from the tourists, who rarely venture there but who sometimes find themselves affected by the conflict brought to them.

With the exception of the New People's Army communist movement in the Philippines, these are all ethno-nationalist conflicts: struggles by an ethnic minority to achieve a measure of meaningful autonomy, if not independence. The insurgent groups leading these struggles are well armed, sufficiently financed, and enjoy a significant measure of popular support in their areas. In the case of the ethnic armed groups in Myanmar and Mindanao, they hold significant expanses of territory and have organised, formally-structured armed forces. When I visited the Moro Islamic Liberation Headquarters at Camp Darapanan, outside Cotabato City in Mindanao, I was taken aback. Not only does the MILF hold territory a few minutes' drive outside a provincial capital, but it is permitted to arm and defend the area with its own troops. The camp's neat lawns and mundane office buildings suggest an established state within a state. The camp even has a dedicated Facebook page. Many of the armed groups of the region trade in drugs and contraband or export valuable gems and timber, their struggle for freedom serving as a convenient cloak for profitable criminal machinery. In the Kachin Hills of northern Myanmar, the profits from mining jade, the cool green stone valued by the Chinese, are estimated to exceed $30 billion a year. These benefits flow to the Kachin Independence Army as well as to the Myanmar Army they have been fighting for decades. Yet apart from the singular case of the Tamil separatists in Sri Lanka, military action alone has failed to defeat any of these insurgencies.

Up close, the armed movements are not what they seem from afar. After decades of underground struggle in forbidding environments on the edges of developed, urban society, their fighters look care-worn and haggard. They have abandoned families and carry their meagre rations on their back. By contrast, their sometimes urbane, well-spoken leaders often get to travel overseas or live in exile, inhab-iting a shadowy world of friendly liberation movements, lobbying susceptible liberal governments for support, shelter and welfare, or equally susceptible, less reputable ones for weapons and money. They join meetings of the Unrepresented Nations and People's Organisation in The Hague and the Organisation of Islamic Con-ference in Jeddah. Some of them lead otherwise ordinary, mundane lives, working as bus drivers or postal workers in dowdy suburbs of Sweden or Norway. A professed leader of a liberation struggle I have known for almost a decade lives and works openly in a suburban Swedish town. He has a Facebook page and is fond of racking up air miles; in meetings he wears a smart suit and is always neatly turned out. Yet he is the man whose organisation is suspected of planting and detonating a bomb in a hotel next door to the one where I was conducting a meeting in southern Thailand. Luckily, the bomb blast caused only minor injuries.

He and I have shared countless lunches and dinners – broken bread. Still, he is a trained guerrilla fighter, who learnt his trade at the hands of the Palestine Liberation Organisation in Libyan training camps back in the 1970s. Whenever I meet his henchmen, with their wide smiles and emotional man-hugs, I ponder the violent acts they have committed, as well as the victimhood they suffer themselves, from losing family members. Another former fighter I knew lost his son in what we all at first assumed to be a hit by the security forces somewhere along the Thai–Malaysia border. In his anger, the man sent me a file of detailed photographs showing his son's mutilated, broken body. But it turned out that his son had died in a drug deal that had gone wrong. When I spoke to him about this he shrugged, and said: 'I have other sons.'

People are driven to violence. They grow accustomed to it. It becomes a business, a way of life.

The seeds of sub-national conflict in Southeast Asia lie in the pro-cess of modern state formation, which involved the disruption of pre-colonial autonomous principalities and the birth of the cohesive, centralised nation state. The majority of violent internal conflicts in Southeast Asia today are situated in marginal princely states that were independent before the colonial period. Some of these principalities had long histories. The Patani Sultanate, situated in modern southern Thailand, conducted trade directly with China and the Arabian coast in the fifteenth century until it was subdued and became a tributary state of the Siamese king in 1786. The Acehnese Sultanate at the northern tip of the Indonesian island of Sumatra was one of three countries that supported the Dutch declaration of independence from Spain in the sixteenth century.

When armed rebel movements raised the flags of rebellion in the latter half of the twentieth century, they used these fading memories of sovereignty to justify their armed struggle. Ibrahim Syukri, a local historian of Patani in southern Thailand writing just as the nationalist struggle first erupted in the 1940s, relates how the Kingdom of Patani developed into a rich trading hub by the seventeenth century 'constantly frequented by ships which carried trade goods from foreign lands'. Aside from Arabs and some Chinese, the pocket sultanate attracted first Portuguese then Dutch and English traders who established factories at the mouth of the muddy Patani River. By the end of the sixteenth century, the 'Raja' of Patani was sending trade missions to Japan. Boldly, the historian claims that 'Ayuthya, the centre of government of Siam during that period, could not equal the commercial progress of Patani. Seeing the progress of Patani, the Raja of Siam was inspired with intense desire to subjugate Patani.' Much as this surely exaggerates the importance of one among a myriad of tiny ports that foreign ships called on to provision or seek shelter from the monsoon, the narrative of prosperous autonomy from marauding powerful kingdoms laid a strong foundation for the ideology of modern irredentism across Southeast Asia.

Acehnese rebel leaders were keen to highlight the treaties the old sultanate had signed with European powers in the seventeenth century. They, like the Muslim Malays of Patani, were always grateful when presented with copies of these original treaties, long eclipsed and forgotten, but cherished as the memory of sovereignty from another age. To take another example, the Mon-speaking people who today populate the eastern littoral of Myanmar constituted a powerful kingdom until the sixteenth century. The first European traders who travelled there established warehouses in the ancient Mon trading port of Martaban and embassies in the capital of Pegu. When Burma won independence from Britain in 1948 the Mons demanded self-determination, which was refused. As a result, the Mon National Liberation Army, which can muster at most a thousand men under arms today, has been fighting for independence ever since. Before the colonial period, flexible forms of autonomy were the norm in Southeast Asia. Allegiance and loyalty were paid to distant kingdoms, but limitations on the mobility of armies meant this tended to be symbolic. A sense of pride lingers in these areas that once figured prominently in global trade and diplomacy. Memories of long-faded glory and importance are significant props to the claims on statehood and demands for independence that underpin the violent insurgent movements of the region.

The colonial powers brought the means and mechanisms for centralising power over territory, from the telegraph and railroad to the district officer. The introduction of effective administrative power and authority upset the unequal balance between imposition and neglect that had allowed marginal areas to govern themselves until the late nineteenth century, or even later. European and American interlopers disrupted the isolated upland societies of mainland Southeast Asia; if not fastidious colonial administrative officers, then loggers from the originally Scottish-owned Bombay Burmah Trading Company and Christian missionaries from the United States, who traipsed the hills of mainland Southeast Asia in search of teak and souls, and found plenty of both. It was Christian missionaries who first recorded the languages of these upland people, often lending them the Roman script so they could remain distinctive from the lowland kingdoms they feared and shunned. Lieutenant Colonel Alexander Ruxton McMahon typified the leading edge of this disruptive force. McMahon, a deputy commissioner in British Burma, travelled the remote hills of the country in the last quarter of the nineteenth century classifying, recording and (albeit unintentionally) annexing people who had roamed free of any sort of rule and governance for centuries. He writes in the 1876 preface to *The*

Karens of the Golden Chersonese: 'I was able by intimate communication with the people in my tours through the district, sometimes in jungles where a white man had never been seen before . . . to collect much matter which had not been noticed by former observers.'

As a student in northern Thailand in the early 1980s, my research focused on the ethnic minority groups populating the upland borderlands and occasionally migrating to the cities in search of commercial opportunity. Distinctive groups such as the Akha, Karen, Lahu, Lisu and Hmong had migrated originally from Western China to the sparsely populated hills of Burma, Laos and Thailand. On my frequent trips to their villages in the hills around Chiang Mai and Chiang Rai, I was treated to simple meals of mountain pig stewed in pungent forest herbs accompanied by bowls of pink hill rice, washed down with fermented rice wine served up in porcelain tumblers. Afterwards, around a flickering fire, I listened to their old stories about a free-spirited people roaming across the lush, green hills stretching from the borders with India to the valleys of Yunnan in China. The conversations lasted much of the night, after which I would collapse on a split-bamboo floor and be wakened before dawn by the sweet scent of pine kindling and the sound of padding feet as the women prepared the morning kettles. I was struck by their ingrained sense of independence, oblivious to the encroachment of modern government and authority.

At the end of the colonial era the blunt force of unifying, central authority replaced the more tolerant expediencies of divide and rule. The newly independent nations were established on ambitious ideals of brotherhood and unity. 'Let us rejoice at the independence which has come to us today,' declared Sao Shwe Thaike, an ethnic Shan prince in his maiden speech as the first president of the Union of Burma in January 1948:

> For a long time, the principal races of Burma – the Kachins and the Chins – have tended to look upon themselves as separate national units. Of late, a nobler vision, the vision of a Union of Burma, has moved our hearts, and we stand united today as one nation determined to work in unity and concord for the

advancement of Burma's interests and for the speedy attainment of her due position as one of the great nations of the world. It is unity that has brought our struggle for independence to this early fruition and may unity continue to be the watchword for every member of the Sovereign Independent Republic to be henceforth known as the Union of Burma.

But the shallow basis for this unity was built on an administrative framework steeped in colonial exigency and historical prejudices. Imperfect integration and forced assimilation became the conductors of grievance that eventually generated violence across large areas of Burma, Indonesia, Thailand and the Philippines soon after the end of the Pacific War. As new states struggled to establish themselves, rebellions erupted along poorly defined borders and fault lines of social and ethnic division. Many of these groups, such as the Karen and Kachin of Burma, felt abandoned and betrayed, as they had been pawns in the colonial game of divide and rule. Others, such as the Muslim Moro in the southern Philippines, and to some extent the Acehnese in northern Sumatra, had evaded subjugation altogether and were not about to change their independent mindset just because of modern statehood. The Muslim Moros and the Acehnese were among the most difficult people the Western imperial powers found to subdue. The occupying United States army developed the .45 calibre automatic pistol for the Philippine jungles of Mindanao, so that marauding Moro could be blown away as they charged out of the trees with swords and spears. Casualties were high as the Moros were determined to fight to the death. The Indonesian writer Mochtar Lubis told me he recalled hearing as a child in the 1940s about Acehnese who would walk up to Dutchmen on the street and stab them because they hated them so much. The Acehnese used suicide tactics similar to modern-day jihadists, inspired by their nationalist cause. The Dutch only subdued Aceh after a thirty-year war in 1904 that cost 60,000 lives. Seventy years later, a vicious internal conflict erupted after the Acehnese were disappointed with the benefits of joining the modern Indonesian republic.

Careless management of the decolonisation process helps explain the genesis of the most deadly internal conflict in Southeast Asia today, one which I have had a close working experience over the past decade. The Patani Sultanate, which ruled the largely Malay and Muslim people of the area, had been independent or at least semi-independent until the late eighteenth century, after which it was finally subjugated by Siam in 1786. Historical accounts from the period attest to a violent suppression of resistance during which Siamese forces roped together men, women and children and had them trampled by elephants: contemporary reports indicate that at least 50,000 refugees fled south into the neighbouring Malay states. To this day a massive seventeenth-century bronze cannon that belonged to the sultanate sits outside the defence ministry in the heart of Bangkok, like a piece of lawn art.

At the end of the Pacific War, the former Patani Sultanate appealed to allied forces to consider their case for separating from Thailand. Under the terms of the 1909 Anglo-Siam Treaty, the Muslim Malay majority areas of modern-day Patani, Narathiwat, Yala, Satun and Songkhla were ceded to Siam. Even so, the Patani Malays were banking on a favourable hearing because Thailand had refused to declare war on Japan, which occupied the country without opposition. However, the British ignored their pleas, possibly because they had their hands full with the Malay states further south. Shortly after the war ended, Tengku Mahmud, a British-educated Malay prince descended from the Patani royal family, started running guns into the three southernmost provinces of Thailand to arm a fledgling rebel movement and the revolt began.

By the mid-1960s, violent internal conflict simmered across much of Myanmar, southern Thailand, the southern Philippines and Indonesia, fuelled by increasingly repressive forced integration and armed by a steady stream of modern weapons flowing out of the Indochina War and procured on the black market. These conflicts have proved pernicious and protracted because central governments have stubbornly resisted responding to the rebel demands and granting autonomy. Yet they have been unable to defeat these insurgent armed movements. The British army developed one of the earliest modern counter-insurgency strategies in the late 1940s, struggling in the jungles of Malaya to contain the Malayan Communist Party. The main tools for doing so were the denial of any kind of legal rights to those who were caught and the ruthless treatment of local inhabitants accused of harbouring what were known then as terrorists. National approaches to counter-insurgency in Southeast Asia have adopted some of the extra-judicial characteristics of their former colonial masters, including torture and detention without trial. These conflicts being for the most part out of sight, security forces in Southeast Asia have an appalling record of brutality towards insurrection. Common methods include punitive killings of civilians thought to be sympathetic to rebel forces, destruction of homes and livelihoods, and the widespread use of torture and extra-judicial killings. Even so, security forces have conducted poor and long-drawn-out military campaigns designed to pad defence budgets rather than secure victory.

In contemporary Myanmar, Thailand and the Philippines, long-running security operations against separatist guerrilla armies have served to boost military prestige and justify the need for the army to act as guardians of the state – in the absence of a clear external threat. In the case of the civil wars in Myanmar, the army developed profitable businesses dealing with the ethnic minority groups who control large areas on the borders of India and China. In southern Thailand, the past decade of virulent internal conflict has justified significant increases in the Thai army's overall defence budget and the awarding of additional per diems for those who serve in the deep southern region, also known to be a major transit point for smuggled goods. According to informed officials, the army's view of 'success' with regard to this conflict is for the violence to continue, but at a manageable level. Resolution is *not* the goal, as this would mean giving something away.

The preface to a long-forgotten report on reconciliation in southern Thailand completed in 2007 quoted a former King of Thailand in the early twentieth century, Rama VI, as saying that the key to managing the south was to 'send good people to govern'; there was no mention of integration. 'The goal is not the happiness of the people,' I was told by one of the senior members of the committee that produced the report. The insurgents, too, impose on local inhabitants, often raising taxes to fund the armed struggle or imposing heavy levies on trade. The violence they perpetrate kills innocent civilians, like the female Thai teacher who was gunned down on 28 October 2016 by two young men riding a motorcycle who were caught on a security camera. They left a note that read: 'For you bastards that kill Malays'. In southern Thailand, both sides carry out targeted shootings of civilians.

At the same time as finding these conflicts hard to win – or too profitable to end – governments have baulked at peace talks, citing threats to sovereignty. This is perhaps the most fundamental reason why lives continue to be lost in these archaic conflicts; there is simply no will to settle them using the tools of peaceful dialogue. It is only in the past twenty years that governments have started to hold talks with rebels. The conflict in Aceh, northern Sumatra, ended after a short period of dialogue and negotiation when the Indonesian government agreed in 2005 to giving both a significant measure of autonomy to the province, and to the armed resistance movement forming a political party whereby they could contest local elections. This uncomplicated compromise ended thirty years of low-intensity insurgency that had cost the lives of an estimated 50,000 innocent villagers in skirmishes and army-led reprisals.

After seventeen years of negotiation, the conflict in southern Philippines was settled with a comprehensive peace agreement signed with great fanfare in March 2014. And in Myanmar, after just two years of negotiation between government negotiators and an alliance of ethnic armed groups, a nationwide ceasefire agreement (NCA) was initialled in March 2015, paving the way for a national-level political dialogue on a future framework to grant federal rights to the ethnically non-Burman areas that comprise about one third of the country and its population.

Yet despite such hopeful, hard-won agreements, the peace is fragile and hard to implement. In Myanmar, only eight of the twenty-one ethnic armed groups ended up formally signing the NCA. Meanwhile, the army continued military operations in areas not covered by the ceasefire, sustaining a deep reservoir of mistrust. In the Philippines, the Comprehensive Agreement covering the Bangsamoro in Mindanao languished after a botched raid in February 2015 to capture an Islamic terrorist suspect in Mindanao resulted in the deaths of forty-four Philippine police commandos – killed in a defensive counter-attack by the MILF who retaliated because of the violation of a long-standing ceasefire agreement. The larger issue was that, with a presidential election looming, no one was prepared to defend the peace process. Often, with each change of government there comes a fresh approach to tackling internal conflict. Not only is there money to be made from waging war internally, but also political capital from playing at making peace. Over the ten years I have worked in Indonesia, Thailand and the Philippines on internal conflict, each new government has effectively undone the achievements of its predecessors and taken a fresh approach, which leaves the armed groups sceptical about commitments to peace and untrusting of government emissaries. Back in 2005, a National Reconciliation Council was established in southern Thailand to explore and discuss the local grievances fuelling the conflict. I attended many of its sessions and saw how open some Thai officials were at that time to listening and shaping policy to address the causes of the conflict. The recommendations were ignored and then buried after the military coup in 2006.

Add to this the tendency of centralised states in the region to ignore conflicts on the margins. Unlike many of the small wars of Africa and the Middle East, which bring death and destruction into their capital cities, the small wars of Southeast Asia tend to remain localised. Nevertheless, the economic damage must be taken into account: the World Bank estimates that the thirty-year-long Aceh conflict cost the country $10 billion, double that of the 2004 tsunami, which claimed almost 200,000 lives. The estimated cost of twelve years of conflict in southern Thailand is in excess of $3 billion. Then there are the lives disrupted and dislocated, the education interrupted or prevented, the provision of social services, and justice, denied – the incalculable human cost of conflict carried over from one generation to the next.

I saw this for myself most vividly in a charming island province called Sulu in the southern Philippines, notable for being the first community to embrace Islam, introduced by Arab traders in the fourteenth century. Yet despite its charm and beauty, Sulu is one of the most dangerous spots in the region, plagued by endemic violence associated with a form of traditional clan conflict that demands fierce battle until honour is restored. Small wars employing heavy mortars and machine guns have been sparked by something as insignificant as a casual glance at another man's wife.

While other remote islands in this colander of an archipelago have stabilised and developed as lucrative tourist destinations, Sulu's endemic violence has deterred development. High up on a jungle-clad hill that overlooks the capital, Jolo, sits a Philippine military camp with a commanding view of the city below. In the 1970s the Philippine army invaded the island to retake it from Muslim Moro rebels in a bloody fight that saw the destruction of the historic downtown area. Not much has changed, arguably not since Joseph Conrad cruised through the Sulu Sea on a schooner, encountering well-armed bands of Tausug pirates. In one evocative short story, Conrad described the Tausugs as an 'ornamented and barbarous crowd . . . [the] frank, audacious faces of men barefooted, well-armed and noiseless'. Today these same men pass, unimpeded, through the jungles. Several notable Islamic terrorists from Indonesia found safe haven among them, and set up camps to train and develop their bomb-making skills. In recent years evidence has surfaced of recruitment in the name of IS. The Moro insurgency, coupled with the proliferation of weapons and poor or non-existent law and order, has spawned ever more violent clan conflicts leaving thousands living in poverty and fear.

When I visited Sulu I was guarded by police officers almost falling over with the weight of automatic weaponry and extra ammunition. As Conrad found, the Tausugs form a bond with weaponry, boasting that they value their guns above their women. Images of mafia-style shootouts with small arms do no justice to the barrages of heavy mortar and .50 calibre-machine gunfire that characterises clan warfare in Sulu. Add to this lingering resentment towards Manila over arrangements for the return of the now Malaysian State of Sabah, which the heirs to the Sultan of Sulu claim, and incessant demands for autonomy, and it's little wonder that the Philippine marines based there huddle in their hilltop camp, which boasts the only Starbucks on the island.

So why are these conflicts so hard to resolve? Why have the Moro in the Philippines struggled since the 1960s? Why have the Malay

Muslims of southern Thailand fought Thai rule since the 1940s? And why have the Karens, like the Mons, waged a civil war with the central government of Myanmar since 1949 – two years after the country gained its independence?

Virulent sovereignty is one of the most obvious explanations. It is clear that one of the least complicated resolutions of sub-national conflict is the granting of some form of autonomy. But for most of the governments of Southeast Asia, sovereignty remains a highly sensitive issue, in part because most of the nation states are relatively young, and memories of their nationalist struggle remain fresh. For the archipelagic states, Indonesia and the Philippines, granting autonomy to far-flung islands is seen as inviting secession. As a result, states are seized with a paranoid fear of partition or the loss of territory, and retain strong impulses to impose authority and compel people as subjects, rather than have faith in their loyalty as citizens. This speaks to an astonishing degree of short-sighted selfishness; what kind of national leader or official calculates that it is worth the deaths of three people a day (the average loss of life in the southern Thailand conflict until 2012) to preserve sovereignty? At the same time, many of the societies that feel imposed upon or subjected are equally determined to maintain their identity and a degree of autonomy – even to the point of choosing debilitating war over peace.

This duality lies at the heart of the ethnic conflicts that have plagued Myanmar since 1948 and which together constitute one of the world's largest landscapes of internal conflict stretching from the borders of India to China. The non-Burman ethnic groups, which constitute one-third of the country's population and more in terms of land area, secured an early promise from the newly independent government of a federal system and known as the Panglong Agreement. This wasn't much beyond a vague promise, though. Initially, ethnic leaders placed their faith in the benevolence of the country's first prime minister, U Nu, under a constitution giving them some say in how the country was administered. They did so in the hope that reform would follow. But in the course of fighting rebellious ethnic warlords and communist insurgents on the margins shortly after independence, the Myanmar army strengthened, and under its strongman, General Ne Win, acquired a structural cohesion not matched in civilian political circles. When in 1962 the army stepped in and seized power, all hopes of a federal system collapsed. The army viewed the ethnic groups on the margins as subject peoples who were fighting to secede, and who needed to be suppressed by force. Disappointment, fuelled by harassment and abuse at the hands of the army, tipped the ethnic groups into open rebellion.

When I was a student in Chiang Mai in the early 1980s I lived next door to one of the leaders of the Shan Nationalist Movement. Chao Tzang Yaunghwe, born in the Shan princely state of Yaunghwe, was the son of one of the many Shan princes granted administrative power under British rule. As mentioned earlier, his father, Sao Shwe Thaike, was a Shan noble who had served as the first president of the Union of Burma. He lived with his mother, known as the *Mahadewi*, or 'Great Queen' of Yaunghwe, in a modest house near the northwestern wall of the city. We all called him Eugene – a name he probably acquired at one of the Catholic seminaries he attended as a child. I learned of his past over long evenings and delectable Shan dishes served by the grand and imposing but charming *Mahadewi*, who was an excellent cook. Eugene wasn't exactly the picture of a rebel insurgent leader. Already in his late forties when I met him, he was a slightly built, bookish and bespectacled man racked by a congenital heart defect. He told his war stories with mild reluctance and a complete absence of bravado, and I learned of the many trials and disappointments he faced after he abandoned his studies to join the Shan State Army after the Shans rose up in rebellion against the government shortly before the 1962 military coup. He later wrote a compelling memoir of the uprising, relating the story of dashed hopes and bitter betrayals as the Shan leadership, including his father who later died in prison, tried in vain to negotiate a fair and just status for his people within the framework of the Union of Burma.

Although she never spoke of her husband's fate, or of her son's disillusionment with the nationalist struggle, the *Mahadewi* once pulled me up over my academic interest in ethnicity. 'You need to be careful,' she said in her haughty tone, diffused by the mischievous gleam in her eyes. 'Identity is simply a convenience. You see, I have no identity any more: I am like a kite without a string.' Both Eugene and his mother died in exile in Canada.

The Burmese army grew stronger at the expense of idealistic, edu-cated politicians like U Nu and Sao Shwe Thaike, who lost power and influence. With them died the vision of a federal union where people of different races were treated equally under the law and could feel proud of their identity. This gave way to fanciful aspira-tions to restore the glory of pre-colonial Burmese kings. The most successful of these historical kings spent their reigns conquering the margins and filling their treasuries with loot and their palaces with slaves. Blinded by this gilded vision of glorious militarism, the Burmese army allowed the ethnic areas to become war zones where they committed violent atrocities involving forced labour, rape and summary execution. Local warlords, taking advantage of a power vacuum, imposed an opium-based economy, demanded both labour and levies and executed people accused of being disloyal to the ethnic cause. Eugene, when describing his role as commander of the first military region of the Shan State army, told me that one of his main challenges was preventing his own troops from harassing the people they were fighting for. Writing in 1986, a decade after he left the battlefield in the mid-1970s, he reflected: 'There is little basis for optimism about the future because in so far as Rangoon is concerned, it will probably continue to treat ethnic rebellions as common banditry and will continue trying to wipe them out militarily, as it has been doing all these years since 1949.' Despite continued peace efforts, this very much remained the case in 2016, and by early 2017 the government's efforts to invigorate the formal peace process were clearly challenged by ongoing fighting.

Decades of war, punctuated by semi-peaceful periods brought about by fragile ceasefire arrangements, have entrenched the social and economic aspects of armed conflict in these Southeast Asian societies, perhaps more pervasively than in any other war-torn region of the world. While countries like Somalia, Mozambique and Sudan have also experienced decades of civil war and strife, they have enjoyed periods of unity and relative peace in the modern era. And though its horrific memory remains vivid, Lebanon's civil war was relatively brief, spanning the mid-1970s to the late 1980s. Larger numbers of people have been killed in some of the African and Middle Eastern civil wars, where military aggression is better armed and less hampered by mountainous jungle terrain.

The startling difference is the longevity of these armed conflicts in Southeast Asia. In terms of enduring protracted wars of attrition where peace and security is but a distant memory possessed by ageing relatives, there is almost no parallel in the modern world. Fear of losing territory drives Southeast Asian governments to refuse to acknowledge or address the basic grievances underpinning protracted internal conflicts. The case of Papua, the easternmost province of Indonesia that constitutes about one half of the island of New Guinea, is a good illustration of the folly of governments when it comes to dealing with protracted grievance that fuels conflict. Successive Jakarta governments have denied native Papuans any redress with regard to the way in which the territory was incorporated as part of Indonesia in 1969. The Papuans for their part demand an acknowledgement that the UN-assisted plebiscite was flawed – most of those who voted were selected by the Indonesian military and told what to choose under duress. This failure to address a single historical grievance is a powerful driver of popular resentment today that fuels violence.

Yet Jakarta insists that the solution is development and a heavy military presence. Decades of a harsh security response to low-intensity resistance in Papua have bred hatred towards the government on the ground. Scarred by the experiences she had as a journalist, seeing her friends arrested and even killed, Aprila Wayan, who lives in the Papuan capital of Jayapura, carries a heavy burden of bitterness. When I suggested a dialogue with Jakarta might be possible, she spat: 'Dialogue is bullshit.' I was met with the same wall of mistrust and hatred when I met with Benny Wenda, the self-styled exiled leader of the Papuan resistance movement, in the modest council house he and his wife Maria live in on the outskirts of Oxford. Wenda escaped from an Indonesian prison and relates being tortured to within an inch of his life; as a young man he witnessed Indonesian forces bombing a highland tribal rebellion. Unsurprisingly, Wenda can see no use in holding discussions with the Jakarta government. Instead he places faith in a burgeoning coalition of pro-independence activists, many living abroad, known as the United Movement for the Liberation of West Papua. In mid-2016, the grouping came close to being recognised as a full member of a group of South Pacific Nations known as the Melanesian Spearhead group.

For all the progress that Indonesia has made over the past two decades, throwing off the burden of authoritarian rule, replacing rubber-stamp democracy with a genuinely accountable elected government, and enshrining universal values of human rights, not one government since 1998 has effectively addressed the grievance of the Papuan community, which with each passing year becomes a minority in its own land thanks to the influx of non-Papua immigrants from other parts of Indonesia. President Joko Widodo, elected in 2014, went further than many when he promised to investigate human rights abuses. Just as some progress was being made towards this goal, he installed a conservative former armed forces commander as the minister responsible for Papua.

The failure of governments in Southeast Asia to address these internal conflicts makes violence an everyday occurrence across huge swathes of the region, inhibits democratic freedoms through the use of martial law and military occupation, and perpetuates the kinds of injustice and infringements of human rights that should by now have been put aside as the majority of countries enjoy middle-income levels of prosperity. It also leaves many of these marginal conflict areas exposed to buffer-state strategies and proxy wars, as can be seen along the border between Myanmar and China. In both socio-economic and geopolitical terms, these conflicts are the soft underbelly of Southeast Asia. I am reminded of the paradox of covering Northern Ireland as a junior reporter at the BBC, where normal freedoms were suspended and the Prevention of Terrorism Act justified suppressing freedom of expression. And just as the British government was prepared to endure lethal terrorist attacks in the heart of London for decades to defend the legitimacy of British rule and the interests of the Loyalist Protestant minority in Northern Ireland, so the Thai government seems prepared to endure double the number of victims in Northern Ireland and higher levels of daily violence. In southern Thailand, the continuing conflict generates 50–80 casualties a month, about a quarter of them members of the Thai security forces. Yet these victims – be they Thai servicemen, civilian teachers or even Buddhist monks – warrant scarcely a mention; it is as if the government wants to sweep the suffering under a rug of silence rather than confront the root causes and make hard decisions that might impinge on sovereignty.

Most visitors to the conflict zone in southern Thailand arrive as I did, via the regional airport in neighbouring Songkhla Province. From Hat Yai with its bustling, mainly ethnic-Chinese-owned businesses, the overland drive to Patani takes about ninety minutes along a well-maintained dual carriageway that forms part of the main artery running from the south to the north of the country. Since 2004, daily shootings and weekly bomb attacks have occurred along this narrow isthmus that connects Thailand to the Malay Peninsula, resulting in close to 7,000 deaths. Yet on my first few visits in 2005, aside from haphazardly spaced army checkpoints and the odd patrol in lightly armoured Humvee jeeps, it was hard at first to sense violent conflict in an otherwise flat and featureless landscape of interminable rubber estates and long sandy beaches. I found a strangely camouflaged war. Conversations in Thai with local people, especially in the presence of officials or security personnel, solicited nothing but ignorance of the war and satisfaction with the status quo. But moving into native Malay language at the back of dark tea shops along the side of the road, a different story emerged. One of my early guides and informants was a young man called Ibrahim, who had studied both at a Thai university and then on an Islamic scholarship to the University of Sudan in Khartoum. Ibrahim had a gentle nature and a broad, winning smile – on the rare occasions he found anything to smile about. He carried a nine-millimetre automatic pistol in the glove compartment of his old Australian sedan and, for reasons I never found out, had one prosthetic leg.

I arrived in the south six months after the conflict re-erupted in mid-2004, when a band of well-trained insurgents launched a raid on an army camp in Narathiwat, south of Patani, netting hundreds of automatic weapons and ammunition. In response, the government initiated a security crackdown that provoked fierce resistance. When thousands of youths demonstrated in the border town of Tak Bai on 25 October 2004, many were arrested and stacked on flatbed trucks, their arms bound, to be transported to jail. Eighty-five died en route. There was little public outcry; no one was held to account, or punished, though an older generation of retired rebel leaders stepped forward to offer an explanation. The Tak Bai incident marked the resurgence of an ugly conflict that sees no end and has been responsible for some of the most violent periods in Southeast Asia's recent history.

The government in Bangkok insisted that the Muslim Malay community was happy to remain part of Thailand, and pointed to the religious freedoms they enjoyed, including the freedom to establish their own religious schools with a Malay-language curriculum. Senior government officials claimed that the rebels and demonstrators were criminals, or delinquents behaving like naughty children. But Ibrahim and his friends spoke about the mounting sense of frustration among Malay Muslim youth, who felt they had no place in Thai society and at the same time no space to assert their own sense of identity. 'The Thai government has always felt this was a problem of assimilation,' argued Wan Kadir Che Man, an avuncular Patani Malay leader now living in comfortable exile in Malaysia, 'and that the Malays had to be assimilated, integrated into the system and "made into Thais" so to speak . . . But the Malays in Patani realise they are not foreigners, and that in fact their territory has been colonised by the Thais who were originally a foreign power.'

Meanwhile the revived insurgency, led by a shadowy group of revolutionaries who would neither identify their leaders nor assume responsibility for their acts of violence, had been indoctrinating a new generation of warriors willing to lay down their lives in the cause of independence from the 'Siamese oppressors'. Ibrahim, like many others, received much of this indoctrination while studying first at local Islamic schools as a teenager, then as a student overseas. The eruption of violence generated concern in Western capitals: this was happening just four years after the 9/11 attacks by Al Qaeda, and just two years after the Southeast Asian affiliate Jemaah Islamiyya had exploded bombs in Bali, killing hundreds of people. Now a Muslim minority in Thailand had launched a small war against a Buddhist majority state: was it a new jihad seeking to establish a caliphate in

Southeast Asia? My resourceful guide Ibrahim recalled attending an
evening prayer meeting with Osama bin Laden in Khartoum shortly before the famous Saudi millionaire-turned-jihadist launched Al
Qaeda. According to Ibrahim, bin Laden was quiet-spoken and not
all that inspiring; he wasn't impressed. But then, that's typical of
the Patani Malays, who have a rather high regard for themselves
and their historical role in spreading the Islamic faith throughout
Southeast Asia.

It was against this background of violence, fear and confusion that
the Thai government, in a hesitant move to negotiate peace, reached
out to the Centre for Humanitarian Dialogue with a request to seek
out representatives of the insurgency. Given my long experience
and contacts in Thailand, both as student and journalist, my new
employers at HDC gave me the task of establishing contact. It was
2006, two years into the resurgent conflict, and I didn't have much
to go on: the insurgents claimed no responsibility; they melted away
from roadside ambushes and issued no bold statements. There was
a cohort of ageing former rebels living on the Malaysian side of the
border and a couple of leads we got from former rebels in Aceh,
who told us of leaders living in exile in Sweden. So we turned to the
Stockholm phone book.

After many months and a few false leads, I made a modest
breakthrough. My first contact was at a secret meeting in Egypt in
2006. I managed to persuade a delegation from the Revolutionary
Nationalist Front (known by the acronym BRN in Malay) to travel
to Cairo, where in a two-star hotel coffee shop along the banks of
the Nile we hunched over bowls of olives and hummus, and sweet
mint tea, steaming away in glass cups too hot to touch. The leader
of the delegation was well educated and intellectually sophisticated
and the rest of the group were predominantly in their forties and
clean-shaven. They seemed a bookish lot, more like a delegation of
visiting scholars – which is how they presented themselves to the
Egyptian authorities. They insisted that jihad was not their game;
instead they were inspired by the left-wing revolutionary ideas of
Indonesia's founding president, Sukarno. They were innately suspicious of all foreigners and outsiders, including me. We spoke
in the Malay language, but at times our meeting felt more like an

interrogation; they refused to give me their names or even stay in the same hotel. Secrecy, they told me, was essential. Each time they had revealed themselves and engaged with the other side, as they put it, their leaders had either been killed or detained. 'Like mowing the lawn,' as one of them described it. Indeed, Thai authorities allegedly murdered the revered Haji Sulong, the man who inspired their movement, in 1954. Their secrecy has worked, for despite billions of dollars spent on defence, a standing army of almost 400,000, and all the modern surveillance technology money can buy, the Thai military has failed to defeat the insurgency.

'The basis of our struggle grows stronger because our people have begun to realise the importance of their separate history,' said Azuddin, an elderly former member of one of the older separatist movements from Patani, and whom I had got to know in the course of my efforts to convene the conflict parties in dialogue. We met often in the musty lobby of the Perdana Hotel in Kota Bharu, built in the 1970s and neglected by time, just across the border in Malaysia. 'Also because of the way the Thais treat us,' lamented Azuddin. 'The way the police and army treat our people; the way they look at us.' Ten years on, after thousands of deaths from daily bombings and shootings, senior Thai officials defiantly insisted that the problems in the restive southern provinces could be solved by a process of fostering 'Thai identity, which would convince people to do good deeds for the nation and to be loyal to the king'. At checkpoints along the well-maintained north–south highway, local Malay Muslim kids glowered at young peasant soldiers sweating under their Kevlar body armour and over-sized helmets. Speaking no Malay, the soldiers struggled to communicate with the locals. For these nervy Thai soldiers, everyone was suspect; for the kids, every Thai was an invader – and a fair target.

And so the violence worsened. I passed flimsy, hastily erected checkpoints along the road leading to the Thai–Malaysia border that looked like afterthoughts, providing scant shelter to the soldiers cloistered within, veiled behind netting meant to protect them from hand-grenades that kids passing on motorcycles could hurl at them. The insurgents themselves were ghosts who never showed themselves. They struck with impunity – one such attack claiming the lives of Thai Buddhist monks in retaliation for a deadly military raid on an Islamic boarding school. 'Everyone is afraid of being arrested,' an elderly Islamic imam told me on a hot afternoon at a rural boarding school close to the border. 'We're afraid to leave our homes at night. Even for us as Islamic teachers it is hard. We have difficulty carrying out our teaching duties.' Who or what were they afraid of, I asked. 'People are mostly afraid of the government, not the movement. People are disappearing.' How many? 'Many thousands have disappeared. Villagers tell us they come across bodies in the rivers and the forest.'

I asked about the insurgent movement. The teacher lowered his voice and mentioned the revolutionary front, BRN, with its shadowy youth wing – by government estimates, 5,000 in strength. 'They have a presence in every village,' the teacher said. The independence movement was rooted in the Islamic religious teaching community, yet theirs was an oddly secular pitch for freedom. No one invoked jihad, or mentioned anything that could be interpreted as religiously motivated. They spoke instead of the suffering of the Patani people, and of their complete loss of faith in the government. Given that this conflict was unfolding in the wake of the rise of Islamic extremism post-2001, it was important to understand this seemingly counter-intuitive motivation. The few fighters I met in the field, or at furtive meetings along the Malaysian border, spoke like guerrilla commandos at the head of a people's struggle, far removed from the dogma of religious faith or ideology of hate. Theirs is a fight for freedom for a culture and a way of life that is predominantly Malay rather than Muslim, although the two are intertwined. 'It will be hard to persuade the people of Patani to compromise while they are still so fearful, and feel so misunderstood,' said one fighter active in the field in the first two years after the conflict re-erupted in 2004.

'The government has no sense of what this insurgency is about,' said the highly regarded former Thai Foreign Minister Surin Pitsuwan, himself a Muslim from a province outside the conflict zone further north. In his view, the Patani Malays were driven by common inspiration over a shared grievance: 'It's like Al Qaeda. There's no need for a coordinated command structure. Everyone is already motivated . . . [much of the time] by revenge.' And there were revenge-motivated attacks from the government, too: with the establishment of a royal foundation to provide arms for Buddhist villagers; with wounded, hospitalised soldiers encouraged to go back to the field to seek vengeance.

Against this bleak background of relentless violence, misunderstanding and intensifying hatred between Muslims and Buddhists, I pursued an effort to broker peace talks. The first meetings were convened in 2006 at the Centre for Humanitarian Dialogue's lakeside villa in Geneva. The insurgents, members of the Patani United Liberation Organisation, were the same men I had met on dark nights in roadside coffee shops; only now they were in dressed in sober-looking suits, resembling an Asian version of *Men in Black*. One of their number had lived in Sweden for two decades and had worked, he told us, as a translator for the police and the courts. He presented himself as the leader of a coalition of armed forces on the ground. 'There are many groups in our coalition – some of which are not known.' With an unnerving air of confidence he related how in the past the rebels had followed a strategy of open warfare against Thai forces, then after suffering serious losses, due partly to infiltration, they had gone underground. There had been earlier efforts to negotiate in the mid-1990s, with talks held in Damascus and Cairo: 'But the Thais were not genuinely interested in discussing a settlement. They used the opportunity to destroy us from the inside.'

The insurgents had come prepared, presenting a memorandum outlining demands for autonomy in a region to be named 'Patani Darussalam', made up of the four southern provinces and several districts of Songkhla. They were willing to consider a limited ceasefire, in return for immunity. The sole representative of the Thai government, a stony-faced army general not long elected to parliament and a close confidant of the prime minister, showed no sympathy. He refused to engage, spoke very little, and left small talk to his wife, a former Thai Airways flight attendant. The insulting behaviour angered the rebels: 'We are treated like colonial subjects . . . they try to avoid calling us Malay. Why do we have to be called Thai?'

Over the following six years we continued to hold meetings in secret, at venues in neutral countries outside Thailand and Malaysia.

Gradually, the two sides began to engage in dialogue, helping to foster trust. Some of the Thai security officials developed an awkward rapport with their opponents – a far cry from the days when they would sit opposite each other in hostile silence, speaking only to deliver rigid and uncompromising statements. Frustratingly, the delegations on both sides were proxies for their respective leaders; thus they could not speak for them and lacked the authority to implement or change policy. The proxies on the insurgent side were often former combatants with a tenuous, easily terminated mandate from the core movement.

After many tedious, long meetings, something of a common understanding of the impasse developed – the Thais recognising the serious intent of the rebels' quest for independence; the rebels realising that their official counterparts would never compromise on sovereignty. In between, it seemed as if both sides were going through the motions, pocketing generous per diems and filling up on lavish hotel buffets. Progress was measured in terms of building a modicum of mutual trust and respect; both sides recognising that they had suffered real casualties. They helped each other move forward in small but symbolic ways – a renewed travel document, or the briefest pause in combat – to facilitate confidence-building.

In the eyes of young fighters on the ground, this kind of dialogue was a threat to morale and spirit. They believed engagement with the state would lead only to surrender and betrayal. More to the point, what sort of dividend would a deal bring? By mid-2016, with progress on dialogue perpetually interrupted by political deadlock in Bangkok, and by the Thai government's reckless insistence on a security-based approach, the armed movement in southern Thailand took their campaign of violence beyond the borders of the ancient sultanate of Patani. In August 2016, a spate of bomb and arson attacks at several tourist spots in Thailand resulted in four deaths and many injured. BRN was responsible, even though the authorities in Bangkok tried to avoid attributing violence on a national level to a separatist conflict on the margins. 'This is different from terrorism,' said a police spokesman in Bangkok, correcting earlier reports that the bombs were all similar to those used by insurgents in the deep south. 'If it was a terrorism act,' he added with an absurd flourish, 'our intelligence office would say which group claimed responsibility.' BRN in fact never claims responsibility for its acts of violence, and as far as the movement was concerned, the trading of accusations between opposing political camps in Bangkok over who was responsible served its ends, which are to encourage the weakening of the Thai State.

In recent years, with some degree of democratic advancement, Southeast Asian governments have come under increasing pressure to engage in dialogue with non-state armed groups: either the military solution has failed, as in Mindanao, or it has become too unacceptably brutal, as in Aceh. Yet dialogue and negotiation hasn't been used effectively, and lingering grievances lurk, even where the conflict appears to have been settled, as in Aceh. For both sides, there are issues of face and pride. After the re-eruption of the conflict in southern Thailand it took the best part of six years for the government to frame a policy making it legal for officials to sit down and engage with members of the armed insurgency. Notably, the insurgents were described as 'people who disagree with the state'.

Ten years after the end of the conflict in Aceh, the remnants of the rebel movement were ensconced in power, under a special autonomy arrangement that allowed them to form their own political party – and a blind eye from Jakarta that allowed them to use strong-arm tactics and intimidation to win. Aceh under autonomous rule by 2016 was effectively a one-party state that supported the harsh imposition of Shariah Law under which offenders were flogged in public. Was this the peace dividend that the world expected? I attended a tenth-anniversary celebration of the peace agreement and found all the old rebel leaders either squabbling among themselves or complaining that the agreement had not been sincerely implemented. 'We were once called the "Verandah of Mecca",' said an Acehnese legislator, his voice filled with emotion, referring to the traditional label bestowed on Aceh by virtue of its geographical position facing northwest towards Saudi Arabia. 'More recently we became known as the verandah of peace. But today we are becoming the verandah of lost opportunity.'

Formal negotiation in Southeast Asian conflicts invariably involves much posturing and rigid position-taking, creating huge levels of mistrust and a lack of sincerity, which in turn prevents swift or workable outcomes. The usual way to address these issues is to harness third-party help, but as my own experience reveals, states in Southeast Asia are reluctant to submit to external mediation. Virulent sovereignty, marginal significance and a deficit of dialogue explain why sub-national conflicts persist in parts of Myanmar, Thailand, Indonesia and the Philippines. Even on the rare occasion when agreement is reached and a peace deal struck, as with Mindanao in the southern Philippines, the drivers of conflict remain. No sooner had the Philippine government settled with the Moro National Liberation Front through a 'final' peace agreement brokered in 1996 by Indonesia, when a splinter group took up the Moro cause and the banner of the Moro Islamic Liberation Front. It seems likely the same fate awaits the Comprehensive Agreement on Bangsamoro signed with the Moro Islamic Liberation Front in 2014. And so the cycle continues, a tragic mandala of violent conflict keeping army officers flush with per diems and kickbacks, the gunrunners fat and happy, and the politicians elected every five years with the help of both the goons and their guns.

Given Southeast Asia's economic and strategic importance, to ignore these protracted sub-national conflicts, or refuse to seek a peaceful end to them, is nothing short of criminally irresponsible. It becomes ever more disastrous and far-reaching, as economic development and infrastructure spreads into once-marginal areas. Many of the conflict areas straddle strategic border zones and conduits of trade – such as in southern Thailand or along the borders of China and Burma; they are also raging at a time when all ten countries of Southeast Asia have declared themselves a community. Following the trail of endemic conflict and violence and trying, without much luck, to talk people into peace over the past decade has been something of an epiphany for me. It has driven me to consider the region more realistically, much more so than when I was a journalist filled with idealistic notions about the struggle for freedom. It is clear that, with or without external encouragement or interference, the most logical approach to resolving these conflicts today would be for states to adopt a progressive, tolerant attitude towards demands for decentralisation and autonomy. Many of the declared motives for fighting ascribed to ideals of sovereignty disguise little more than selfish personal interests – preserving official position or a lucrative source of illegal income, sometimes even justifying military expenditure. The problem with peaceful solutions is that they involve compromise, yet giving ground in Southeast Asia is still regarded as a sign of weakness, a loss of face. Saving face drives people to extreme positions from which they will not budge. Violence ensues and then serves other, more material ends.

The young man and his rusty sub-machine gun in the photo on my office wall would have been the second generation born in a state of civil war along the Thai–Myanmar border. The man who guided me across the border then, a young colonel in the Pa O National army called Okker, is today part of the team negotiating with the Myanmar government for a federal system. As for the young man in the picture, it's quite possible his children, soldiers, too, are carrying more modern weapons and a new uniform, all made in China. Their struggle is endless.

CHAPTER TEN

CLASHING BELIEFS AND
THE NEW JIHAD

'If there are some of you who wish to be an Arab and practise Arab culture, and do not wish to follow our Malay customs and traditions, that is up to you. I also welcome you to live in Saudi Arabia.'

Sultan Ibrahim Ibni Almarhum Sultan Iskandar of Johor

At some point in the mid-1980s male students in the central Java city of Jogjakarta who used to wear ragged jeans and long hair began sprouting wispy beards and wearing white skull-caps; the girls started covering their heads with the *hijab*. By 2004 supporters of a local football club, Slemaniyya, were wearing T-shirts that sported pictures of Osama bin Laden.

'It's nothing to do with the Taliban or Al Qaeda, we just want to support our football club,' one of the supporters told me with a broad marzipan smile. It was like visiting a film studio and wandering off a Southeast Asia set into another recreating the deserts of Arabia. Over coffee in a restaurant overlooking Malioboro Street, the city's main thoroughfare, a soft-spoken Muslim scholar, Muhammad Fajrul Fallah, tried to explain these puzzling changes to me. Like most observers of Indonesia, I assumed that moderate manifestations of Islam were the norm – especially here in central Java, where the refined culture embodies a fine balance between its ancient Hindu–Buddhist roots and the more recent Islamic overlay. But a lot was changing in Indonesia in the post-authoritarian era of reform. I spoke to Fajrul on the eve of the landmark 2004 election campaign, the first direct election for the presidency since the end of the authoritarian era in 1998.

'Young people just took to adopting Islamic symbols,' he said, so softly it was a struggle to hear him over the chaotic cacophony of cars, motorcycles and the clanging of bells belonging to the city's ubiquitous three-wheel pedicabs. 'They never turned violent or anything, they just all went to the same lectures and prayer meetings and, because of the more open environment, they thought it was OK to change the way they'd done things before.'

I was struck by an apparent paradox: a more open political environment that leads to a closing of the mind to other views, a strict adherence to orthodoxy in a more liberal setting, which in turn breeds intolerance and hatred. Was all this numbing Islamic orthodoxy the tragic by-product of Indonesia's transition to democracy? Understanding the changing shape and role of Islam in the world's largest Muslim country is of vital importance to understanding a key driver of conflict in Southeast Asia. In the wider global context, we live in an era of violence associated with Islam – in the name of Islam towards non-Muslims, and by angry non-Muslims towards believers in a faith that, although forged with the sword, professes peace. The Islamic Holy Scriptures contain mixed messages, what Din Syamsuddin, a former Chairman of Muhammadiya, one of Indonesia's largest Muslim organisations, terms 'ambivalent tendencies'. There are messages of peace and accommodation, but also strong calls to arms and exhortations to attack non-believers. This has opened the way for the manipulation of gullible minds by reckless politicians and radical forces. On a more mundane level, as with all Abrahamic religions, there is a tension between traditional paths to piety and modern forms of civic life. 'Being a Muslim in the modern context creates a quandary,' argues jailed Malaysian politician Anwar Ibrahim: 'how can we reconcile modern governance with traditional teachings?' Anwar and fellow liberals would argue that democracy is a moral imperative for all Muslims, as their faith urges engagement with society. The trouble is that this more enlightened, modernist view has been eclipsed by a much darker vision of exclusive identity that rejects democracy on the basis that only God speaks for the people – *vox populi vox dei.*

Southeast Asia suffered from the scourge of Islamic violent extremism years before the 9/11 attacks on New York and Washington DC in 2001. One of the earliest Al Qaeda-backed terrorist plots involved a plan to plant bombs on eleven airliners flying from Asia to the United States in 1995. Operation Bojinka was foiled only because chemicals to be used in the bombs prematurely exploded. The same group of terrorists, led by a man called Ramzi Yousef, a Kuwaiti who was one of the principal planners of the 1993 World Trade Center bombing in New York, considered assassination plots against President Bill Clinton and Pope John Paul II, who both visited the Philippines in the mid-1990s. Al Qaeda established cells in Southeast Asia both because of access to a sympathetic Muslim community and free and easy cities such as Manila and Bangkok, where almost anything could be had for a price and money could easily be transferred because of lax banking rules. According to a US Navy report, Osama bin Laden's brother-in-law, Mohammed Jamil Khalifa, was set up in Manila by the early 1990s.

However, it wasn't Al Qaeda as such that was behind a series of spectacular terrorist attacks launched in the region in the first few years of the new century. Soon after the 9/11 attacks, a home-grown jihadist organisation with roots in a much longer struggle for Islamic statehood in Indonesia decided to align with Al Qaeda's struggle against the West and target Westerners. On 12 October 2002, a car bomb ripped through the popular Sari nightclub in the heart of the Indonesian resort island of Bali's most popular tourist spot, Kuta. 202 people died, most of them Australians, Americans and Europeans, as well as 38 Indonesians. Already struggling to come to terms with the aftermath of the 9/11 attacks, which spawned the US-led War on Terror, as editor of the *Far Eastern Economic Review*, I faced the reality of a new front dominated by a shadowy world of former mujahideen from the Afghan wars and disillusioned clerics. They were people with grudges, having suffered under repressive policies towards Islamic militants conducted by the secular governments of Indonesia and Malaysia; they rode the coattails of Al Qaeda's new violent jihad. But they were the symptoms of a far more serious problem.

One of the chief engines of Islamic extremism, fuelling much of the Jihadist violence in Southeast Asia, is the Wahhabi messianic sect, a social movement that grew out of the Arabian peninsula in the eighteenth century preaching a return to fundamental Islamic values as determined by the traditions of the Prophet Muhammad. Allied with the Royal House of Saud, the Wahhabis underpin the religious basis of contemporary Saudi Arabia. 'Born in massacre and blood,' writes the Algerian author Kamel Daoud, 'it manifests itself in a surreal relationship with women, a prohibition against non-Muslims treading on sacred territory, and ferocious religious laws. That translates into an obsessive hatred of imagery and representation and therefore art, but also of the body, nakedness and freedom.' This seems an unlikely dogma to take root in a part of the world steeped in sophisticated traditions of art and the celebration of nature, and where women command positions of respect and even power. Yet it has. How did this happen and what does it mean, not just for Indonesia and Southeast Asia, but also for the wider world?

Shortly after a terrorist attack in the streets of the Indonesian capital that killed eight people at the end of January 2016, a colleague sent me a short video statement by one of the alleged perpetrators that had been doing the rounds on social media. The man in the video was a good-looking youth sporting a neat beard, a headscarf and an automatic weapon, and speaking to a camera-phone from somewhere in IS-held northern Syria. The background appeared to be the ruins of a building. His voice dripped with hatred as he challenged the army and the police to come after him: 'otherwise we are ready to come and get you . . . ' How did this fellow from somewhere in rural Java end up in a bombed-out Syrian town, serving an organisation that has carried out some of the worst atrocities in recent times, supposedly in the name of Islam? As a journalist in Indonesia and Malaysia, I witnessed some of the early stirrings of Islamic activism before Islam's relationship with the wider world changed irrevocably on 11 September 2001. I wrote about the emergence of Islamic social and political awareness as the shackles on freedom of expression and social activism began to loosen. I was privy to the thinking of Islamic intellectuals and political leaders as they contemplated the implications of a more pious Muslim society.

The experience gave me plenty of exposure to changes in society, the direction of which were uncertain at the time, but with hindsight were profoundly important.

The dominant narrative since 9/11 is one of the spread of jihadist ideology along subterranean networks of alienated Islamic youth, forged in the rugged mountainous battlefields of Afghanistan and the disciplined Deobandist madrasas of Pakistan. For many in Southeast Asia, this was a sudden and unexpected development. Singapore's founding father Lee Kuan Yew, who died in 2015, had strong views on the subject, which he shared with me in an interview in 2002 a year after the 9/11 attacks. Lee typified the generation who grew up alongside Muslims who, although devout and faithful, essentially accommodated non-Muslims in the interests of communal harmony. Lee played golf and drank whisky with Malaysia's founding father, Tunku Abdul Rahman, who was appointed the first secretary general of the Organisation of the Islamic Conference, a global Muslim body. Lee called it 'tropical Islam': 'you know – green trees, green grass, no desert and a very different ethnic mix'. Then, suddenly, he said, these jihadists were making a bid to seize power and establish a caliphate. 'It's absurd. It's not achievable,' Lee told me in the sterile environment of his air-conditioned office.

Fifteen years later, nothing near a caliphate has been established, but Muslim society has become deeply conservative in Indonesia and Malaysia and many other parts of Southeast Asia where Muslims constitute a minority. As a result, you can no longer buy beer at convenience stores in Indonesia. Lawmakers began debating a bill in parliament to ban alcohol altogether in 2015. And in 2016 the province of East Java banned alcohol sales completely. In Malaysia, there is a move to implement Islamic Hudud criminal laws in some areas of the country; Shariah law is now in force in the tiny, oil-rich state of Brunei, where Christmas has been banned. These cosmetic changes tend to draw headlines, but beneath the surface there are strong currents in Muslim society influenced by moves towards the purification of faith, stricter religious observance and, more disturbingly, appeals to lay down one's life for the faith. Much of this can be attributed to the neo-Wahhabi movements, and similarly dogmatic Salafist ideology, that wafted through the region on a cushion of charitable donations from the Arabian peninsula and which mushroomed after the oil boom of the mid-1970s, just as the authoritarian landscape started to change.

This thinking of Islamic extremism as an alien virus in Southeast Asia has been reinforced by the new incarnation of radicalism represented by IS in Syria and Iraq. However, compared with Europe, North Africa and the Middle East, Southeast Asia has contributed tiny numbers of disaffected Muslims to the ranks of IS – compare 3,000 militants from Tunisia, or half that from France, with around 300 from Indonesia, the largest Sunni Muslim country in the world. That doesn't make the situation any less dangerous in Southeast Asia, as the 2016 attacks in Jakarta and Kuala Lumpur claimed by IS show. Put simply: the assertion of Islamic piety and the spread of conservative Islamic mores in societies once considered 'moderate' or 'tolerant' threatens to undermine the basic assumptions of pluralism that underpin this region's stability. There are also political implications. As Muslims in Southeast Asia become more influenced by Wahhabi thinking about the Islamic underpinnings of the state, so they are less likely to believe in democracy. My late father P. J. Vatikiotis, an Arabist and scholar of Islamic political theory, put it like this: The whole notion of the legitimacy of modern statehood derived from popular sovereignty runs headlong into Islamic insistence that sovereignty belongs to God 'and that the legitimacy of earthly authority in the state rests on the implementation of the sovereign God's will and Sacred Law'. This dichotomy, as he saw it, gives rise to 'periodic demands by Muslims for the realisation of the Islamic political ideal by the rejection or overthrow of the temporal or mundane reality'. My father died in 1997, just shy of the spectacularly violent debut of radical Islam. It is possible that, given the strong state prevailing in Southeast Asia, we will never see the collapse of state structures that in the Middle East have allowed IS to establish a territorial base. But as we saw in the previous chapter, there are ungoverned spaces in the region that offer permissive environments for violent extremism to incubate.

External influence and stimuli from the Middle East have

always been important factors in the rise of Islamic fundamen-
talism. The oil boom that started in the mid-1970s led to massive
investment in Islamic education emanating from Saudi Arabia,
Kuwait and the Gulf States. By one estimate Saudi Arabia has
invested at least $100 billion over the past few decades in Islamic
education overseas. Despite the heavy hand of the state in all other
areas of society, religious education is surprisingly open to private
funding. In Indonesia about 90 per cent of the 40,000 or more
religious schools are run privately – only around 10 per cent by
the state.

Another important factor has been the general advance of religiosity in societies subject to rapid social and economic change.
Religious faith is a refuge from poverty and uncertainty, encouraged
when there are funds available to offer a means of escape. Piety
therefore becomes a vote-getter in societies where religious faith and
identity has become both a boundary marker and a buffer against
uncertainty. It is important to understand the changing dynamics
of religion – Buddhist and Christian faiths as well as Islam – because an alarming sectarian divide is fast evolving in the region as
the resurgence in religiosity provides a fertile seedbed for violent
extremism.

Across much of Southeast Asia, people have managed over time to
adhere to their respective faiths in a climate of tolerance. In the
towns and cities of Java, churches sit next to mosques, and traces of
ancient Hindu practices suffuse the rituals of Muslims, Christians
and Buddhists. In the traditional plural societies of Southeast Asia,
freedom of worship was guaranteed by law; in Indonesia, for example, Article 28 of the country's constitution states that 'every person
shall be free to choose and to practise the religion of his/her choice'.
The boundaries of religious faith were well observed, but not to
the point where the faithful felt the need to cordon themselves off
from outsiders. When I was a student in Chiang Mai in the 1980s,
I would regularly duck into the Sikh temple for a free lunch, or sit
in the city's mosque on a hot day to cool off and reflect. Nowadays,
if someone recognisably foreign walks into a mosque in Southeast
Asia they most likely will be asked to leave if they are not Muslim.

At the funeral of a Muslim friend in Malaysia a few years ago, I was politely requested not to enter the mosque.

There have been other signs of the erosion of tolerant coexistence. Hardline Sunni Muslims have exploded bombs at Buddhist temples, vandalised Christian churches and attacked Catholic worshippers in central Java. Towards the end of 2015, Catholic church burnings in northern Aceh resulted in the displacement of 10,000 people. In a recent attack, Molotov cocktails were thrown into the yard of a Catholic high school in Jakarta. Minority Muslim sects have also been targeted; members of the Ahmadiyya sect in west Java have been subjected to persecution, and in 2013 there were violent clashes between Shiites and Sunnis in east Java. Surveys show a 20 per cent increase in violent attacks on religious minorities in 2012 compared with the year before, and a 50 per cent increase since 2007.

The Indonesian government and the courts seem powerless when it comes to enforcing constitutionally guaranteed freedom of worship. In one prominent case, local authorities in the town of Bogor ignored a Supreme Court ruling ordering a building permit for a protestant church to be unfrozen. In early 2016, when agitation against a small religious sect known as Gafatar (Gerakan Fajar

*Protestor from the Hizbut Tahrir group
in Jogyakarta, 2009.*

Nusantara) in East and West Kalimantan displaced several thousand people, the authorities accused the sect of being a separatist movement and herded the community into detention centres.

Muslim pressure groups such as the Islamic Defenders Front (FPI) have forced city and district administrations to curb the sale of alcohol and enforce strict observance of Islamic law, thereby undermining tolerance, which should have the backing of the law. In November 2016 over 150,000 people mobilised by FPI flooded the centre of Jakarta clad in white and waving black flags; they were protesting against the elected Governor of Jakarta, a Christian of Chinese descent, who was accused of insulting the Holy Koran by citing a passage that warns Muslims about being governed by non-Muslims. The government looked on powerlessly as police questioned the popular governor and eventually determined that he would be charged with blasphemy.

In Malaysia, where Islam lies at the heart of the Malay majority identity, there has been a steady drift towards intolerance of non-Malay communities of Indians and Chinese. Hindu temples and Christian churches find it harder to get official operating permits and their places of worship come under attack. In mid-2015, the Malaysian Islamic Development Department issued new rules for entertainers, stressing the need to be of good morals and to avoid provoking 'extreme laughter'. At the same time, the Malaysian Tourist Board launched a campaign promoting Malaysia as a land of festivals. At the end of 2014, Brunei banned Christmas decorations and declared the full implementation of Shariah law.

Just as alarming has been the recent emergence of acute intolerance in the majority Buddhist communities of Myanmar towards long-established Muslim minorities. Theravada Buddhism, predominant in Southeast Asia, is perceived to be a benign, peaceful faith. But as in other religious faiths, the ideals of human kindness can mask a strong protective instinct. 'It is also our duty to protect the faith,' the Venerable Ariya Wun Tha Bhiwunsa, an abbot from the central city of Mandalay, told me at his monastery on the outskirts of the city. In the shady grounds of his pagoda, he is trying to teach his followers the basics of mediation because he sees conflicts within the community over land and identity growing more serious as the country becomes more open. His main tools are a small library and the charisma of his teaching.

Rakhine State, the modern name for the old region of Arakan, perches on the west coast of Myanmar and borders Bangladesh, facing the Bay of Bengal. Remote from the rest of the country, Rakhine has long been one of Myanmar's least-developed states. It is also home to the world's most unwanted community of Muslims and the largest group of stateless people in Asia. The Buddhist Rakhine majority has lived in awkward but mainly peaceful coexistence with a Muslim minority who call themselves Rohingya for generations, but the Rohingya have never been officially recognised as an ethnic group in Myanmar, where Muslims have long been viewed with suspicion. They are therefore denied citizenship. As of early 2018, an estimated 400,000 Rohingya in Rakhine State, plus another 1.5 million or so outside, mainly in neighbouring Bangladesh, constitute 10 per cent of the world's stateless people. The problem was regarded as just one of many challenges Myanmar faces on a halting path to democracy and better government. But when communal violence erupted in 2012, it highlighted a dangerous religious divide in the country and threatened the rest of the region. The violence has not only forced the two communities apart and created a humanitarian crisis for Rohingya forced to live in terrible conditions in poorly

Rohingya refugee in Sittwe, Rakhine State, 2015.

equipped camps, but more than 700,000 of them have now fled
– almost half the Rohingya population. Some end up being smuggled or trafficked as cheap labour in Thailand and Malaysia. The
Rohingya stand out as a single group persecuted for their identity
with nowhere to go. Some of them have even showed up in the flow
of migrants reaching Europe's shores.

One hot October afternoon in 2015, in the main refugee camp
of Khang Doke Khor in Sittwe, the capital of Rakhine State, I encountered the makeshift community centre beside a dusty stretch of
ground that serves as a football field. This was where I met the camp
leader and a few of the men telling stories about being evicted from
their homes, losing their right to vote, and the long wait at a nearby
beach for a boat that will carry them off in search of a new life. I
was introduced to a wiry man with red-rimmed eyes calling himself
Mohamad Thayeb, who related the story of his son. Two months
after his son clambered aboard a boat bound for Malaysia, Thayeb
received a call from a trafficker demanding $2,000 to ensure his son's
safety. The anguished family could only raise $700, so the traffickers
beat their son and left him for dead. It was only the kindness of another Rohingya refugee that nursed him back to life, said Mohamad
Thayeb, holding back tears. Such is the plight of Rohingyas today.
Something of the security and prosperity they enjoyed in the past
as diligent fishermen and farmers is faintly visible in Rakhine State;
not far from the fire station on the main road in Sittwe there's an
abandoned mosque, crumbling and overgrown, its stuccoed min-
aret a forlorn reminder of a proud faith.

Arguments on either side of this religious divide are extraordinarily passionate: the Buddhist Rakhine majority cite British records
from the nineteenth century to prove how the Rohingya were
brought over from Bengal as immigrant labour and are therefore not
indigenous. The Rohingya, who speak a language almost identical to
Bengali, insist they are indigenous to Rakhine. Attempts to engage
the two communities in dialogue provoke fury and indignation,
and international NGOs have been attacked in Rakhine State for
trying to address the situation with humanitarian aid and counsel-
ling. To make matters worse, what began as localised anti-Muslim
sentiment has since spread to other parts of Myanmar, fuelled by

Buddhist nationalism encouraged via social media. Facebook and Twitter have been used to spread hate, and in at least one incident of violence against Muslims in Mandalay in 2014, accounts of an alleged rape spread via social media turned out to be false. Much of this incitement of religious hatred has been politically motivated as Myanmar struggled to manage a hesitant democratic transition.

So why has religious sectarianism and extremism reared its head in a region long proud of its traditions of tolerance? The answer is a mixture of several factors. On the one hand, people of all faiths have become more religiously observant, their lives subject to greater social and economic uncertainty as Southeast Asia started to take off economically in the last quarter of the twentieth century. Prosperity and development have also disrupted traditional village-bound societies and loosened the moorings of cultural identity. Huge numbers of people have moved to large cities, or overseas and across borders as migrant workers. The tight-knit rural communities they were born in were places bound by ties of family and multiple layers of cultural and animistic tradition that tended to dilute religious orthodoxy. I saw this for myself in Jakarta in the course of the 1990s when middle-class Muslims with family histories in traditional villages across Java and the islands were drawn to Islamic teaching and immersion in religious faith as the bonds of local culture and tradition were loosened and forgotten.

This attraction to religious affiliation generated friction between faiths. Muslims and Christians, who lived alongside one another in Java, or Buddhists and Muslims, who lived similarly alongside one another in Myanmar, were respectful of one another's faiths because they enjoyed the familiarity and tolerance born of proximity and daily interaction, as well as a common sense of local identity. For a more atomised society, with ties of family or tradition of place diffused or lost in the surge of development and urbanisation, religion often becomes a refuge, and therefore a stronger marker of identity.

At the same time, more openly contested politics in the age of democratic transition has, for better or worse, created the need for attractive platforms to mobilise voters. In Indonesia there are

religious faith-based parties that don't command huge majorities –
the most that the two avowedly Islamic parties could win was 10 per
cent of the vote in the 2004 elections. They have not done much
better since. More alarmingly, though, political parties professing
secular ideals have exploited religious identity to attract support.
This explains why democratic transition in both Indonesia and Myanmar has proceeded hand in hand with the assertion of religious
politics: parties tend to form around individuals dispensing patronage, rather than leaders with ideas. Faith and religious identity
present themselves as useful surrogates for aspiration and affiliation
based on secular ideals. The steady infusion of external notions of
a purified faith prone to radical thinking and extremist action has
taken advantage of both these factors over the past two decades.
Buddhist monks that I have spoken to in Myanmar complain that
Muslims in their communities have become more aloof as they have
been influenced by imported conservative Sunni orthodoxy. They
have grown apart, and when Buddhist women marry into Muslim
households, they disappear from view. This pronounced differentiation has bred fear and suspicion and fuelled communal friction.

The same can be said of Indonesia, where the first neo-Wahhabi
elements embedded themselves in society in the late 1960s, becoming more pronounced after the end of the Suharto era in 1998.
Mosques that were once almost indistinguishable from churches
but for a loudspeaker attached to a rudimentary tin cupola were
replaced by brash multicoloured Moorish affairs complete with tiled
domes and soaring minarets. This was a physical manifestation of
the vast amount of money pouring into the country, much of it
from wealthy Islamic foundations in Saudi Arabia and Kuwait. Several local institutions act as a conduit to help channel this money,
the most prominent being Ilmu Pengetahuan Islam dan Arab (the
Institute of Islamic and Arabic Studies, or LIPIA) established with
Saudi support in 1980, and Dewan Dakwah Islamiyah Indonesia
(the Indonesian Society for the Propagation of Islam, or DDII).
At LIPIA students learn about Islam in Arabic and wear traditional
Arab garb; many go on to study in Saudi Arabia on Saudi government scholarships. More insidiously, the Saudi money has begun
to alter the faith, replacing the sedate Shafi'i school of Sunni Islam

with the more orthodox Hanbali in religious school curricula, thus paving the way for hardline Salafist teachings supported by the Saudi Wahhabi sect. Saudi money was used to train religious teachers in Middle Eastern centres of learning. They returned to Indonesia with more intolerant, even radical views of the primacy of the Islamic faith, which in turn has inspired hatred towards non-believers. The militant Islamic Defenders Front (FPI) is led by Habib Rizieq, a graduate of LIPIA who went to Saudi Arabia on a Saudi government scholarship and modelled the FPI on the Saudi religious police, a body that enforces the moral strictures of Islam in society. Indeed, Indonesia is perhaps the single best and most important example of these shifts from tolerance towards religious tension and conflict.

Bandung in the late 1980s was a hotbed of incipient Islamic activism. This bustling provincial capital of west Java is nestled in the hills and was much appreciated by the Dutch for its cooler climate. They built long boulevards lined with grand hotels like the Savoy Homann, which employed Bauhaus and Art Nouveau architecture; they lived in stately, steep-roofed villas on streets shaded by graceful ficus and plane trees. With the establishment of the Institute of Technology (ITB) in the early twentieth century, Bandung became a seat of higher learning. Sukarno, the country's founding president, was an engineering graduate of ITB. The focus on higher education prospered in the modern era and Bandung today is home to hundreds of thousands of students. No surprise therefore that Bandung has long been a hotbed of student activism. But after the mid-1970s, President Suharto stifled all normal outlets for student expression – except for the mosque.

I travelled to Bandung frequently in the late 1980s and early 1990s, often taking the afternoon train from Jakarta's Dutch-era Gambir Station and enjoying the lush mountain views on the two-hour journey up. At Salman Mosque, built to an angular modern design in the city centre, I came across groups of intellectuals who were at the leading edge of Islamic revival. One of them, Jalalludin Rakhmat, introduced me to his followers and helped explain what was going on.

Jalalludin was a bookish man of considerable intellectual passion, who just as easily could have been a leftist. These were heady days for Islamic revival, with young idealistic preachers influenced by the 1979 Iranian revolution (which coincided with the dawn of the fifteenth century in the Muslim calendar). In other parts of the Islamic world at this time there was growing restiveness among a new generation of Muslims who resented the wealth of secular elites and who were attracted to the reassertion of Islamic dogma advocated by groups like the Muslim Brotherhood, which questioned the supremacy of Western civilisation. The broader context, combined with the more repressive atmosphere in Indonesia and a ban on student politics, was a compelling invitation for young people to explore the limits of defiance. 'Our main advantage are all the students,' Jalalludin told me. 'Ever since the ban on student politics, the mosque has become a sanctuary for them, a place where they can express political dissatisfaction and frustration. When they talk about Islam, they're talking about social and political issues – just using Islamic packaging because it's safe.'

In my discourse with the students over many months it was clear they were frustrated with the lack of channels for expression. At this stage, a little over two decades before the explosion of Islamic extremism that targeted the West, embracing Islamic dogma seemed a safe way for young people to struggle for more freedom and democracy. I was drawn to the Bandung crowd in their scruffy jeans and long hair – very few wore beards or donned Arab garb at this stage. We sat and exchanged views on notions of social and political struggle for hours over strong black coffee and pungent *kretek* cigarettes. There was no sign of the hatred or polarisation between Muslims and non-Muslims that prevailed in later years. In my eyes, they were students struggling for freedom. They just happened to be Muslims.

At the same time, another trend was emerging in society: a tendency to seek comfort in Islamic mystical beliefs and ritualistic practices, and an increase in middle-class interest in Sufi mysticism, both rooted in growing reactions to the side effects of growth and development such as rampant consumerism, chronic unemployment and pervasive corruption. Nurcholis Madjid established the

Jakarta-based Paramadina Foundation in the mid-1980s. Nurcholis, who died in 2005, received a traditional Islamic education in east Java, but won a scholarship to study modern social science at the University of Chicago. He was respected for advocating tolerance and moderation, yet his foundation played a significant role in drawing middle-class Muslims in Jakarta to seminars and training sessions in luxury hotels where modernist Islamic scholars spoke about the nexus between business and Islamic values. As much as Nurcholis himself projected an image of tolerance and moderation – one of his slogans was 'Islam yes, Islamic parties no' – he nonetheless supported the instilling of proper Islamic values in everyday life.

With no outlet for mass mobilisation to channel or express their concerns about the pressures of modern society, embracing religious faith served as a source of relief for Indonesians at all levels of society. As the scholar Stephen Headley points out, the marginalisation of Islamic political parties by Suharto's New Order regime elevated the appeal of the ethical ethos of Islam as 'the only source of *civilitas* available to Indonesians'. Islamic teaching therefore filled a void. Charismatic Islamic teachers imparted values of honesty and purity on cassette tapes and in popular magazines that circulated in the millions; their pure and pious image set against that of venal bureaucrats and politicians.

I visited one such teacher in his *pondok* – a place of religious learning derived from the Arabic word *funduk*, meaning rest house – outside Jakarta in the early 2000s. His name was A. A. Gymnastiar, or AA Gym in short form. He wore long, expensive silk robes, a neat turban and reeked of cheap cologne. His hands were dry, soft, smooth, his handshake gentle but assured. Thousands attended his sermons, listening to him speak in reassuring, lilting tones of the values of honesty and purity, often employing simple epithets such as: 'Change befalls those who live their lives better . . . ' Yet over the holy month of Ramadan it was reported he collected tens of thousands of dollars for a single sermon, eventually earning him the sobriquet 'The Britney Spears of Islam'. His many businesses and publishing ventures churned out copies of books and DVD recordings of his sermons, which were broadcast on a radio station he owned. Purification achieved through religious observance offered peace of mind and was a big business in the Indonesia of the 1990s. I was reminded of the business empires built by Christian charismatic preachers in the US. It appealed to the prevailing Javanese culture, in which pressure to maintain outwardly peaceful relations between individuals in an overcrowded, hierarchical society was balanced by escape into the realm of mystical speculation to seek release from the heavy burden of social responsibility. For the students, embracing Islamic rituals offered a path to empowerment in a situation where their voices were not heard, their aspirations unmet, perhaps unattainable: 'When you have no control over the environment and feel powerless, so people defer to supernatural forces and the assumption of spiritual power over the environment,' said my friend Jallaludin, who was worried, even before the emergence of the violent strand of Islamic extremism. 'People are embracing this kind of religiosity uncritically. You have graduates in physics and chemistry preferring to devote their energies to Islamic teaching by rote and the rigours of Koran memorisation in Arabic. They should be more rational. They're our future.'

All this more orthodox observance of Islam was happening in the world's largest Muslim nation at a time of political ferment and profound social and economic stress. It was around this time that the circulation of certain Islamic magazines like the popular weekly *Sabili* started to take off. Right before my eyes, Indonesian society started to look physically different: women covering their hair, men growing beards and wearing white caps – a style of dress that, in the past, only those who performed the Haj had worn. Department stores like Sarinah in the heart of Jakarta, established by the secular left-wing President Sukarno in the 1960s, removed a whole floor of traditional colourful batik cloth to make room for more sober monochromatic Islamic headgear and prayer paraphernalia. It was a reminder too of how lucrative an industry piety had become, trading not just in Islamic *haute couture* but also halal food. If the authoritarian state considered this advancing Islamisation a threat, it was hard to tell. Almost 90 per cent of Indonesia's 260 million people are Muslim, making it the largest Muslin nation in the world, and while Suharto was careful to use neutral terminology when invoking God, he himself finally went on a Haj in the 1990s.

Yet there were those who believed in the need to counter the head-long rush towards the irrationally pious. There were half-hearted attempts to balance religious curricula in the *Pesantren* (as Islamic religious schools are called in Indonesia). Suharto initiated a pro-gramme for training Islamic clergy at McGill University in Canada. But ironically some of those educated in the West came back with more dangerous ideas of political activism and left-wing notions they cloaked in Islamic dogma. Simultaneously, Suharto's New Order regime, having emasculated Islamic political parties, turned a blind eye to the development of Islamic missionary activities, which provided a convenient channel for those excluded from promoting Islam on a political platform. And as oil prices rose in the 1970s, the Saudi kingdom's proselytising zeal seemed to increase; thus, the Saudi-based Muslim World League became a key source of funds for Islamic missionary activities in Indonesia. The exact amount of money is next to impossible to measure, but given that per capita GDP in the mid-1980s was less than $500 (compared with $3,500 today), it's not hard to imagine the impact.

As the Australian historian Merle Ricklefs points out in his magisterial study of Islam in Java, the success of private missionary activities prompted the government to compete with an accelerated programme of mosque building, thus reinforcing piety. By the end of the twentieth century, Islamic identity in Indonesia had become more pronounced among middle-class urban youth; Islamic mis-sionaries trained in Saudi Arabia under the influence of neo-Wahhabi scholars had infiltrated the campuses, and huge sums of money flowed in from the Middle East. Almost undetected, Indonesia was set on the path to adopting an antagonistic Islamic identity that the left-leaning, European-educated founders of the republic had hoped to avoid using constitutional safeguards of tolerance and pluralism.

It was virtually the same story across the Malacca Strait in Malaysia. Islamic political activism was already established on campus in the 1970s, spearheaded by the Malaysian Muslim Youth Movement led by the young activist – later the reforming politician – Anwar Ibrahim. As in Indonesia, the moderate, secular inclinations of the British-educated Malay elite who led the nation at independence were gradually influenced by Islamisation at the grass roots in the mosques and religious schools of village society. The foundations of fundamentalist activity in Malaysia developed out of the competition between the ruling United Malays Nationalist Organisation (UMNO), which had liberal, modernist leanings, and the Islamic Party of Malaysia (PAS) threatening UMNO's supremacy using a platform of conservative Islam and demanding the implementation of Sharia law. UMNO briefly shared power with PAS in the mid-1970s, but after parting ways, the two parties started competing for votes in Malay Muslim areas where Islamic faith and tradition are powerful influences over everyday life. To win in these mainly rural constituencies UMNO started to outdo the PAS conservatives with both the rhetoric and practice of more conservative Islam. In a bid to co-opt the Islamic agenda, Prime Minister Mahathir Mohamad invited Anwar Ibrahim to join UMNO, which he did in 1982. By the time I was posted to Malaysia in the early 1990s as a correspondent, the annual UMNO assembly was less a rally to stir up nationalist sentiment and more a platform for aspiring Malay leaders to litter their speeches with Koranic verse and boast of their Islamic piety.

Until then, my perception of Malay culture and society was influenced by my long Indonesian sojourn: Indonesia is a country where religious faith and ethnic identity are more loosely associated. One day as I travelled in to Kuantan from a small airport in Terengganu on the east coast of Malaysia, the taxi driver complimented me on my Malay-language skills and asked: 'Why aren't you a Muslim?' There and then, I recognised how far Malay society had moved in the direction of association with Islam, to the point where the pre-Islamic culture of Malays on the peninsula is now almost completely obliterated. To thundering applause and standing ovations, UMNO politicians made their bid to climb the ranks of power by promising to protect the faith, which in turn prompted PAS to campaign for stricter application of Shariah law in their grass-roots constituencies.

Not surprisingly, this frothy competition for votes based on faith rather than secular programmes provided fertile ground for more radical elements to evolve and shelter. With national leaders refusing to unequivocally deny that Malaysia was on the verge of being declared an Islamic state for fear of being attacked by their more devout Islamic rivals, the non-Muslim Chinese and Indian population grew spooked and feared that the bonds of pluralism and tolerance, like Indonesia enshrined in the constitution, were weakening.

The more pronounced stress on faith, reinforced by these social and political factors, has helped sharpen differences of identity, which in turn highlights differences between communities across Southeast Asia that were less evident in past generations. Islamic piety in particular has a transformative effect on mixed communities: mosques grow bigger, the call to prayer louder, clothing and the appearance of people becomes more distinctive. Communities that once considered themselves Indonesian or Malaysian, Thai or Burmese, now seem more starkly differentiated. In conversations with Buddhist leaders in Myanmar and Thailand, I heard concerns about this differentiation. They asked: 'Why do Muslims look and act so differently today when they did not yesterday?' This fear of the pronounced difference piety has generated leads to moves to govern interaction and erect safety barriers, often by institutional means. In Myanmar there have been moves to prevent intermarriage between Muslims and Buddhists. Malaysian Muslims have objected to the use of the word 'Allah' as a generic term for God by Malaysian Christians and used a court order to prevent them from doing so.

The problem with this widening religious divide is that it is very hard for moderate voices to prevail. Islamic orthodoxy has this astonishing ability to prevail in Muslim society because of the threat of apostasy to those who deny the word of God. When just recently a group of prominent Malays raised their voices to express concern about the threat to pluralism posed by disputes over the application of Islamic laws in the country, conservative Muslim scholars insisted that since Muslims were the majority in Malaysia they had a right to be governed by Islamic law. So much for the constitution that guarantees freedom of religion.

In Myanmar, those Buddhists who questioned the harsh rhetoric against Muslims were deemed unpatriotic; in the run-up to the November 2015 elections, to criticise the shrill Buddhist nationalists could be damaging. In June 2015, Htin Lin Oo, a columnist and former information officer for the National League for Democracy, was arrested and jailed on a charge of insulting religion. He had been urging Buddhist nationalists to be more tolerant of minorities from other faiths. Even more alarmingly, in Indonesia, a newspaper that published a cartoon critical of the Islamic State in Syria resulted in the editor being officially accused of blasphemy.

All this points to the emergence of a worrying fissure between Southeast Asia's two main religions which could divide the region just as it moves awkwardly closer towards social and economic integration. The majority of Buddhists live in the mainland states, while Muslims dominate the island states. Muslims make up around half the total population of Southeast Asia. Movements on a micro-scale are already detectable. Muslims from Myanmar's mainly Buddhist Rakhine State are finding their way to Muslim-majority Malaysia; Buddhists from the three southernmost provinces of Thailand, where Malay Muslims are a majority, are leaving after a decade of ethnic conflict in which Buddhist monks and Islamic preachers have been targeted. That's not to say that Southeast Asia will inevitably transform into the polarised, violent landscape that we see in the Middle East and parts of Africa, but the fabric of the plural society that has served the region well in terms of providing a basic foundation of stability is torn and in need of repair. This becomes a real challenge in a context of freewheeling and contested politics.

The three decades I have covered Southeast Asia span the period in which society has vigorously embraced religious faith, displacing the refuge many took in secular ideologies such as communism until the 1980s. While the developing socio-economic environment was conducive to reinforcing religious piety, politics has been a key driver.

The Darul Islam revolt in Indonesia, which sought to establish an Islamic state, was violently suppressed in the 1960s and for the next twenty-five years Islamic activists associated or sympathetic to DI were jailed or treated like pariahs. Suharto's New Order regime did everything it could to emasculate Islamic political aspirations. This changed unexpectedly at the start of the 1990s after Islamic sentiment was endowed with a political channel. With growing unease in the military ranks over the excesses of his rule, notably the monopolistic practices of his family, President Suharto decided he needed to shore up popular support. At the time, after decades of relegation to the political wilderness, Suharto's embrace of the 'greens', as the Muslim lobby was termed, seemed a balancing act to counter military influence in politics. But for Muslim intellectuals who felt their weight in numbers was not properly reflected in the power equation, it was a long-awaited opportunity. 'We Muslims are weak because we have failed to unify,' lamented an old Muslim scholar I met in the Al Falah Mosque in Surabaya in mid-1990. 'A political role is the only way for us to forge effective unity,' he said. Abdurrahman Wahid, then head of the largest Muslim organisation, Nahdlatul Ulama, echoed this sentiment: 'We are big and Suharto needs us,' he told me during one of the regular meetings I held with the nearly blind cleric who was destined to become president a decade later. A year later, in Malang, a charming hill town in east Java known for its delicious apples, the much sought-after basis of unity and a political role for Islam was established with the inauguration in 1991 of the Association of Islamic Intellectual and Scholars (ICMI), under the sponsorship of Suharto's trusted minister of technology and future president B. J. Habibie.

Just as Sukarno, the country's founding president, had embraced the Communist Party in the 1960s to forge a mass base of popular support and fend off the army, so Suharto at the start of the 1990s adopted Islam to shore up support for the same reason. This need for a man who rose to power on the back of the military to acquire Islamic legitimacy is not unlike the path taken by Pakistan's military strongman Zia-ul-Haq, who overthrew a civilian government in a military coup in the mid-1970s, and then embarked on a rigorous Islamicisation programme. By doing so, Zia laid the foundations for the strong influence of political Islam in Pakistan today. For Suharto in Indonesia, it was clear by the mid-1980s that the army was growing concerned about the concentration of power and patronage in his hands. To offset the army's power, Suharto established ICMI and began cultivating political and military figures with Islamic leanings – classic divide-and-rule tactics – and when the portly president went on a Haj in 1991 he adopted a new name: Haji Mohammad Suharto, to the delight of many Muslim intellectuals.

Suharto co-opted the Islamic intellectuals almost certainly because he was more interested in the short-term goal of securing his power base rather than changing the fundamental secular basis of the Indonesian state. He was also tapping into a source of ready support within certain sections of the army considered 'green' in the Islamic sense – in contrast to the situation in Turkey, where the military was avowedly secular and was moving against Islamic parties at around the same time. But the Islamic support base Suharto now patronised had other ideas. 'Our concern is the potential Lebanon-isation of Indonesia; the economic elite are Chinese and Christian, the military leadership is Christian and the rest are Muslim. This is very dangerous and the balance needs addressing,' a leading Muslim intellectual told me at the time. The army and many of the Christian elite, and Chinese Indonesians, grew alarmed. Opening the door to the assertion of fundamentalist Islamic values that were already brewing in Indonesian society as a result of the influx of Saudi money had in their eyes empowered the Muslim majority in a dangerous manner. Given what we see today, with a Muslim mob agitating against a Chinese Christian city governor, how right they were to be concerned.

At first the manifestation was symbolic, but then a powerful wing of the military emerged under Muslim patronage; leading Muslim figures started to play politics, and soon it was hard to question or roll back the parallel spread of piety and dogmatism. All this was happening in an era where the Saudis were actively campaigning for a revival of Sunni as opposed to Shiite Islam. In a broader sense, the Saudi compulsion was to roll back what it saw as the successful spread of Shiite influence emanating from the Iranian revolution. In Iran, a decade of war with Iraq left the country weak and isolated; the mullahs were preoccupied with internal consolidation. This meant that the only source of external support and influence was Wahhabism, profoundly intolerant and divisive.

In Malaysia, the politics of religion has played out in much the same way, with the Islamic faith harnessed to jockeying for power within the context of more competitive politics. As mentioned above, the interplay between advancing religiosity and political posturing was manifested in the rise of the Pan-Malaysian Islamic Party, known as PAS, established in 1951, and which for many years competed with the mainstream establishment: UMNO. It sat on the left of the political spectrum and its espousal of Islamic faith was no different than that of UMNO. This started to change from the early 1980s, reflecting the spread of more fundamentalist ideas emanating from the Iranian revolution – the same ideas that galvanised the students and young Islamic preachers like my friend Jalalludin in Bandung. From this point onwards, PAS started using the promotion of a purer Islamic dogma to undermine UMNO support in its rural Malay constituencies, reflecting a feeling that Malays should go beyond paying lip service to Islam as a way of life.

Covering by-election campaigns in the 1990s, I was impressed by the power of their oratory and compelling appeal of their ideas. In small villages, notably in the north, where a basic agrarian existence magnified the values of faith and tradition, PAS leaders presented themselves as simple men of faith interested in the welfare of the people. Their message was that UMNO had allowed Malays to become corrupt and dominated by *kafir* (read: Chinese interests). Many of these ideas were vague and it was hard to envisage their implementation without tearing up a constitution guaranteeing pluralism and ruling out the more exclusive aspects of Islamic statehood; nevertheless, in 1990 PAS won a majority in the autonomous state of Kelantan on the northeastern coast of the Malay Peninsula. Led by Ustaz Nik Aziz Nik Mat, a quiet but charismatic preacher of immense humility who refused to take a salary and shunned official protocol, Kelantan initiated the slow, steady trajectory towards Islamic statehood, pushing for the implementation of Sharia law.

To counter these moves and a significant loss of political ground, UMNO was forced to adopt a holier-than-thou approach, and embark on a process of Islamisation itself. As the Singaporean scholar Joseph Liow points out in his masterful study of Islam in contemporary Malaysia, 'the primary dynamic has been one of competition.' To show there was meaning to their polemic

countering PAS, UMNO leaders used their control over the machinery of government to inject Islamic values into the bureaucracy,
turning an easy-going approach to practising Islam into a battery of
enforcement agencies that started hauling off unmarried couples,
cracking down on Muslims who chose not to fast over Ramadan,
and, more recently, judging any criticism of Islam liable to prosecution under harsh sedition laws. The late Malaysian writer and
journalist Rehman Rashid observed in his lyrical book *A Malaysian
Journey*, 'an awful obsessiveness, a faith on the brink of fanaticism'.
Rehman, who was himself a Malay and a Muslim, goes on to quote
an Indian taxi driver remarking on a crowd of worshippers outside
a city mosque: 'These people are followers. With good leaders, they
will be good people. With bad leaders, they will be bad people.' The
reality was that under strong leaders like Mahathir Mohamad, who
could effectively use government muscle to muzzle the mullahs, the
non-Muslim minorities were safe. But the muzzles came off after
Mahathir stepped down in 2003, handing power to his deputy Abdullah Badawi.

It was around this time that governments on both sides of the
Malacca Strait were forced to confront the rise of radical Islamic movements and pay serious attention to the concerns of the
non-Muslim community. In the 1990s the Malaysian government
banned an innocuous ascetic Islamic sect known as Al Arqam. They
were harmless eccentrics living off the mainstream grid, making
money to support their numerous wives by selling pickles and pre-
serves. But for all the apparent vigilance in multiracial Malaysia for
extremist groups, it was the ability of a small group of Indonesians to
seek refuge in Malaysia, where Islamic piety and scholarship enjoys a
pronounced degree of protection, that nurtured the movement that
came to be known as Jemaah Islamiyya (JI), later held responsible
for terrorist attacks in Bali and Jakarta.

Abu Bakar Bashir and Abdullah Sungkar – both Indonesians of
Arab descent – were among those who sought to revive the struggle
to establish Indonesia as an Islamic State that had been so effectively
crushed in the 1960s. Using latent networks of religious teachers
and activists loyal to the Darul Islam movement, they led Islamic

revivalist programmes that became progressively radical, influenced by the Muslim Brotherhood teachings of Sayyid Qutub and Hassan al-Banna, among others. Jailed by the Indonesian authorities in the late 1970s, the pair escaped to Malaysia in 1982. From there, working as religious teachers, they made contact with Malaysians and Indonesians who had fought in Afghanistan as mujahideen. It was these men who spearheaded recruitment for JI, which the American researcher Sidney Jones described as a series of unconnected cells. Initially, the aim was to carry out revenge attacks against Christians following religious conflicts in the eastern Indonesian provinces of Maluku and Sulawesi. From there, it was a very short step towards jumping aboard the global jihadi bandwagon after 9/11.

On an intellectual level, the appearance in 1993 of Samuel Huntingdon's article on the clash of civilisations in the US-published journal *Foreign Affairs* was met with critical alarm. Huntingdon's piece captured the shift away from the ideological divide of the post-Second World War era towards one defined more by ideas of faith and culture. Although factual in his analysis, Huntingdon imparted a sense of renewed division in the world, one that carried the menace of conflict just a few years after the end of the Cold War. This went against the euphoria about the end of history and a new globalised society. Huntingdon's article, it was predicted, would 'confirm the Muslim view of what Americans think of them and confirm the feeling that Islam and Muslims will be a target of the West. Negative feelings towards Islam and Muslims will increase.' This divide might have been bridged if it had remained firmly planted in the academic realm, or in the hands of sophisticated political actors with a modern vision. It was a struggle that Anwar Ibrahim and the young Muslim intellectuals he fostered in the mid-1990s tried very hard to win.

Anwar spoke to adoring crowds on the campaign trail about the Muslim *umma* needing to balance traditional dogma with modern technological and industrial achievement. He railed at PAS: 'They talk of jihad and then go home to sleep.' Anwar tried to be a little bit of everything to everyone: his aides liked to say he retained his radical roots, albeit tempered by experience; in reality he was good at pleasing everybody, something of a political chameleon. But with one eye on his growing international stature, he was genuinely interested in finding a path to a less disruptive or divisive way of implementing Islamic principles and dogma in a mixed and modern industrial society – in other words, to bridge Huntingdon's civilisational divide. Writing three years after Huntingdon's article appeared, Anwar called for a Consortium of Cultures: 'As Asia renews itself, it must have the confidence to appreciate and learn from Western civilisation, inasmuch as the West has to learn from the East.' Anwar's ideas were electrifying and refreshing at a time of bruising rhetorical jousting between those who said that, to modernise, Asia must embrace Western notions of democracy and law, while the recalcitrant authoritarian leaders like Lee Kuan Yew in Singapore and Mahathir in Malaysia used their colonial-era British education to hammer away at Western encroachment using flimsy and poorly articulated 'Asian values'. More importantly, Anwar's vision of Islam was broadly inclusive and civilisational, as opposed to blinkered and exclusive.

The power of Anwar's polemic and inspiring leadership might have helped stem the tide of what was coming if he hadn't been abruptly removed from the scene. In 1998, following a clumsy bid to topple Mahathir on a wave of calls for reform, Anwar was stripped of his deputy prime minister's position, hauled into court and jailed for corruption and sodomy. His voice was absent when the planes slammed into the Twin Towers, and when he was released from prison in 2004, he penned a diary piece for the *Far Eastern Economic Review*, musing:

> I have often wondered whether there was a mystical reason for my being put out of circulation during one of the most turbulent periods of human history, at least in my lifetime. Given my contacts in both Muslim and Western worlds, I would have been expected to play some diplomatic role in the so-called war against terrorism. And I would have been loath to shirk it.

Prone to hubris as Anwar was, he had a point. For when the bombs started going off in the wake of 9/11 in Bali, Jakarta and elsewhere, there was a mad scramble to identify and eliminate those responsible. Little thought was given to the need for the kind of civilisational dialogue Anwar and his friends had proposed in the 1990s. From Anwar's diary again:

> There are cynics who scoff at the idea of dialogue, pointing to the futility of decades of talks to resolve the Middle East conflict. But dialogues among cultures are not the same as peace talks. According to a popular song from the 1970s, 'most of us will hate anything we don't understand'. The Koran gives a similar message [about dialogue] in positive language, telling us that God created nations and tribes so that we would learn from one another. And when we do, we shall not only understand but indeed appreciate each other's values – for I am certain of this – we shall then realise that no single culture can claim a monopoly on morality or justice.

It was too late. Whatever happened to Lee's 'tropical Islam' of green trees, green grass and no desert? Huntingdon's divisive vision has materialised with ghastly impact. Hatred of the West has transcended the old authoritarian promotion of Asian values; Muslims in Southeast Asia have absorbed more fundamentalist manifestations of the faith from its Arab hearth – Arab values born of a desert existence in the seventh century, no less. This in turn has physically transformed communities that once blended harmoniously, and peacefully coexisted with non-Muslim neighbours. So now the Buddhists and the Christians feel threatened, and they in turn embrace and reinforce their own fundamentalist narratives to protect their space and shore up their boundaries. In Anwar's absence – he is serving yet another term in prison – the mantle of civilisational dialogue has fallen on his daughter, Nurul Izzah. Now a member of parliament and deputy leader of the opposition People's Alliance Party that Anwar established, Nurul Izzah stared at her hands when I asked her recently in Kuala Lumpur who could lead the Muslim world towards a more tolerant, reasonable discourse with non-Muslims. 'We had put a lot of faith in Erdogan and the AKP,' she said. She was speaking in July 2016, a week after the failed coup attempt in Turkey and the emergence of Erdogan as an Islamic strongman bent on veering away from the West. Not much of an ideal model, she conceded.

My friend Jalalludin Rakhmat was right to worry when he saw his student followers in Bandung burying themselves in Koranic study as a means of finding the freedom to think. How ironic that the struggle for freedom ended up breeding more tyranny and violence.

CHAPTER ELEVEN

THE DRAGON APPARENT

'China is a big country and other countries are small countries, and that's just a fact.'

Yang Jiechi, Chinese State Councillor

'Small countries destined by geography to live on the periphery of big countries are always going to experience a degree of anxiety.'

Bilahari Kausikan, senior Singapore diplomat

Brigadier General Aung Thaw leaned forward in his chair to make the point as forcefully as the formality of the setting allowed: 'Myanmar is not at all like other countries in Southeast Asia.' The general's dark, thickset features suggested a stereotypical military enforcer, belying the strong intellect and open manner of this deputy minister of defence. 'You see,' he continued, 'we are surrounded by powerful neighbours. Indonesia is lucky, it's a group of islands and faces no overland threat.'

Myanmar, the general was at pains to point out, shares a 2,192-kilometre eastern border with China and a 1,331-kilometre western border with India.

Just a few months after our meeting in the country's soulless, modern capital, Naypyidaw (built in the middle of the country, some say, to better protect the government from invasion), the general's strategic concerns became a reality. In the first months of 2015 a virulent insurgent force, comprised for the most part of ethnic Chinese under the umbrella of an organisation called the Myanmar

National Democratic Alliance Army (MNDAA), attacked the Myanmar army close to the Chinese border in what is known as the Kokang region. In the months of fighting that ensued, close to a thousand Myanmar army troops were killed, including around 200 of officer rank who the Myanmar military say were targeted by snipers using sophisticated rifles that could only have been procured from China. The MNDAA boasts a fighting force of 5,000 and allegedly recruits some of its soldiers from inside China. Most of its modern weaponry is Chinese. Just a few months later, over on the western border, an Indian army Special Forces attack squad crossed over with a helicopter-borne force in early June 2015 to intercept a group of insurgents alleged to be responsible for a spate of ambushes on Indian forces in the northeastern state of Manipur. For a country with two powerful neighbours, worrying about their influence is bad enough, but Myanmar faces armed clashes and incursions.

At the start of this book I described the serendipity of Southeast Asia's location betwixt and between busy trading routes 'below the winds'. Historically, this accessible geography has served the region well, ensuring an abundance of trade and the technological as well as cultural by-products fluid commercial exchange brings. That ease of access also made the region vulnerable to intrusion and invasion. Modern Southeast Asia has spent nearly a century recovering from the two last invasions, one by Europeans expanding eastward and which lasted some four hundred years; the other by Japan expanding southwards between 1941 and 1945. Both these imperial intrusions were epoch-forming. To read any contemporary opinion or analysis of Southeast Asia is to become aware of the threat of a new invasion, from China. In this chapter, I will explore the dynamics of modern Southeast Asia's relationship with China and the region's vulnerable proximity to the largest and increasingly powerful nation on earth. Apart from sparsely populated Central Asia, the similarly lightly populated frozen eastern provinces of Russia, or India, or Pakistan and Nepal's high-altitude Himalayan margins, there is no region of the world closer and more exposed to China's rise than Southeast Asia.

There is also today perhaps no more significant fault line of superpower rivalry in the world than the complex interface between

Southeast Asia and China. For as the US looked for a way of disengaging from two decades of entanglement in the Middle East, the rise of China goaded Washington into making a strategic 'pivot' back towards the Asian theatre. Southeast Asia lies, much as the Balkans did in the nineteenth and twentieth century, along the edge of a geopolitical plate that is increasingly contested by the larger powers. To the west there is India, which although preferring non-alignment and inclined to pursue interests close to the sub-continent, finds it expedient to cosy up to the US because of its own border issues with China. To the east lies China, which in the words of one of Singapore's more senior diplomats 'wants to reclaim something of its centrality in East Asia'. For the legions of academics and strategic thinkers who make a living out of geopolitical alchemy, something of a Great Game in Asia is apparent.

China is umbilically tied to Southeast Asia by demography and history. For centuries, people moving along swift-flowing rivers and over gently undulating hills peopled the mainland of Southeast Asia from what is now the Chinese province of Yunnan. The Mongols secured Yunnan for the Chinese empire in the thirteenth century and the province subsequently became the staging area for successive Mongol invasions of Burma. Today, with a population of 45 million people and a $200 billion economy, Yunnan is the staging area for China's push to extend lines of communication through Southeast Asia to the sea. As the renowned British scholar of China, C. P. Fitzgerald, noted: 'Chinese influence, Chinese culture and Chinese power have always moved southward since the first age of which we have reliable historical influence.'

The Chinese have a word to denote the warmer southern reaches encompassing the sea and land borders with Southeast Asia: 'nanyang'. Deceptively pacific, the term is also used to refer to the Chinese, who over centuries have migrated to Southeast Asia and established successful communities engaged in commerce. Unlike almost any other geopolitical threat to Southeast Asia, that posed by China is more than simply one of military might; it also involves the logic of demography – 1.3 billion people living just next door. There's also the question of what if anything China makes of the 30-plus million people of Chinese descent who live in Southeast

Asia and who account for the lion's share of its wealth. It is this subliminal, unspoken fear of mass migration from China, as well as China's putative extra-territorial claim over the ethnic Chinese communities of the region, rather than the threat of an actual naval or overland invasion by military forces, that keeps a lot of Southeast Asian governments worried about their sovereignty.

There hasn't been a real shooting war between states in Southeast Asia since the 1960s. The pernicious internal conflicts described earlier are tucked away behind thick curtains of isolation and neglect, and rarely spill over borders. No one seems to want to threaten the region with outside military force, and the United States serves as a reliable sentinel, despite the legacy of the Indochina Wars. Memories of US Air Force B52s carpet-bombing Cambodia and North Vietnam have faded, replaced by a genial, impermanent presence characterised as 'places not bases'. Replacing the Cold War menace of US military forces in the region was the sight of US amphibious ships and helicopters dropping food and water to the victims of the 2004 Tsunami in Aceh. This benign security profile served the region well until the end of the first decade of the twenty-first century. It began to change after 2010 when then US Secretary of State Hillary Clinton delivered a speech in Hanoi that intentionally threw down a gauntlet of sorts at China's door. Based on a calculated view in Washington that the US needed to assert its strategic presence in the region more forcefully, Clinton took aim at China's active claims of sovereignty in the South China Sea, particularly in waters claimed by Vietnam to the north, and by Malaysia, the Philippines and Brunei to the south. 'We believe claimants should pursue their territorial claims and the company and rights to maritime space in accordance with the UN convention on the law of the sea,' Clinton said. 'Consistent with customary international law, legitimate claims to maritime space in the South China Sea should be derived solely from legitimate claims to land features.' This was a barb aimed directly at China's wider claim to the whole of the South China Sea as depicted in all official Chinese maps, and even on Chinese passports, as the famous nine-dashed line.

China's response was to aggressively ramp up its assertion of sovereignty, using physical force as well as rhetoric, and to create a new and destabilising threat of conflict in the region. By mid-2016, China had built several runways capable of handling modern fighter jets and massive transport planes on small coral features in the middle of some of the busiest sea lanes in Asia. These islands have also seen the temporary deployment of high-frequency radar and high-altitude missile batteries. US ships or planes probing the air or sea around these islands have been aggressively told to buzz off.

It has always been difficult to precisely gauge the Chinese threat to Southeast Asia in military terms. For all the hyperventilation about its rise from an isolated and impoverished totalitarian state to global giant, China hasn't actually gone to war with anyone since the 1970s, and even then it came off worst after launching a poorly planned invasion across the Vietnam border in 1979. Neither properly trained nor adequately supplied, the Chinese army was beaten back by battle-hardened Vietnamese artillery units fresh from victory over US forces. A former artillery office in the Vietnamese army, who was a veteran of the campaign, told me it was like a 'duck shoot'.

Chinese military capacity and strength has significantly improved since then. China now spends around 10 per cent of its GDP on defence, making its military budget the second-largest in the world after the US. Direct Chinese military intervention is, at least for now, not what concerns the region, however. The bigger challenge for Southeast Asian governments is dealing with China as a super-power in economic and therefore political terms. General Charles de Gaulle once said that there is no political reality in Asia that is not of interest and concern to China. Today, this would seem truer than ever, with China accounting for one-fifth of the world's population and a $10 trillion economy.

China's economy began to grow after Deng Xiaoping inaugurated free market reforms in 1978, allowing the country to offer a proximate market for Southeast Asian goods and services. By some accounts, Deng was inspired by the success of thriving entrepôt Chinese majority states such as Hong Kong and Singapore. He recognised the enterprise of overseas Chinese-dominated societies, and was able to foresee the transformative effect this would have on China's peasant-driven agrarian economy. Equally, opportunity to invest in and trade with China has been a considerable driver of growth and prosperity for Southeast Asia, with trade now valued at $500 billion between the ten countries of ASEAN compared with just $32 billion in 2000. China is ASEAN's largest trading partner; the US is only the fourth-largest. There was once concern that China's lower cost of labour would draw off investment from Southeast Asia; however, this seems less of an issue today, given China's increased wages (now averaging over $1,670 per month compared with around $1,100 in Indonesia, Myanmar and the Philippines in 2015). Some low-end manufacturing is even moving away from China to lower-income countries such as Indonesia.

Of course, a collapse of China's economy would hit the regional economy badly. China is the largest rice importer in the world. Falling demand because of declining growth in China over the past two years is already hitting Southeast Asia's top rice exporters such as Thailand and Vietnam. Should recession morph into crisis, the unspoken fear in Southeast Asia is of an influx of Chinese migrants, much the same way that hundreds of thousands of impoverished Chinese poured out of the old treaty ports into Southeast Asia at the end of the nineteenth century, shortly before the final collapse of the Qing Dynasty in 1911 – as they did on a smaller scale after the collapse of the Ming Dynasty in the mid-seventeenth century. Dynastic transition in China has historically been the primary push factor of Chinese immigration to Southeast Asia. The latest wave of Chinese immigration is propelled by Chinese investment in large infrastructure projects such as ports and high-speed trains. Chinese labour scrambles over construction projects and seeps into Southeast Asia via special economic zones that now dot the border areas of mainland Southeast Asia with the look and feel of Chinese towns.

In diplomatic and military terms, Southeast Asia has mixed experiences with China. As mentioned above, the Mongols invaded Burma in the thirteenth century. They overreached and the invasions failed. Later the Ming repeatedly tried and failed to seize Vietnam in the early to mid-fifteenth century. The Qing dynasty under the Qianlong emperor launched four invasions against the Burmese Konbaung dynasty in the mid-eighteenth century – they may have originated as punitive expeditions to go after Ming refugees who sought refuge and support at the Burmese court. These invasions failed either because the Chinese armies were overextended, or the disciplined soldiery from the plains of the Yangtze became entangled in the region's inhospitable jungle, falling prey to tropical diseases. The Qianlong emperor's fruitless forays into Burma in the mid-eighteenth century were the last significant Chinese invasions of Southeast Asia.

Nor it seems was China all that committed to developing as a maritime power. Wang Gungwu, one of the most erudite and accomplished scholars of China in Asia, argues that at various points in dynastic time, notably under the Ming Dynasty (1368–1644), the Chinese dominated the East China and South China Sea; the famous Ming admiral Zheng He, a Muslim and a eunuch, set forth from the coast of China with a vast armada of ships and men at the start of the fifteenth century, and even attempted to invade Java. 'But they gave it up,' Wang argues, 'because in a way they were being traditional. They decided there was no real threat . . . so why waste resources?'

Set against these brief and not very successful expansionist episodes is an otherwise benign and beneficial relationship with the Middle Kingdom. The Chinese imperial court viewed the outer world as a forbidding place full of barbarians, and was content to receive token assurances of subjugation from far-flung kingdoms in the lands below. Tributary missions involved official visits to the imperial capital, a ritual kowtow to the Dragon throne acknowledging the emperor as the lord of the world, and the delivery of presents as tokens of allegiance. In return for these annual or biannual tributary missions, the emerging princely states were given rights to trade, usually at a hefty profit. As one ship's captain noted in 1725: 'Three years ago we made a tributary voyage to the Great Qing on behalf of the Siamese Court. We were advised at the time that because rice was very cheap in Siam, 4,200 tons was to be exported to the provinces of Guangdong, Fujian and Ningbo . . . ' China's isolated scholar mandarins, walled up in their Forbidden City, never seemed to worry that they were at the losing end of this arrangement, valuing above all else the comforting conceit of their centrality in the world. This was the basis of what famed Harvard China scholar

John Fairbanks termed the 'reasoned pacificism' of old China.

More recently, by Chinese measures of history, there was also a good internal reason for the absence of a palpable threat: China, once the dominant power in pre-colonial Asia, has slumbered or been distracted by dynastic decline and disarray for two centuries. The long decline of the Qing dynasty, which ended in humiliation at the hands of the West following the Opium Wars, was succeeded by decades of strife as the fractured imperial realm fell victim to warlords and then the predations of imperial Japan. After the Pacific War and the defeat of the Kuomintang Nationalists led by Generalissimo Chiang Kai-shek, there followed almost three decades of isolation as the communists consolidated power in a frenzy of violence and propaganda, killing millions. China was effectively shut off from Southeast Asia during this period spanning almost a century. It was not until the start of the Cold War in the 1950s that China started to present a tangible threat to Southeast Asian security. Communist insurgencies erupting across Southeast Asia received ideological and material support from China, most notably in Burma, Laos, Malaya, Thailand and Vietnam. In the early 1960s there was the possibility of a communist takeover in Indonesia, which China stood to gain from, but oddly did little to physically support.

It is debatable to what extent China believed in the possibility of much of Asia turning communist, or if it was merely exercising prudent strategic counter-moves to limit Soviet influence in the region. The two communist giants split in the 1960s over doctrinal differences and – more significantly – because of territorial concerns. By the late 1970s Deng Xiaoping had other ideas, and in 1978 he embarked on a ground-breaking tour of Southeast Asia, launching a new, more constructive relationship with the region. Beijing's primary concern was to keep other major powers out of its neighbourhood, specifically Soviet Russia; hence, it was thought the 1979 Chinese invasion of Vietnam was meant more as a sharp message to Moscow than a bid to seize Vietnam.

In any case, countering US influence in the wake of the Indochina war wasn't so hard, as Washington withdrew forces from Vietnam and Cambodia after 1975 to lick its wounds. By the 1990s the US was preoccupied with military adventurism in the Middle East, from which it has struggled to extricate itself. However, perhaps to ensure a measure of border security and a definable zone of influence, China remained a staunch supporter of the Burmese Communist Party in its long war against the Burmese army that only ended in 1989. The Malayan Communist Party sheltering in the jungles of southern Thailand surrendered the same year. By the late 1980s China had declared that it was withdrawing support from armed rebellions conducted by communist parties in the region. Thailand was told that China would withdraw support for the Communist Party of Thailand so long as it would turn a blind eye to China arming the Khmer Rouge.

What remained ambiguous were China's feelings towards the millions of overseas Chinese living in the region. China had a first taste of extraterritoriality when the British humiliatingly imposed a strict exemption from Chinese law on British subjects residing in Hong Kong, ceded to Britain under the 1842 Treaty of Nanking after China's defeat in the first Opium War. China continues to recognise the principle today, almost twenty years after Hong Kong was returned to China, as the people of Hong Kong are treated separately under the one country, two systems formula in place until 2047. But this acknowledgement of extraterritoriality swings both ways.

For the wider Chinese diaspora, China at first made a distinction between ethnic Chinese living overseas with Chinese citizenship and those who had acquired foreign nationality. Those with foreign nationality, Beijing stated in the late 1970s, could not be called overseas Chinese. Yet as China's economy grew, there were increasing appeals and campaigns to attract ethnic Chinese help from overseas. Overseas Affairs offices were established in many of the areas of southern China from where migrants had left in the nineteenth century, tempting their descendants to return to and/or help their ancestral towns and villages. In fact, the lion's share of inward investment to China in the first three decades of market opening came from overseas Chinese living in Hong Kong, Taiwan and Southeast Asia. By 1989, overseas Chinese investment in China amounted to some $30 billion – as much as 10 per cent of this from ethnic Chinese in Southeast Asia.

No sooner had China ceased supporting land-based insurgencies struggling to establish communist rule than it began asserting sovereignty over islands and features in the South China Sea. In late January 1988 a group of Chinese naval vessels attacked a small Vietnamese garrison on an atoll known as Johnson Reef in the Spratly Islands. According to the Vietnamese, its poorly armed soldiers bravely defended the patch of coral and beat off the Chinese with heavy loss of life. By the end of 1988, China had occupied half a dozen small features in waters close to the coasts of Malaysia, Brunei and the Philippines. It was only in 1990 that Chinese Premier Li Peng announced in Singapore that China was ready to join efforts to develop jointly the Spratly Islands area and set aside issues of sovereignty. Wang Gungwu somewhat apologetically takes the view that China's need for security in the South China Sea stems from memories of Japan's imperial reach in the mid-twentieth century. The Pentagon considers that China's active pursuit of these claims, which revolve around small specks of coral upon which China has now effectively built fixed aircraft carriers, will deny the US Pacific Fleet, ironically based in Japan, unrestricted access to the area. Like it or not, argues senior Singapore diplomat Bilahari Kausikan, Southeast Asia 'will draw conclusions about American resolve and Chinese intentions from the South China Sea issue'. Bill Hayton, in his detailed history of the disputes, argues more pungently that 'in our era, what happens in the South China Sea will define the future'. In July 2016 the Permanent Court of Arbitration in The Hague delivered a landmark ruling after a Philippine government submission on Chinese encroachment of its waters. The ruling effectively dismissed China's legal control over what it calls islands upon which it has historical claims by defining them as low-tide features around which no extended boundary limits could be drawn. China furiously rejected the ruling and nothing changed.

As a mediator, I was drawn to the issue and started to explore in 2015 how to de-escalate a situation that was clearly a proximate *casus belli*. My conversations with Chinese security officials in Beijing indicated that effective control of economic exploitation zones encompassing sea-based resources was less important to them than the security imperative of planting the flag and military material on specks of coral. This in turn appeared to stem, at least partially, from the Chinese Communist Party's need to strongly assert claims of sovereignty to bolster political stability at home. As the China scholar Linda Jacobson points out: 'Chinese people today feel that it is high time that China become less submissive and cease acquiescing to outsiders, especially Japan and the United States. Many Chinese regard their government's diplomacy as "weak-kneed".' This suggested to me a rather emotional imperative; a big power game not easily addressed by conventional means of negotiation and arbitration and with Southeast Asia cast as the nut between two giant arms of a geopolitical nutcracker.

On land, China may have nominally abandoned support for long-defeated communist insurgencies, but its subsequent interventions have been just as intrusive, only subtler. The fierce border war in Kokang State along the China–Myanmar border mentioned earlier is apparently well armed and funded from the Chinese side, and seems to have the backing of local officials and shadowy companies in neighbouring Yunnan province, from which Beijing officially distances itself. India accuses China of arming rebels in its northeastern states through a web of private trading companies and underground intelligence contacts. When pressed, Chinese military officials scoff at the idea of official backing for these cross-border actions, yet they will admit that when ethnic Chinese populations on their margins ask for help, as was the case along the Burma–China border, they feel 'public pressure' to respond. It is also possible that, much like the way the US conducts its wars these days, small bands of former Chinese military personnel are fighting for money. One is reminded of the old refrain from Washington that it backed military uprisings against dictators in Latin America at the request of the people. Superpowers do as superpowers do, and China would appear to be following a playbook compiled by the US in the 1950s.

To counter the threats – real or perceived – from powerful neighbours such as China, Southeast Asia has long been urged to develop a strong and cohesive regional identity, serving both to enhance its own security and to develop as a common market. As a result, the Association of Southeast Asian Nations (ASEAN) was born in Bangkok in 1967 after a Western-backed NATO-like alliance named the Southeast Asian Treaty Organisation (SEATO) aimed at countering communist aggression fell apart. For much of its first four decades, ASEAN grew and developed as a group of like-minded nations interested in common security and economic issues. A free-trade regime was established, and in 2015 ASEAN was declared an economic community with plans to open borders to the free movement of capital and labour. In fact, almost nothing has changed; tariff barriers and obstacles to labour movement remain in place. That the promise of a cohesive region sharing the burden of security and enjoying the benefits of a market place of half a billion souls has not really materialised says much about the virulence of sovereignty in the region highlighted earlier, and underlines the threat of its powerful regional neighbours.

ASEAN is much misunderstood by outsiders, who imagine a vision of an integrated community of nations on a trajectory towards union. Nothing could be further from the truth. As Bilahari Kausikan puts it: 'In Southeast Asia, sovereignties are relatively new and often still tender; historical enmities not yet forgotten and the region lies at the intersection of major power interests.' To help keep ASEAN the sum of its parts, all decisions are strictly reached through consensus, which means that nothing very much is achieved in policy terms and it takes close to a decade to reach any decision of substance.

For all its impotence, almost every major power in the world has become a dialogue partner with ASEAN; and most have signed the bedrock treaty of amity and cooperation that underpins the organisation. From the mid-1990s, at the urging of Western powers and Japan anticipating China's rise, ASEAN launched a broader security forum that meets annually to discuss matters of common security – and even includes North Korea as a member. After ARF, argues Bilahari Kausikan, the Singapore diplomat who has been at the heart of regional security discussions for the past three decades, 'who can now reasonably or credibly argue that major powers have no legitimate interest in the security of Southeast Asia?'

Yet for all of ASEAN's supposed centrality in this web of security mechanisms, the past decade has seen all the major powers that ring ASEAN – China, the United States and, to a lesser extent India, essentially push for exclusive access. In many ways, a sort of mini-

Cold War is already under way, with the aim to hold sway or at least deny exclusive domination over what remains one of the world's most important corridors of trade. The problem for Southeast Asia is that historically each of its states has preferred to balance external forces rather than select one over the other. The United States initially tried through the hapless SEATO experiment to create a carbon copy of the North Atlantic Treaty Organisation in Southeast Asia, back in the early days of the Cold War. In fact, ASEAN only formally engaged with China as a dialogue partner in the mid-1990s, allowing a decent interval after China ended its support for communist insurgencies. Indeed, most of the larger Southeast Asian states normalised relations with China in the 1990s – although both Thailand and Malaysia, with their sizeable Chinese population, took the daring step in the mid-1970s.

As US power and influence in the region faded after the end of the Vietnam War and later with Washington's growing preoccupation in the Middle East, so China started building a new framework for relations based on what its diplomats like to call 'win-win', or mutual benefit. Initially, Beijing focused on soft targets like Laos and Cambodia. Laos, with its communist-led government and long border with China, has been at the sharp end of China's strategic infrastructure drive, conceding to road, rail and dam-building projects that have secured logistical access and water resources for China, but which have exposed Laos to Chinese immigration and natural resource degradation. The signature project, a $6 billion rail connection between China and Laos, has the cash-strapped Lao authorities complaining that they have been forced to take a 30 per cent stake. With $5 billion worth of investment and 300,000 Chinese workers in a country of less than seven million, the Chinese presence looms large. A number of special economic zones clustered close to the border with Yunnan begin to look like territorial land grabs. There have been scattered outbreaks of violence against Chinese citizens in remote areas of Laos close to Chinese mining projects, where popular resentment runs high.

Cambodia's ties with China run especially deep both because of the need for a counter-force to neighbouring Vietnam, towards which Cambodians display instinctive animosity in part because the

Khmer Rouge grew out of the Viet Cong, and the historical relationship that King Sihanouk, an early pioneer of the non-aligned movement, enjoyed with Chinese leaders. Even though Beijing also supported the Khmer Rouge, and therefore bears some responsibility for the genocide, the emerging post-civil war order led by former Khmer Rouge fighter Hun Sen rapidly developed close political and economic ties with Beijing after he shed his royalist coalition partners in the late 1990s. In many ways, it was the successful international and regional diplomacy that Chinese participated in to help rebuild Cambodia in the late 1980s that generated an initial sense that rising China would be, in the parlance first adopted by former World Bank President Robert Zoellick, a 'responsible stakeholder'. Today, however, Cambodia is the primary example of concerns about the snugness of China's embrace, which Beijing describes as a 'comprehensive strategic partnership'. China has provided Cambodia with as much as $15 billion in aid since the late 1990s. The flow of Chinese military aid and assistance, which includes equipment and the provision of training, is close to $20 million and rising, and the number of Chinese immigrant workers is estimated at 500,000, and rising, in a country of just 15 million. Symbolic of China's growing presence in Cambodia is the erection of a massive shopping and condominium complex in the heart of Phnom Penh, just a stone's throw from the iconic Cambodiana Hotel built in the 1960s. Armies of Chinese workers crawl all over the construction site of the Sino Great Wall development below a giant banner that declares: 'Sino Great Wall building for the Cambodian people'.

China's impact on the region is increasingly being felt economically. As Southeast Asia's biggest trading partner, Chinese investment in the region grew sluggishly throughout the boom years of the 1990s, even as China's growth and development grew an average of 10 per cent since 1978. Inward investment from Southeast Asia to China was initially the prevailing trend, at least until the financial crisis of the late 1990s. Ethnic Chinese conglomerates from Southeast Asia such as Thailand's CP Group, Malaysia's Robert Kuok and Indonesia's Lippo all benefited handsomely from these forays into the China market – even if they met some resistance from local Chinese competitors. However, since 2005, Chinese investment in the region has grown an astonishing 50 per cent a year, and will soon overtake the pace of Japan and the US.

In some parts of Southeast Asia, unpalatable regimes or instability provided a fertile investment environment for China's state-owned companies. For much of the past two decades Western countries imposed sanctions on Burma's military government, keeping Western companies out and giving China's state-owned enterprises a free rein. Much of this investment is focused on big-ticket infrastructure projects such as pipelines, railways and ports as well as hydroelectric power. Two pipelines are being constructed to carry oil and gas from ports on the Bay of Bengal across the country to Yunnan. Chinese state companies such as engineering giant CITIC have poured into the country to develop dams, ports and build real estate in the vicinity of the pipeline terminal in a spate of deals that critics say were rushed and need to be revisited by the new democratically elected government of Aung San Suu Kyi.

These investments may serve to forge closer economic ties with Southeast Asian countries – and line the pockets of their governments – but they are intended to develop sources of cheap power and reliable overland routes from continental China through Southeast Asia to the sea. These are needed so that China's energy supplies don't solely rely on the Malacca Strait, the main east–west sea lane that could easily be choked and blockaded in any major power conflict with China. As the American strategic thinker Robert Kaplan observed: 'China is propelled abroad by the need to secure energy, metals and strategic minerals in order to support roughly a fifth of humanity.' Southeast Asia may not be the best source of raw materials, but it does provide a secure access to the sea by which to import them from further afield – hence the focus on infrastructure. Wang Gungwu points out that China has a long tradition of engaging and pacifying people along the routes it needs to satisfy its needs. Just as the overland Silk Road of ancient times stretching from China to Europe was made secure by engaging with the nomadic tribes of Central Asia, so the modern Belt and Road initiative envisaged by Chinese President Xi Jinping must be ensured by reliable relations with all the Southeast Asian states along the way.

Modern forms of capitalist engagement have replaced traditional models of fealty and tribute. China has offered to lend the region $10 billion to facilitate these deals and set up an array of funds and investment mechanisms. China pledged an initial $40 billion for a Silk Road Fund established in 2014. The same year China launched the Asian Infrastructure Investment Bank (AIIB), which is meant to rival the Bretton Woods lending institutions such as the World Bank, which China considers is geared towards the interests of Western donor countries. Using capital disbursed through AIIB in Indonesia, Malaysia and Thailand, China can also count on feverish interest from their overseas Chinese communities to partner with Chinese companies. But rarely noticed in the scramble to secure deals and infrastructure projects is the demand for land acquisition or the stipulation that imported Chinese labour be used. Somewhat startlingly, almost one quarter of new migrant workers in Indonesia in 2015 came from China – most of them were working on Chinese-funded infrastructure projects.

This is where the notion of 'win-win' starts to unravel. For if China manages to build deep-sea ports as well as the roads and railways to connect them to overland routes heading north to China, and at the same time insists on importing tens of thousands of Chinese workers to work on these projects, what's in it for Southeast Asia? The rustling of ghosts from the past can be heard.

The long reach of China into Southeast Asia is most clearly evident in the Kachin state capital of Myitkyina. Situated in a valley only some 100 kilometres from the Chinese border further north over the Kachin Hills, the town is a major trading centre for jade, a semi-precious stone highly valued in Chinese culture. To reach the place takes almost two hours by plane from Yangon, and on arrival there is a frontier feel to the town, which lies along the sleepy Irrawaddy River. The shabby hotel I stayed in was dominated by photographs of the vast open-cast mines situated around the nearby town of Hpakant where labourers toil under dangerous conditions, often at night, to mine the jade, which is then exported by Chinese companies operating through Myanmar or Kachin front men in a business that the UK-based NGO Global Witness estimated earned annual revenues exceeding $30 billion in 2014. A sense of that wealth was evident at the vast Chinese banqueting hall where

I was invited to a multi-course dinner that included exotic Chinese delicacies that had been procured at considerable cost. The sole reliable mobile phone signal when I visited in 2014 was one beamed in from China. Many of the Japanese SUVs had Myanmar plates tacked over Chinese ones. It was here also that the new President Thein Sein decided in 2011 to fire a shot across China's bow. Bowing to months of protest by Kachin civil society groups, Thein Sein unexpectedly suspended the almost $4 billion Myitsone Dam project, which China was counting on for cheap electricity in neighbouring Yunnan.

While the new Myanmar government was looking for badly needed popularity at home, it was probably also courting the West; the move against the dam project came as the United States and other Western countries were making the first moves to lift sanctions and bring investment to the country. The Burmese were clearly eager to signal their readiness for a more balanced external relationship. And though Thein Sein's bold move may have been something of a wake-up call for China, subsequent moves to forge similar patterns of infrastructure investment in Cambodia, Indonesia and Thailand suggest it has had little lasting impact. China is now the largest foreign investor in Indonesia, mostly conducted through countries such as Singapore and Hong Kong. Much of this investment is focused on mining and power projects that bring with them many of the same environmental concerns as the Kachin-made plain around Myitsone dam.

Beyond the environmental concerns that lay at the heart of the Myitsone dam debacle, a much deeper fear is what China could possibly do with a bigger stake in the economies of Southeast Asia. Western commentators have breathlessly warned that China's overarching aim is to tie its economy more closely to those of its neighbours, 'not only to accrue economic benefits, but to expand its economic penetration of Southeast Asia, with associated increases in influence and power,' wrote Michael Mazza in *The National Interest*. The concern for many governments in the region is that, having established a concrete stake in their economies by building new roads, railways and ports, often in league with local conglomerates run by overseas Chinese, it won't be long before China starts to demand cooperation – if not fealty – from its overseas Chinese. After centuries of interaction with a distant, aloof imperial China that seemed to have no interest in directly meddling in Southeast Asian affairs, could it be that the logic of more closely intertwined economics and demography changes this dynamic into one of incipient control and dependency?

In May 1998 angry mobs began attacking ethnic Chinese businesses as the fires of protest erupted across major cities in Indonesia in the dying months of the Suharto regime. The reason? Ostensibly shortages of food and other staples brought about by a steep devaluation of the Indonesian currency as a result of the Asian Financial Crisis beginning in July 1997. Indonesia's wealthy Chinese community, which numbers close to eight million people, keeps bolt holes and bank accounts in Singapore or Hong Kong and has long been subject to periodic attacks. Many of them live in high-walled gated communities, but the last significant outbreak of violence against the Chinese was in 1965, a by-product of the anti-communist killings. The difference in 1998 was that China and the global Chinese community protested against their mistreatment. As television footage showed the burning and looting of Chinese-owned stores, and as reports came in of the rape of Chinese women, China's foreign minister Tang Jiazuan appealed to the government in Jakarta for the protection of Indonesian Chinese. Earlier, Chinese President Jiang Zemin had stated clearly, and significantly, that: 'Chinese Indonesians will not only serve . . . the long-term stability of Indonesia, but also . . . the smooth development of the relationship of friendly cooperation with neighbouring countries.'

Likewise, Chinese communities globally expressed concern, including those of Hong Kong and Taiwan, yet what all governments in the region picked up was Beijing's claim of responsibility for the welfare of overseas Chinese. This was in stark contrast to a few years earlier, when Prime Minister Li Peng drew a line under China's claim over its former citizens by declaring that the *Nanyang* Chinese owed allegiance to their host countries. Now, as a senior Chinese foreign ministry official scurried to Jakarta at the height of the rioting to oversee the evacuation of Chinese passport holders, suddenly the distinction seemed less clear.

The role and influence of the ethnic Chinese in Southeast Asian society is of paramount importance. From the earliest sojourners who came in search of trade as early as the ninth century, to the tens of thousands who were brought as indentured labourers in the nineteenth century, or who arrived with only a 'pillow and mat' to find their fortune in the twentieth century, the Chinese have long been a recognisable and significant component of Southeast Asian society. Today they number around 30 million living in all ten countries of Southeast Asia. The majority came from the coastal southern provinces of Guangzhou or Fujian, in large numbers after the establishment of regular steamship routes from the ports of Amoy and Canton in the last half of the nineteenth century. Singapore is preponderantly Chinese, the descendants of coolies imported by the British to work the docks. In Malaysia until recently the Chinese comprised a third of the population – six million people. They came to work in the tin mines or on tea and rubber estates. In Thailand, where Chinese immigrants came in search of a better livelihood and fortune, they account for 10 per cent of the population of around 68 million people and a majority of the population of Bangkok.

Predominantly involved in commerce and living in urban areas, the ethnic Chinese have a disproportionately significant influence on their communities due to their wealth and assiduously cultivated connections with those in power. In addition to Thaksin Shinawatra, no fewer than six of the prime ministers who governed Thailand in the past twenty years were of direct Chinese descent. Although many of them have taken local names and intermarried, their businesses tend to be family-owned and privately held. To the casual observer, and incidentally also a long-established academic assumption, the communities seem well integrated and have long been on a path to assimilation. Yet my own observations of the past three decades suggests otherwise. Perhaps it's my own ethnic diversity that makes me sensitive to this, but if there's one aspect of any society that is fluid and open to manipulation it is identity.

Ethnic identity and association can be transactional in nature, as much a product of opportunity as a fact of birth and ancestry. I have a Thai friend who is ethnically Chinese, born in the southern

Thailand town of Hat Yai, a graduate of the majority Chinese
Penang Free School and then a prestigious university in the UK. He
came of age at the height of the Cold War, when he suppressed, or
had suppressed, his Chinese cultural identity and language ability
in order to become assertively and unambiguously Thai. He did
well, and worked for several Sino-Thai conglomerates, eventually
becoming a senior executive at a Thai-Chinese bank. Yet for all his
Thai and Anglophone leanings, he encouraged his son and daughter to learn Chinese and supported his son's decision to work and
live in China. By this time, in the late 1990s, it had become legal
again for Thais to learn Chinese. Prompted by fears of a communist fifth column, the Thai government had maintained a ban on
learning Chinese; when I was a student in Thailand in the early
1980s, the only place it was possible to learn Chinese was in the
mountaintop villages in northern Thailand, where remnants of
the nationalist Chinese Kuomintang army had settled after their
retreat from China in 1949. Two decades later, the northern Thai
capital of Chiang Mai was filled with mainland Chinese tourists –
drawn to the place after a popular Chinese romantic film had been
set there – and there were dozens of signs up advertising Chinese
language schools.

Back in the 1950s, an American social scientist by the name of
William Skinner predicted the disappearance of the ethnic Chinese
in Thailand as in other places. At the time, this was a valid prediction: for many of Thailand's ethnic Chinese, the last real contact they
had with their mainland kin was before the communist revolution
in 1949. One of my office assistants when I was a correspondent in
Bangkok recalled her parents complaining of the burden this placed
on them: China was so much poorer after the end of the Pacific
War, and many of the villages of southern China had nothing in
the way of material goods, so their Thai cousins were asked to bring
everything from motorcycles to refrigerators. During the dark years
of the Cultural Revolution there was little or no contact with overseas Chinese communities in Southeast Asia. The next time they
were able to visit their ancestral villages was a full generation later in
the 1980s. By this time, China was a place to make money and find
new opportunities. As the office towers and shopping malls went up

in Beijing, Shanghai and Shenzen, just across the border from Hong Kong, many ethnic Chinese from Southeast Asia, the children of a generation that had all but assimilated, started returning to the motherland, speaking Chinese and acting as Chinese in search of opportunity.

China at first was uncertain how to manage the overseas Chinese and their newfound attraction to the mainland. While India moved quickly to define and institutionalise its 'Non-resident Indians', China's government adopted a mixture of approaches. For the super-rich tycoons, owners of large conglomerates like Charoen Pokhphand and Bangkok Bank from Thailand, Kerry from Malaysia, and Lippo from Indonesia, the doors were thrown open. Joint-venture deals were done to draw on their capital and access to technology. Chin Sophonpanich, the founder of Bangkok Bank, was quick to establish a branch near his hometown of Suzhou. But little was done to facilitate returning ethnic Chinese unable to bring capital. Care was taken not to claim these people as citizens, despite China's rather liberal regulations on permanent residency. There was even some pushback from local Chinese entrepreneurs who did not share their government's view of these *Nanyang* interlopers, convinced they had little to offer beyond competition. All the same, as China's economy grew, so did the economic and cultural links with the overseas Chinese.

Southeast Asia's proximity to China has made this one of the more remarkable diaspora success stories. Robert Kuok, who made his original fortune as a sugar baron in Malaysia, magnified his wealth on the back of the companies he established in China, chiefly Kerry Logistics. In 2015, *Forbes* estimated Kuok's wealth at around $10 billion, making him at the age of ninety-two the richest man in Malaysia. Many of these grateful tycoons returned the favour by helping China manage its interface with the outside world in the initial market-opening years. Kuok, for example, took shares in Citic, a giant mainland-trading conglomerate with ties to the Chinese leadership. They helped build much-needed infrastructure and logistics networks and assisted in the forging of closer diplomatic ties between China and their home countries; they also helped manage the barbarian outer world. In many ways, these modern-day Tai-pans have acted as go-betweens for China as it charted its rise, reflecting a longstanding tradition of leaving the dirty business of commerce to outsiders. To what extent their wealth has been ploughed back into Southeast Asia is an open question. Meanwhile, in mid-2015, China quietly launched a scheme whereby overseas Chinese could acquire an identity card for use in China.

None of this would matter very much were it not for fears of what China could do with the leverage it now has over Southeast Asia's leading corporations and, by extension, their governments. For China, the stakes are clearly much higher now than they were when it supported speculative communist insurgencies in the mid-twentieth century. Today, and notably under the leadership of China's current President Xi Jingping, Beijing considers that the US, Japan and, to a lesser extent India are intent on containing China. To respond, Chinese scholars are looking for ways to justify a more forward policy in the region set against the long-held official creed of non-interference in the affairs of other countries. Phrases like 'constructive engagement' and 'harmonious intervention' have been floated. After almost two decades of distraction in the Middle East, the Pentagon has woken up to the fact that China is acquiring the firepower to challenge its dominance in the Pacific, hence the challenging of China's claims in the South China Sea. Japan, which has its own territorial disputes with China in the East China Sea, is moving towards dismantling the post-war shackles on the role and strength of its military power. India doesn't have a forward policy as such in Southeast Asia, but has in recent years deployed naval ships as far eastwards as Vietnam.

The build-up of tension in the South China Sea, where for now the US navy retains the strategic edge although probably not for much longer, makes it all the more important for China to forge overland routes through Southeast Asia to secure its energy and other resource needs. And as China's economy begins to contract at home (GDP growth fell below 7 per cent in 2015, the weakest performance in a decade), overseas investment in nearby friendly places in Southeast Asia becomes more of a priority for Chinese state companies. In some places, China's overtures have been embraced with alacrity, exposing the risks of drawing too close to the Middle Kingdom.

Thailand after the May 2014 military coup was virtually ostracised by the United States, with whom it has an almost 200-year-old alliance, established by treaty. Washington demanded a swift return to democracy, warning that unless this happened it could not be business as usual: 'Thailand is losing credibility in the eyes of its international friends and partners by not moving more quickly to end martial law, to restore civil rights and to ensure that this effort to engineer a new constitution and hold elections is not purely a top-down affair,' declared US Assistant Secretary of State Danny Russell in January 2015. The Thai military establishment was furious, and Beijing was quick to offer support. At first it looked as if Thailand was heading unambiguously into the China camp, with talk of high-speed rail projects from Bangkok and northeastern cities within striking distance of the Chinese border. Some of Thailand's military leaders were even willing to oblige the Chinese government's request to repatriate refugees from the restive Uighur province of Xinjiang – allegedly in return for sweetening the business deals in Thailand's favour. In July 2015 a group of around 100 blindfolded Uighur men were bundled on to a plane and forcibly repatriated to China, a move that shocked international refugee agencies and was apparently carried out over the objections of the normally careful Thai Foreign Ministry. Weeks later, on 17 August, a terrorist bomb planted at a famous shrine in Bangkok killed 21 people, most of them ethnic Chinese. The police investigation revealed that the bombers were Uighurs, some of whom had flown in from Turkey to organise the attack. Their main target was Chinese tourists, some 8 million of whom flocked to Thailand in 2015. To make matters worse, China's close ties with the military government in Bangkok also facilitated the rendition of at least two Chinese dissidents, Hong Kong residents who had been holidaying in Thailand.

Thailand's recent experience demonstrates the ugly side of China's embrace – the opportunistic support of tyranny, the unseemly rush to secure business deals, the quid pro quo linked to China's security concerns, and the long arm of the Chinese public security bureau. There were faint echoes here of American foreign policy adventurism of the 1960s – 'he may be a son of a bitch, but he's our son of a bitch,' as Franklin Roosevelt reportedly said about Nicaraguan dictator Anastasio Somoza in the 1930s. Washington lent overt support to distasteful dictators in South Vietnam and turned a blind eye to the massacre of those deemed to be communist sympathisers in Indonesia all within the last fifty years. Indeed, it is remarkable how closely China appears to be emulating the US from its own bygone era of geo-strategic expansion. The message? China has risen, is now a global power and has wider interests to defend. China may not share what Robert Kaplan characterises as the United States' 'missionary approach to world affairs' but, as he puts it: 'China is merely re-establishing after a fashion its imperial domain.'

That Thailand was so willing to allow all this to happen in so short space of time, abandoning the traditional balanced approach to major powers, sent tremors through the region. Malaysia was next in line: with Prime Minister Najib Tun Razak's back to the wall over the alleged misuse of money from an investment fund that was in serious trouble, China appeared as a white knight with a bailout plan in early 2016. Using normal bidding channels, Chinese state companies paid close to $4 billion dollars to buy up assets in power and property from the debt-laden and troubled 1MDB Fund chaired by Prime Minister Najib. Eyebrows were also raised in September 2015 when, after a pro-government rally that accused the opposition of being dominated by the Chinese and Indian minorities and therefore not significant, the Chinese ambassador to Malaysia made an appearance in downtown Kuala Lumpur's Petaling Street, part of the old city's Chinatown, and publicly called for calm. 'Business is good here. There are many tourists. I am proud to see Chinese traders working closely with Malay and Indian traders in harmony in developing this area,' the ambassador was quoted as saying after handing out moon cakes. There were echoes here of Chinese assertiveness when ethnic Chinese were attacked in Indonesia almost two decades earlier.

All this has made Southeast Asia very much aware of the dangers of China's rising status and economic might. China's declaration that its pursuit of claims in the South China Sea is part of a new 'regional order' echoes the Monroe Doctrine used by the United States in the nineteenth century to justify its domination of the American continent. On the economic front, Singapore commentator Victor Savage tartly wrote in early 2016: 'The rising dragon is using economic bribery to win over Southeast Asia and its task is being made easier by weak national governments, disparities of wealth and corrupt politicians.' Reflecting these fears, some Southeast Asian countries have sought to balance their China ties and even challenge some of China's claims in the region. After Myanmar's President Thein Sein's suspension of the Myitsone dam, the Philippines lodged a daring challenge at the Permanent Court of Arbitration in The Hague to China's claims in the South China Sea – which the Philippine government prefers to call the West Philippine Sea. And after China built a Chinese cultural centre in Singapore, the Singapore government swiftly built one of its own. In terms of trade alone, it seems unlikely that Southeast Asia has a viable alternative to reliance on China. Washington's Trans-Pacific Partnership, which aimed at sweetening terms of trade for all of its Asian partners, yet excluded China, was a brave gesture, but was one of the first victims of President Donald Trump's 'America First' policy. The Trump administration, with its apparent tilt away from multilateralism and the mantra of free trade, abandoned the Obama administration's stress on pivoting to Asia for which the TPP was an important instrument. Chinese officials were privately gleeful. However, with the Chinese – and also Russian military presence – making itself felt in formerly close US allies like Malaysia and the Philippines, it seems likely that some kind of forward policy will continue, probably with the US military in the vanguard.

Singapore thrives on its ability to offset the embrace of China, as a kind of hedge against China's growing corporate heft and geopolitical clout. That's why the tiny island republic has been so shrill and insistent about the need for the US to maintain its economic and military edge in the region. Singapore was a primary supporter of the Trans-Pacific Partnership; it allows US naval ships to visit frequently and has a basing agreement for the new littoral combat ships the US navy has deployed to Asian waters. But the relentless advance of Chinese capital and investment threatens Singapore's position as a sort of 'non-China'. Jack Ma is CEO of China's largest digital trading and e-commerce platform, Alibaba. Worth almost $30 billion, Ma has steered Alibaba to a dominant position in China's vast consumer market. Its micro-messaging app WeChat has over 700 million users in China, who use it to speak to each other, message one another, and pay for almost everything from a taxi fare to a bowl of noodles. Indonesia and Malaysia competed to lure Jack Ma to become a digital economy adviser – Malaysia won. Thailand is wooing Ma to host a global e-trading centre. Southeast Asia seems poised to become the next market for Jack Ma's highly profitable digital platforms for payments and shopping that already dominate the China market. Meanwhile, Singapore, desperately trying to shore up its non-China credentials, raced to design and implement comprehensive e-payment schemes of its own to pre-serve some independence for its banking system. As 'Ali Pay' and other Chinese-owned e-trading platforms proliferated, it was clearly too late.

The choice appears stark: a new Cold War with Southeast Asia as a fault line, or embrace China's terms and accept a new and hitherto unforeseen form of economic and cultural domination. This has long been the view of Western strategists who, like the journalist Brian Crozier writing in the mid-1960s, saw post-colonial Southeast Asia as a 'battleground in an uncomfortably "hot" cold war . . . a battlefield of the great powers.'

Full-blown Cold War is the less likely scenario. For all the sabre-rattling and nerve-racking confrontation in the South China Sea, neither China nor the United States wants a hot war and regards the current tensions as a threat to commerce and trade. Something in the order of $6 trillion in trade passes through the South China Sea annually – mostly benefiting China.

I had a close-up view of the dynamics trying to fashion a crisis management initiative for the South China Sea over the course of 2015–16. Not being a China expert, it came as something of a shock to me on visits to Beijing to discover how little Chinese officials know of the wider world. As one senior foreign ministry official put it to me as we sat side by side in comfortable armchairs in the manner that the Chinese prefer for formal meetings: 'You have all the advantages of area specialisation and long exposure to a wide range of scholarship; we on the other hand are only just discovering things. I get all these foreigners coming here and accusing us of being a major player in far-flung places like the South Pacific, yet we don't even know where half these places are and have to look them up on Google!'

By contrast, the People's Liberation Army has a very strong sense of its destiny as a major military power in the world. 'You know China's next war won't be fought at sea but on land,' remarked a senior PLA Officer to me in Beijing. Really? I responded. Not the South China Sea? The pace of modernisation of the Chinese navy has been marked in recent years. 'No,' my PLA friend said emphatically. 'Like the United States we have a lot of interests in Africa and the Middle East. Someday these will be attacked and, like the United States we shall be forced to defend them.' Ignorance was once the hallmark of the American seersucker-clad, crew-cut policy types who designed coups and counter-coups in the early years of the Cold War. Yet there are differences in the Chinese superpower strategy. Albeit subtle ones.

Southeast Asian nations first registered their concerns about China's claims in the South China Sea as early as 1992 and, after agreeing with some difficulty on a Declaration of Conduct, consultations started on a more formal Code of Conduct in 2013. Like other superpowers including the US, China is allergic to multilateral negotiations, preferring to pick off smaller powers bilaterally to exercise the most leverage. By mid-2017, a draft framework emerged, but nothing of substance that could be seen as binding. The negotiations will be 'protracted, if not interminable', as the Australian scholar and expert Carl Thayer puts it. Meanwhile, China has accelerated its landing-strip programme on a series of small features that, as The Hague ruling has made clear, cannot be classified as islands and therefore are not subject to a corresponding 200-mile economic exploitation zone. China has done its best to turn them into islands, though. One of the most commonly cited, Fiery Cross Reef, now has a three-kilometre runway China has used for both civilian and military aircraft. These are the unsinkable aircraft carriers the US is so worried about; Fiery Cross Reef, which the Chinese pointedly call Yongshu Island, sits adjacent to one of the busiest shipping routes in the world. What if China declared sovereignty, and an air exclusion zone, as it did so recently in the East China Sea?

To ease the pressure, as well as the imminent threat of war, China has played a double game – prevaricating on the formal negotiations over a Code of Conduct, while offering joint exercises and other confidence-building measures to friendly states in the region. Observing some of these interactions close-up, it is striking how useful China finds the informal 'track-two' setting to help allay fears. For all the concerns about the lack of a formal arrangement to manage security, China seems content to make full use of an informal security forum known as the Council for Security Cooperation in the Asia Pacific (CSCAP). Here, Chinese officials and scholars (who are normally also government officials) can interact informally with peers and colleagues from twenty countries of the region, including all of Southeast Asia, and discuss shared challenges to security without any commitment to changing official policy. The CSCAP and other informal forums involving defence officials are a convenient buffer, helping to defuse tension through regular engagement and buying China the time it needs to increase its military strength.

The annals of historic engagement with imperial China are filled with the intrigue and dilatory tactics used by inscrutable scholar mandarins to evade decisions that could be interpreted as a slight to the emperor and to the dignity of China. Appearances are everything. 'The Chinese insistence on the value of maintaining appearances runs through all their life and statecraft,' wrote Maurice Collis in a forgotten gem of a book entitled *The Great Within* and published the mid-twentieth century, two decades before the beginning of the Cold War. 'Even when those appearances are transparently absurd they consider them worth keeping up.' But filibustering and delusion have their limitations. The problem for China is that, since at least 2010, with encouragement if not pressure from the United States, ASEAN has started to ask China for more assurance than cosy conferences and informal chit-chat in five-star hotel ballrooms. But China is not good at collective bargaining that isn't done on its own terms. Here lies the danger.

The current Chinese epoch matches no other in the country's history. For despite the long-range forays of the Manchus with their nomadic roots in the central Asia Steppes and the grand diplomatic dreams of the Ming emperors, China's reach has always had limitations. Yet these limitations are disappearing with China's embrace of modern technology and engagement with the global economy. Close to 100 million Chinese citizens now roam the globe. Soon much of Southeast Asia will be as shackled to Jack Ma's internet finance platforms and mobile phone application as they are to Google and Mark Zuckerberg's Facebook. The influx of Chinese tourists mobbing Buddhist temples in Thailand has forced the erection of safety barriers. And they are increasingly present as opportunistic migrants: no longer with pillow and mat, but with iPhones, credit cards and cash, and an acquisitive appetite. Safety barriers have also been erected outside the Louis Vuitton outlet in Paris. It must be remembered that when earlier waves of migrants from China streamed out of the coastal areas in the mid-nineteenth century it was a capital offence for the Chinese to leave the boundaries of the empire except on official business. Today, the Chinese government positively encourages migration from the crowded coastal cities towards the less developed western periphery, from where it is a short trip across the borders to Laos and Burma on roads built by Chinese companies using Chinese labour.

China now has the means to project power by hard means and soft: its developing blue-water navy can deploy well beyond the South China Sea and was used to evacuate Chinese citizens from conflict zones in Libya and Yemen. Its heavily armed coastguard vessels – essentially converted naval destroyers – provide protection for ever more aggressive fishing fleets making forays even into Indonesian waters well beyond the nine-dashed line within which China claims the South China Sea. A new infrastructure bank is providing billions in loans to build ports and roads across Southeast Asia. And what of moves to extend protection to overseas Chinese who have lived in Southeast Asia for centuries? Obviously, the old paradigm of 'reasoned pacifism' has its limitations in the modern era. China under the leadership of Xi Jinping has embarked on an aggressive, forward defence of sovereignty, flexing its muscles as a newly established superpower. China expects Southeast Asia to accept this new power equation with equanimity and never tires of pushing the argument that the presence of American military power in the region poses the threat to peace in Asia. This is a huge change in posture compared with Deng Xiaoping's dictum of keeping a cool head and a low profile. Or for that matter the charmingly naïve proposal of China's 'Peaceful Rise' propagated by Xi's predecessor Hu Jintao.

China today is no longer hiding its strength or sheathing its power. As Yang Jiechi, China's former foreign minister, now a powerful state councillor responsible for foreign affairs, put it at an ASEAN ministerial meeting in 2010: 'China is a big country and other countries are small countries, and that's just a fact.' For now, the US is pushing back, wherein lies the risk of a war in which Southeast Asia would be the battleground, much as it was the last time a rising Asian power decided to challenge the West. But looking ahead to what the future holds in Southeast Asia, one underlying assumption must be that the power and interest of the West to counterbalance the rise of China, despite the rhetoric, is probably in decline.

CHAPTER TWELVE

THE ROAD AHEAD

'Slowly, the city empties. The lap of seawater and the yowl of cheshires replace the call of durian sellers and the ring of bicycle bells.'

Paolo Bacigalupi, *The Windup Girl*

They came in their tens of thousands. Clad in white and waving black flags with Arab script declaring their loyalty to God, they demanded the arrest of Jakarta's popular elected Governor Basuki Tjahaja Purnama, who is a Christian and ethnically Chinese. The protest, which trapped me in the centre of Jakarta one day in early November 2016, was mobilised around remarks the Governor, popularly known as Ahok, allegedly made that cited a Koranic verse prohibiting Muslims from electing non-Muslim leaders. The chief organiser was the Islamic Defenders Front, a militant pressure group that has allegedly received funding from politicians and the security forces, which accused Ahok of insulting Islam. The Front mobilised at least 150,000 people who flooded on to the streets. Politicians said to be behind the rally may have thought they could control these rent-a-mobs – by some estimates the Jakarta protest rally cost around $1 million to mobilise. But the turn-out of militant hard-core elements who burned police cars and repeatedly charged police lines protecting the presidential palace indicated a reservoir of popular anger and frustration about low incomes, rising prices and state-backed evictions. In one shocking statistic of how hard it is for the average Indonesian household, the World Bank reported in October 2016 that: 'Indonesian consumers are paying very high prices for foods rich in protein and micronutrients, including most fruits and vegetables and poultry products . . . prices of these higher nutrient foods are substantially higher in Indonesia than in Singapore, a country which lacks an agricultural sector and imports nearly all of its food.' Food inflation aside, the protest that day showed how easily popular resentment and social discontent could be channelled into ethnic and religious hatred. As I watched the long columns of white-robed men waving flags similar to those associated with IS in Syria and Iraq, I was shaken; for they symbolised both the promise and the threat of newly won rights and freedoms in a divided society.

The political reverberations of this sudden and unexpected whirl of protest will be felt for some time. On one level, the 4 November protest and a much larger one on the 2 December sprang from political manoeuvring around the Jakarta gubernatorial elections, with an eye on national elections in 2019. Competing candidates were eager to dent Ahok's image of incorruptible efficiency. The strategy worked: Ahok was beaten in the polls and later jailed for blasphemy. They were also bent on undermining the position of the popularly elected president, whose approval ratings two years after being elected were still in the range of 60%. Attacking duly elected leaders on ethnic and religious grounds is a cheap but nonetheless effective way to conduct politics in modern Indonesia; it dispenses with the need for costly campaigns and the hard work of persuading people based on campaign promises or an actual programme of work. It reflects the manner in which race and religion can so easily be harnessed to political campaigns. But in doing so, Indonesia was confronted with a disturbing reality. Despite constitutional guarantees of freedom of religion and inclusive Indonesian identity, the past few years have seen the emergence of the ugly face of prejudice, albeit politically motivated, which is eroding the tolerance, pluralism and diversity that lie at the heart of Indonesian identity.

For me, this fleeting encounter with politically orchestrated hatred was a stark reminder of the country's enduring fragility. For all the opportunities offered by democratic pluralism, the fruits of a protracted transition over two decades, hard-won freedoms were blatantly used in this situation to channel ethnic and religious prejudice for political ends. The ease with which such issues were taken to the street and turned to violence also spoke to a constant concern in this book – the lack of institutional integrity and development or respect for laws. Why weren't the political parties responsible for upholding the values of tolerance and equality more vocal? Why wasn't it possible to debate the issue in a more rational manner on the floor of the country's national assembly? Where was the president that day? Apparently, he chose to inspect a railway project just outside the city. His leadership was sorely missed that day. Indonesia's constitution, one of the most enduring in the region, safeguards the rights of non-Muslims; yet an angry mob was able to trample on these rights with alarming ease.

President Joko Widodo struggled in the days after the protest to assert his authority. My Indonesian friends clung to the optimistic belief that the strength of the democratic system would right itself and that the moderate core of Indonesian society would push back the tide of hatred and bigotry. I wasn't so sure. Two weeks later, at a conference of Muslim democrats, an Indonesian member of parliament, Eva Sundari put it well: 'Our tolerance principle is under threat and is being tested.' Sadly, she noted that the moderate 'silent majority' was staying silent.

Given the cycles of change and regression I have described in this book, what then will Southeast Asia look like in the space of another generation, say by the year 2050? As much as Southeast Asians live for the present and easily forget the past, they are also preoccupied by the future, because it has a bearing on the wealth and fortune of their families. 'The past is painful, the present is easy,' writes the Malaysian novelist Tash Aw. 'It's a matter of practicality: they just want to get on with their lives.' Yet many of my Southeast Asian friends regard the future with apprehension. I notice a distinct contrast between Pollyannaish Westerners all agog over the glitz and growth in the region, predicting its glorious future, and anxious Southeast Asians, rich and poor, who harbour worries of lurking catastrophe.

Thais and Burmese in particular are obsessed with determinations of the future, resorting regularly to the services of professional soothsayers and mediums. The most famous of these, until her death in 2017, resided in Rangoon and went by the sobriquet ET. The physically disabled middle-aged woman, so named because of her resemblance to Steven Spielberg's friendly alien, offered advice to Myanmar's former military dictator General Than Shwe and to former Thai Prime Minister Thaksin Shinawatra, amongst many others. She reputedly earned millions of dollars doling out predictions, which because of her disabilities and a speech impediment were interpreted by her sister. Although blessed with a natural abundance and well connected to the modern world, Southeast Asia is beset by calamity precipitated by human folly and greed. Frankly, Southeast Asians have good reason to worry.

Before peering into the crystal ball, let me offer a brief distillation of the themes explored in this book. First, the one constant I have experienced over the last forty years is the perpetual selfishness of Southeast Asian elites and their wilful subjugation of the rights of citizens to their own considerations of wealth and power. We have seen this reflected in the turbulent course of political change, the failure to address enduring drivers of conflict in society, staggering disparities of wealth and the chronic impunity towards injustice and loss of life perpetrated by the state. More than any other part of the world today that claims to adhere for the most part to democratic principles of government and has the GDP to do so, Southeast Asia fails chronically to deliver on the promise of popular sovereignty. The latest map of freedom generated by the US-based Freedom House shows that, apart from Japan and India, the whole of Asia is considered either 'not free' or 'only partly free'. That includes the Philippines and Indonesia – both semi-democracies, only partly free. Remarkably, this democracy deficit cannot be explained away by the kinds of chronic war and related social dislocation afflicting troubled parts of Africa and the Middle East. Quite the reverse, for the past four decades Southeast Asia has been at peace and growing a solid 6 to 8 per cent per year.

Second, there has been a loosening of the bonds of tolerance and inclusion underpinning social stability in Southeast Asia. Identity politics is on the rise. Following a global trend, growth in religious orthodoxy has hardened the boundaries between different religious communities and generated high degrees of intolerance and exclusivity that increasingly fuel violent conflict. Degraded pluralism creates a permissive environment for violent extremism to take root. If we look around the region there has been a serious uptick in ethnic and religious intolerance leading to tension and violence that has opened the space for extremist activity. In addition, the large numbers of people crossing borders in search of refuge and economic opportunity make this region one of the hardest to protect from violent extremism. Meanwhile, deteriorating social conditions driven by alarming income inequalities ensure there are cohorts of young people susceptible to violent ideology.

Rather than address this challenge with policies aimed at shoring up traditions of tolerance, Southeast Asian governments have become prone to conservative impulses serving the ends of power. Malaysia has allowed Muslim clerics to declare liberal Muslims deviants and non-Muslim Chinese who question Islamic law worthy of being slain; a senior Indonesian security official quite recently said that lesbians and gays constitute a threat to national security. In a statement that sounded more like a clerical pronouncement from Saudi Arabia, the Malaysian minister in charge of Islamic affairs told parliament in March 2016 that among the liberal beliefs outlawed are: 'holding on to the concept of pluralism, believing that the human mind is a revelation, doubting the authenticity of the Koran, questioning the interpretation of the Koran and Hadith, pushing for new interpretations on the concept of worship, questioning prophetic morals and having their own methods of referring to *Fiqh* [Islamic jurisprudence] punishment.' Together with the alienation and fragility generated by protracted sub-national conflicts and the chronic impunity with regard to abuses of power and human rights, little wonder that Southeast Asia is becoming a haven for violent extremists feeding off social division and disaffection.

Third, the flux of external environments affecting Southeast Asia: the spread of conservative Islamic dogma and extremist ideology fuelled by the contest between Saudi Arabia and Iran and the rise of China as an economic and military power are two of the most significant developments Southeast Asia has experienced since the Pacific War and the end of the colonial era in the mid-twentieth century. Saudi Arabia and Iran seem determined to escalate their struggle for domination of the Muslim world, which can only mean continued funding for religious schools that spread conservative preaching, which in turn creates a Petri-dish environment for the incubation of hard-line extremist thinking. It is a waste of time for governments to make efforts to prevent violent extremism through programmes of de-radicalisation if at the same time a blind eye is turned to the steady erosion of the legal and institutional moorings of tolerance that Saudi Arabia in its existential struggle with Shiite Iran is underwriting. Muslim nations in Asia have little or no influence over either country – though they should, since the majority of Muslims in the world now reside in Asia. But if there is no political will to defend constitutional rights and freedoms and instead manipulate race and religion for political ends, there will always be a steady stream of people attracted to violent extremist ideology.

Meanwhile, efforts by Western powers, principally the US, to balance and moderate China's burgeoning influence are generating geopolitical friction and turning Southeast Asia into a cauldron of superpower rivalry. And even if China's growth grinds to a halt, or if the country suffers a catastrophic internal collapse – not unprecedented over the long arc of Chinese history – Southeast Asia will be affected due to the probable migration of Chinese to the region, much as they did at the end of the Ming dynasty in the seventeenth century and then more spectacularly after the collapse of the Qing dynasty at the end of the nineteenth century. Bearing these three findings in mind, what then can we make of the immediate future?

Indonesia could be regarded as a political weather vane. Its modernity forged in the fires of an idealistic nationalist revolution, the country managed also to adopt some universal guiding principles, including diversity and democracy. Every year on 17 August, Indonesia celebrates the declaration of independence with a formal ceremony at the presidential palace with the raising of the simple red and white flag. As someone who has never really felt attached to any particular country in the patriotic sense, watching the simple ceremony, I catch myself feeling a tinge of attachment, a desire to belong to this ambitious, somewhat improbable nation. Although the course of Indonesian history has been rocky and is strewn with tragic, unreconciled setbacks, Indonesia is at last on the path to becoming a proper democracy. Four successive elections have freely elected a president who can serve a maximum of two terms and its courts have sentenced senior officials including ministers to lengthy jail terms for corruption. All this progress in terms of free and open government is jeopardised by the laziness of politicians and poorly qualified officials. This makes them prone to the kind of rent-seeking and crony capitalism that keeps restrictive trading policies in place, which in turn drives up prices and means that poorer Indonesians can't afford a balanced diet and close to 40 per cent of children under five suffer from stunted growth. As indicated above, these same politicians and officials seem to be willing to challenge legal and institutional safeguards of ethnic and religious harmony in the interests of short-term political gain. In the immediate future there is the real possibility that as ambitious political players use the forces of Islamic dogma and prejudice for their own selfish purposes, they may in the process so weaken Indonesia's plural foundations that the country is set on the road to the kind of ethnic and religious sectarian strife we see in the Middle East today. Strong leadership asserting the founding vision of Indonesia as a country of confounding diversity as well as reform of the bureaucracy and the judiciary to protect pluralism is needed; sadly, it is nowhere in sight.

Myanmar and Malaysia are somewhere in between. In these countries the legacy of colonially engineered ethnic pluralism has proved an enduring obstacle to effective nation building and held up democratic progress. The situation is particularly egregious in Malaysia, which has had ample opportunity to foster an inclusive Malaysian identity over the past three decades of sustained growth and development. I am profoundly saddened when I visit my friends in the country and see them shake their heads in dismay over the slow disintegration of the multiracial compact. More disturbing still is the erosion of the majority Malay culture, which is now all that stands between tolerance and a harshly conservative conceptualisation of Islam with roots in seventh-century Arabia. 'You wouldn't believe,' a former businesswoman turned activist told me: 'I receive messages advising me to drop the Malay word for "thank you" and as a good Muslim use the Arabic term *shukran* instead.' To my mind, the Malay culture and language, with its syncretic roots in the Hindu and Buddhist world, is an enabler of religious harmony and tolerance. But the riot of colour and lithe ritual the Malay culture embodies is being bleached out by the drab garb of those who pursue a vision of Islam as laid down in the Koran, a literalist view that has no bearing on modern existence other than to serve as a guide to personal spiritual salvation. So, with heavy hearts, many of my Malaysian friends – some of them Malay and Muslim – make plans to leave and encourage their children to find opportunities elsewhere.

In Myanmar, the immediate future will see the challenges of integrating a multiplicity of ethnic minorities in a truly federal manner continue to exert a drag on progress as efforts to make peace with the ethnic periphery make slow headway. Working with members of the ethnic armed groups over the course of the past few years, I have been impressed by their willingness to engage with the government in an effort to forge lasting peace. But they have also shared with me their fears of entrenched inequality and the tendency, of the Burma Army in particular, to fall back on tactics of divide and rule to reinforce the majoritarian rule of the ethnic Bamar. Ending Myanmar's civil wars, some of the longest in contemporary history, would be a landmark achievement, but this won't happen as swiftly as many hoped after the November 2015 elections that brought Aung San Suu Kyi to power. Even as she pursues an inclusive political dialogue with the armed ethnic groups, she will be hamstrung by deep reservoirs of mistrust between the ethnic armies and the Myanmar army that are perpetually replenished by continuous skirmishing in the beautiful but remote hills that constitute the ungoverned margins of the country.

Thailand on the other hand is a singularly archaic state that has managed to perpetuate the power and privilege of a narrow-based courtly elite by curbing growing demands for popular sovereignty with strong, insurmountable bureaucratic and military power. Some eighty years after absolute monarchy was replaced ostensibly by democracy in 1932, the monarchy remained the fulcrum of power, protected by ultra-conservative judges and blindly loyal soldiers guarding a privileged network of courtier-officials. The passing of King Bhumibol Adulyadej in October 2016 seemed at first to portend a significant weakening of the crown. However, just a few months into the new reign, Thais remained transfixed by the power and influence of the monarchy, as the new King kept everyone guessing about who he favoured, and whether he supported democratic elections and curbs on military power. In one of his first acts, the King promoted a group of hard-line military generals to his Privy Council and demanded changes to the constitution that enhanced the power of the throne. At the time of writing, there appeared to be little prospect of the military willingly giving up power. Politicians feel marginalised and bitter, knowing they are at least partly to blame for the demise of democracy. They allowed their quarrels to tip into violent conflict in the streets, providing the military with an excuse to intervene, which has found a measure of popular acceptance and support that can't be solely explained by repression. An opinion poll in August 2016 found that 70 per cent of people expressed confidence in Prime Minister Prayuth Chan-o-cha, who seized power two years earlier in a military coup. And even if many believe that when elections are eventually held, popular sovereignty will be restored, this in itself compels the army to stall the process as long as possible.

Sadly, Cambodia is moving in the same direction. Despite the country's astonishing rescue and recovery from the dark period of genocide that followed the extension of the Vietnam War in the mid-1970s, political stability has come in the shape of a strong leader who, rather like the god-kings of ancient Khmer civilisation, sees himself and his survival as the embodiment of the nation. As elections approached in 2018, there were widely expressed fears that the ruling Cambodian People's Party led by Prime Minister Hun Sen would use all kinds of undemocratic and even violent means to stay in power whatever the results of the election. The opposition Cambodian National Rescue Party established by exiled politician Sam Rainsy also inspired little confidence. Drawing on extensive support from the Khmer diaspora in Europe and the US, the opposition was prone to using ugly racist and hyper-nationalist sentiment to stir up hatred towards Hun Sen and his allies. 'They really don't care if there is a civil war,' one well-placed foreign adviser to the government told me in Phnom Penh.

With populations in excess of 80 million, the Philippines and Vietnam are countries with huge social and economic potential bridled by inhibitive political cultures. The Philippines is a prisoner of oligarchy; its leading families have a lock grip on the institutions of government across the country and thus prevent meaningful social and economic reform, which is why an armed communist insurgency thrives on the fringes. Even if outsiders like President Rodrigo Duterte ride popular waves rejecting this monopoly of power, imperial Manila always finds a way to undermine these insurgent power grabs, if not by impeachment then by military force.

As he embarked on his six-year term in mid-2016, the enigmatic and foul-mouthed Duterte seemed intent on rocking the boat. His opening salvoes were aimed at the United States, the former colonial power. Completely reversing his predecessor's policy of strengthening security ties with Washington in order to push back China's aggressive exercise of sovereignty over islands in Philippine waters, Duterte sidled up to China with offers of dialogue and accommodation. The previous administration led by Corazon Aquino's son Benigno Aquino had secured a new agreement with Washington to establish a light US military presence in several strategic locations around the Philippine archipelago. All of a sudden Duterte was calling President Barack Obama a son of a whore and declaring the cancellation of long-planned joint military drills. On the domestic front, he made good on his promise to tackle the scourge of drugs; more than twelve thousand people, most of them poor and living in urban slums, have died in a new war on drugs that saw gangs of masked gunmen roam the urban slums targeting people local officials had placed on lists of alleged drug dealers. Many of the victims were just unemployed men using drugs. Pictures of their discarded bodies, some hung with signs, others with their faces covered in duct tape, horrified rights groups and the international community – to which Duterte said: 'I don't give a shit.'

The disruptive, clattering debut of this former city mayor of Davao, who only decided to run for election late in the day, was bound to upset the Philippine establishment, who saw him as an unstable and narcissistic figure bent on dismantling their wealth and privilege. Perhaps most disconcerting of all to the oligarchy and the military was Duterte's embrace of negotiations to end the communist insurgency. He made his intentions clear initially when he appointed four Communist Party sympathisers to his cabinet. Then he moved swiftly in his first weeks of office to revive a moribund peace process that hadn't gone anywhere for a decade. When I spoke with members of the Communist National Democratic Front late in 2016, they seemed optimistic of a deal within a year. One of their conditions for ending the armed struggle was sweeping social, economic and political reform; but it was hard to imagine so ambitious a reform agenda – specifically carving up large landed estates for redistribution – getting much further than a discussion around the peace table, let alone being implemented. Unless, that is, Duterte's real intention, something his opponents very much feared, was to get behind their radical agenda for change.

One of Duterte's early accomplishments was to finally bury the dictator Ferdinand Marcos. Marcos died in exile in 1989, but was refused a proper burial at home. Instead, the embalmed body of the dictator lay under a glass case in his home province of Ilocos Norte for almost thirty years until November 2016 when, amid a hail of protest, Duterte allowed Marcos a proper burial at the national Heroes' cemetery in Manila. For a country that had supposedly pushed aside dictatorship and has developed a lively, devolved democracy over the past thirty years, there was bitterness in the air. 'Thirty years, on many Filipinos feel they are still in the same place,' commented Maria Ressa, a prominent Filipino journalist, 'the oligarchs still get everything, they keep the spoils.'

Vietnam's remarkable stability and sustained economic growth have set the country apart during the more recent period of political upheaval in the rest of the region. 'In the last thirty years, Vietnam has become one of the world's development success stories, rising from the ranks of the poorest countries. On the strength of a nearly 7 per cent average growth rate and targeted government policies, tens of millions of people have lifted themselves out of extreme poverty,' crooned World Bank President Jim Yong Kim in early 2016. But this remarkable stability and growth belies the influence of the Communist Party, which continues to monopolise power using often-harsh measures of repression with no sign of a counter-revolution. According to Human Rights Watch, in 2016 the Vietnamese authorities 'restricted basic rights, including freedom of speech, opinion, association, and assembly. All religious groups had to register with the government and operate under surveillance. Bloggers and activists faced daily police harassment and intimidation, and were subject to arbitrary house arrest, restricted movement, and physical assaults.' When US President Barack Obama visited Hanoi in May 2016, the authorities detained dissidents who tried to meet him, and the most spontaneous moment of this carefully choreographed visit seemed to be when he ate noodles at a roadside stall with an American celebrity chef.

Singapore's brand of constrained, carefully moderated representative government has worn the test of time surprisingly well, buoyed by good economic fortune and a remarkably cohesive governing elite clustered around Prime Minister Lee Hsien Loong. In many ways, Singapore's stability has been assured by the palpable absence of intra-elite struggle and conflict – unlike neighbouring Malaysia. Despite the pressures of immigration and the rising costs of supporting Singapore's well-developed social services, there seemed to be no threat to the island republic's social and political stability. The threat of Islamic extremism was dealt with in a clinically efficient manner, although the government warned that attacks were possible. Singapore escaped reliance on flighty hi-tech manufacturing and established itself as Asia's premier offshore banking hub. As Singapore warned Hong Kong, with which it competes as an entrepôt, to avoid confronting Mainland China, it stood to gain from the former British colony's insecurity. However, by 2016 economic insecurity hovered over the island republic's shimmering skyline. Despite the allure of its banks, the effort made to upgrade services and provide a conducive environment for an array of professional niches, there was no escaping significant global economic headwinds. Demand for high-end property and retail services was falling in Singapore by the end of 2016 and there were the first signs of a recession on the horizon as growth fell to its lowest level in a decade. Down the road this could lead to popular pressure for a leadership more in touch with the needs of the people, a finger on the popular pulse that the past two elections have showed the ruling People's Action Party sometimes struggles to maintain.

Representative democracy has shallow roots in Southeast Asia; the demi-democracy that prevails instead builds neither effective institutions to protect rights and freedoms, nor does it create certainty or stability. When I first arrived in Southeast Asia in the late 1970s, there were high expectations of political progress in tandem with social and economic development. Almost four decades later in 2016, the Malaysian opposition MP and human rights advocate Charles Santiago wrote that 'we are witnessing a deteriorating regional human rights situation, as governments – both elected and unelected – crack down on critics, opposition politicians and independent civil society. The state institutions intended to protect and look after people's interests,' he wrote 'are being cowed by strongmen and forced to do the bidding of ruling parties.' This limitation of the space for people to voice their concerns or seek justice is steadily breeding alienation from the strong centralised state. The failure of elites to provide welfare and happiness to the majority, irrespective of the quality of democratic government, has led to alarming disparities of wealth. The yawning social gap, plus mounting pressures on the environment, and the hardening of ethnic and religious boundaries mentioned above, will, I believe, eventually mobilise communities to take matters into their own hands. Historically, as James Scott has shown, Southeast Asians evaded bad or oppressive government or rulers by escaping it and moving to the periphery. This option is no longer available, even in the upland areas that once offered a haven. As Scott writes: 'in the contemporary world, the future of our freedom lies in the daunting task of taming Leviathan, not evading it.'

Fortunately being demi-democracies, as opposed to totalitarian states, there is a degree of empowerment that is slowly changing the distribution of power, affecting the shape of states and the geopolitical landscape. At the national level, the state of quasi-freedom has allowed Southeast Asians to identify and affiliate either with ethnic and religious groups that challenge state power, or across these groups around issues of transparency and good governance.

Examples include the Coalition for Clean and Fair Elections in Malaysia known as Bersih, which means 'clean' in Malay. In spite of tough security laws that require police permits for every gathering, Bersih has managed since 2007 to mobilise hundreds of thousands of protesters, braving rain and tear gas, to demonstrate for fair polls and action against government corruption. In response to Bersih rallies in 2011, the government was forced to establish a parliamentary select committee on electoral reform. In Indonesia, a variety of civil-society coalitions have sprung up to monitor local development, and specifically to address the issue of corruption. The liberation of civil society of course cuts both ways: the militantly intolerant Islamic Defenders Front can and does pressure the state to constrict freedom of worship and freedoms for non-Muslims in Indonesia. Meanwhile, at the grass roots, civil society shows tenacity and brings about change at the community level.

In Thailand, despite the imposition of military rule, small groups of activists have prevented the rampant seizure of land and resources by irresponsible corporate or state-owned companies. This is what Thai scholar Attachak Sattayanurak of Chiang Mai University calls democracy on the move, the product of a more networked society. A friend of mine who is a publisher and entrepreneur in Chiang Mai saw her participation in a protest to prevent the development of a piece of land next door to her elite girls school as a significant measure of progress; the project, owned by a rich property developer, was stopped. In mid-2016, as the military cracked down on free expression and political mobilisation, closed down 1,000 websites and threatened to tap phones in national security cases, the government caved in to community groups campaigning to halt the issue of licences for gold mines and permits for special economic zones that encroached on privately owned land. This, another Thai scholar, Thanet Charoenmuang, told me, is 'democracy you can eat'; it bypasses the political parties that have failed to deliver to communities at the grass roots, it ignores the rules and asserts popular will.

Note that this loosening of the role and reach of the state and its affiliated institutions has not sprung from the 'no bourgeoisies, no democracy' maxim of classical structuralism as predicted by the theory of democratisation, whereby economic growth and prosperity empowers an urban bourgeoisie to wrestle power from selfish auto-crats. Rather, in Southeast Asia the prolonged monopoly of power and resources in the hands of the urban elite has sustained strong, authoritarian government. And because popular demands cannot be accommodated in a broadly inclusive way, people are forced into militancy. That is why we see the emergence of pernicious desta-bilising conflict and corrosive divisions in society fuelling extremist views. Instead of allowing more open, equitable government to address these problems, the power holders exploit these dangerous fissures in society in a bid to prevent the leakage of their power.

The immediate future of Southeast Asia therefore looks certain to be characterised by enduring struggles for equality and freedom. The experience of the past four decades indicates that even with im-proved access to the power of modern communications technology and media, the success of these struggles is doubtful, mainly because the power holders have all the guns and control access to justice. So with James Scott's evasion strategy no longer an option, it isn't hard to predict that the only avenue left will be to abandon the state and, if necessary, fight for secession. The slow response of government to grievances and use of divide-and-rule tactics to undermine opposi-tion will force communities and groups to look after themselves and defy the powerful centre. We can see signs of this developing already in Thailand, where the denial of popular sovereignty is currently the most acute.

The results of the August 2016 referendum in Thailand speak clearly of a divided kingdom. That a slender majority of Thais voted in favour of an undemocratic constitution and the possibility of an unelected prime minister came as little surprise; however, if you look closely at the regional breakdown, the country remains divided as ever. Most of the northeast and many parts of the north of the country, bastions of Red Shirt anti-establishment, voted re-soundingly 'no' on both issues. 'The vote shows that people long for democracy,' said a prominent activist in northern Thailand whom the military authorities watch closely. 'The imposition of a sugar-coated semi-democratic regime has stifled struggle for now, but they are ready to rise up at any time, if conditions allow,' he told me over a coffee in Chiang Mai, glancing nervously around him.

The Malay-Muslim deep south also rejected the charter, with local insurgents using a blanket-bombing campaign on the eve of the vote to emphasise their feelings.

The 'Two Thailands' problem – Bangkok and its surrounding areas versus the extremities – has been around for decades. Thailand is the least decentralised country in Southeast Asia, with centrally appointed government officials serving at all levels of society. Contemporary analysts portray the divide as one of socio-economic discrimination and inequality. Bangkok, with just 17 per cent of the population, benefits from 72 per cent of government expenditure, according to Thai academic Veerayoth Kanchoochat; the northeast of the country, with 34 per cent of the population, receives only 6 per cent of public expenditure.

Left unattended, these stark inequalities could breed irredentist sentiment and fuel demands for greater autonomy secession in the north and northeast of the country, as they have in the deep south. Thailand's coherence and unity is easily taken for granted; the results of the August 2016 referendum starkly outline a dangerous divide.

In neighbouring Myanmar, efforts to bring over twenty ethnic armies to the negotiating table are moving forward, slowly. There is little trust and not much advantage that these well-armed groups see to giving up the fight. The Myanmar government has called for a national ceasefire, but the army continues battling up jungle-clad hills to claw back territory and there seems no end to the fighting, especially in Kachin State from where, by the end of 2016, 100,000 people had been displaced. Economic arguments can be made in both Thailand and Myanmar in favour of integration on more equitable terms. But so far, strong, highly centralised governments want all the benefits of integration and state consolidation without offering much of the equity. We should be alarmed by the palpable potential for state disintegration in both Myanmar and Thailand – two of the larger countries of Southeast Asia closest to China.

Wary as I should be of making predictions about a region that holds surprises at every twist and turn of its history, there is merit nonetheless in concluding with a look ahead at the likely shape of society and the state, given all the trends I have presented in earlier chapters. Where does it all lead? How do Southeast Asians cope with chronically poor governance and persistent inequality? Will decentralisation and regionalism fundamentally alter state structures? Here we enter unknown territory, for which the best guide could well be Southeast Asia's pre-colonial tradition of loosely affiliated localities knitted together by voluntary expressions of fealty, and underpinned by commerce and trade.

Southeast Asia by 2050 may well more resemble the region before the invasion of European powers after the 1500s. It will be more decentralised and characterised by pockets of hard-won autonomy. This shift backward in time is driven also by environmental change. Many of the metropolitan centres that have served as the administrative and political locus of state power since the colonial era are situated on seaboards and at the mouths of rivers offering access to seaborne trade. But as sea levels rise, these cities with populations of 15–20 million will begin to experience severe social and economic problems as a direct result of climate change. Bangkok and Jakarta are already visibly sinking. Salinisation is making it hard to provide fresh water. Waterlogged foundations pose a safety hazard. A Thai government study in 2015 issued a dire warning that Bangkok could be partially underwater by 2025. One recommendation was the erection of a high sea wall that could cost as much as $15 billion. Jakarta meanwhile, has been erecting sea walls for years to fortify itself against the waters of the bay. The first phase of a giant sea wall enclosing what is hoped will become a freshwater bay got under way in 2014 and at an estimated cost of $2 billion. This was partly in response to a massive inundation of the city in 2013 that saw inner-city streets under six feet of water. Forced to spend money and devote political attention to their sinking assets, central governments become more susceptible to making deals on the more distant, querulous periphery.

The failure to match aspirations for strong cohesive states with demands for popular sovereignty means something has to give. Much like the irredentist challenge facing the European Union and the Russian federation in the early twenty-first century, as seen in Scotland, Catalonia and across the Caucuses, popular sovereignty in the end trumps national sovereignty. Except that, unlike the situation further west, in the hearth of the Westphalian state, Southeast Asia has a more recent distinct folk memory of state-repelling behaviour, to borrow Scott's terminology, and a long tradition of self-sufficient locality, which ultimately could make this transition a lot easier.

Based on these stark realities, quite possibly by 2050 Southeast Asia will have lost the minimal benefits of trade and security afforded by ASEAN membership. The ten member states will have become more aligned on the basis of geography and economic dependency – mostly with China. Both India and Japan have become more assertive of late, goaded by Washington, using more frequent military exercises and bilateral engagement in Southeast Asia. But it is hard to see either country providing sufficient strategic ballast, as both are rather insular and lack ethnic and economic advantage. In August 2016, after becoming foreign minister and state counsellor, Aung San Suu Kyi made a first official visit to China – she sent the ceremonial president to India. Neither is it realistic to expect the US to expend blood and treasure on protecting Southeast Asia from China's embrace. After two decades of fruitless warring in the badlands of west and central Asia, the current pendulum of US politics has swung back towards a domestic-focused mindset, captured by Donald Trump in his campaign speeches demanding that US allies pay more to be protected. It wasn't surprising then that one of the first comments on relations with China to come from a Trump adviser was: 'I can therefore see the emergence of a grand bargain in which the US accepts China's political and social structure and commits not to disrupt it in any way in exchange for China's commitment not to challenge the status quo in Asia. It may not be a spoken agreement but a tacit understanding that guides the relations in the years to come.'

Most governments in Southeast Asia sense this reluctance to provoke and are not banking on a US defensive shield beyond a token military presence and the odd bout of sabre-rattling from an Aegis destroyer or a Nimitz-class carrier.

China's advantages of geographical and cultural proximity will be magnified by the weakening of strong centralised states and the emergence of smaller autonomous entities relying on trade orient-ed towards the Middle Kingdom's economy, carried along roads and railways built by China. Yet as China's own history suggests, prosperity and stability are periodically hostage to bloody political transition – from which Southeast Asia has always both suffered and profited.

There is something of a coming full circle here, as the six-hundred-year era of Western influence in Southeast Asia wanes to be replaced by something more discernibly Asian. Long before the arrival of Europeans in the fifteenth century, Southeast Asia derived signif-icant material and cultural sustenance from its proximity to India and China. So it begins to do so again; only now with the greater risks to identity and sovereignty that come with the modern tech-nology of interaction. Until the end of the eighteenth century, rulers in Southeast Asia could satisfy China's imperial dignity with annual tribute missions. Today, it is hard to keep demands for 'tribute' at bay when senior Chinese officials can fly in and bang the table with their demands. I suspect there will be strong urges to moderate the pushiness of big Asian powers – China included – with the residual pull of the West. This will depend on decisions made in the Western boardrooms to invest not just with capital but also with human security – hard and soft.

One evening in 2016 over dinner in Bangkok, Kasit Piromya, a former Thai foreign minister and ambassador to Washington, lamented to me the US State Department's distancing from Thai-land because of its military government. Although very much an ally of the conservative establishment, the urbane, Western-educated Kasit is also a fierce critic of military misrule. His point to me was that both Thailand and the US end up as losers. China has gained the advantage, he said, selling more military equipment to the Thai military, including submarines, and securing lucrative infrastructure deals that lock in financial commitments from large Sino-Thai con-glomerates. The West finds it harder to sell close ties with Southeast Asia to domestic constituencies with so much trouble and strife in the Middle East and North Africa. A European government would find it difficult to argue for the maintenance of strategic balance in Southeast Asia when coping with tens of thousands of migrants

from Syria and Iraq and with random terrorist attacks in the name
of IS. It becomes even more difficult when the Southeast Asian
governments have scant respect for the norms and values that increasingly have become conditions for extending aid and assistance.
That's why understanding the dynamics of power and conflict in
Southeast Asia matter.

In the course of writing this book I have thought long and
hard about what prevents Southeast Asia from achieving the level
of social and political development its economic endowment and
achievements warrant. I have highlighted the selfishness of powerful
elites and the quest for security that weakens popular resistance to
greed and the tyranny it breeds. This perhaps explains why Thais
confounded their politicians and voted for an authoritarian constitution. There is also something appealing and emancipating in
the populism that Southeast Asia's modern leaders find increasingly
effective as a means of acquiring power. This could explain why a
poll conducted by the reliable Social Weather Station in December
2016 indicated that 8 out of 10 Filipinos fear for their lives, yet 8
out of 10 also continue to support President Duterte's war against
drugs. However, people are not fooled for very long by demagoguery; in the end they tend to rebel against the yoke of tyranny.
This explains the long history of popular revolt and resistance in
Southeast Asia.

Towards the end of 2016, as I was putting the finishing touches to
this book, I took a stroll along the magnificent waterfront in the
Cambodian capital, Phnom Penh, which sits at the junction of the
Bassac, Mekong and Tonle Sap rivers. It was the start of the rainy
season and the waters of the Tonle Sap, which lap the city's shore,
were a muddy red. For centuries Cambodians have relied on the
swollen waters of the Tonle Sap to do a unique reverse flow at the
end of the rains, flooding vast areas of land to provide sustenance in
the form of fish and plentiful water for irrigation. For this reason,
the Tonle Sap is literally a river of life. It was a Sunday afternoon,
a cooling breeze blew off the water, and Cambodians of all ages
thronged the newly renovated corniche. Some huddled over decks
of cards with fortune-tellers, others brought flower offerings to the

revered Preah Ang Dongker shrine that sits in front of the royal palace facing the waterfront. Young boys dangled fishing rods in the river and surfed their smartphones; nearby their would-be girl-friends preened and snapped selfies. Young mothers propped their babies up on the iron railing facing the river and older men puffed along in bulging T-shirts and trainers.

This colourful tableau of civic contentment left me feeling momentarily upbeat. For how improbable was it that a country reduced to a ruined mass graveyard in 1979, the year I first arrived in Southeast Asia, could within a generation seem so prosperous and peaceful. The country was literally rescued by a huge interna-tional effort and, for all the factional rivalries that accompanied the aftermath, seeds of democracy were sown and appeared to bloom, allowing the economy to boom – at least, that was the outside per-ception. But Cambodia in the democratic era, as Sebastian Strangio, the author of an authoritative biography on Prime Minister Hun Sen, aptly put it, is 'a graveyard of outside perceptions'. For despite the calm and serenity of that Sunday afternoon stroll, sentiment below the surface seethed with anger and people spoke fearfully of the future. There was also a subdued anger, evident when hundreds of thousands of people followed the funeral cortège of a popular political commentator, Kem Lay, who was gunned down on 10 July 2016 – the funeral procession stretched as long as 40 kilometres. 'I know they are angry,' said one senior government official, 'because in this country those in power believe it is their right to have the lion's share of resources – it has always been this way'. So it is with Cambodia's tenacious Prime Minister Hun Sen, so it was with Su-harto of Indonesia in the 1980s and 90s, with Mahathir Mohamad in Malaysia during the same period, and with Thaksin Shinawatra of Thailand after that; all these leaders promised their people happi-ness and prosperity but in the end left them divided and deprived. They brandished the symbols of wise, munificent leadership, but enriched their families and brooked no dissent. They left anger and conflict in their wake.

No longer the most war-ravaged country in Southeast Asia, Cambodia now holds the title of the most corrupt. Is this the fate of Southeast Asia: locked in a cycle of relentless tragedy, partial recovery, then relapse? 'We have a saying in Cambodia,' the senior government official told me over a long breakfast the morning after my stroll; 'when the water is high the fish eat the ants; when the water is low, the ants eat the fish.'

ACKNOWLEDGEMENTS

This book is a distillation of thoughts and experiences over almost four decades of living and working in Southeast Asia. In addition to the huge debt I owe to my friends and legions of Southeast Asians with whom I have interacted professionally, I am deeply grateful for the kindness and generosity of people from all walks of life who have helped me and my family feel at home, and from whom I have learned a great deal about the region. I feel extraordinarily privileged to have lived among a people with an amazing capacity for generosity, tolerance and forbearance. If I have been harsh and overly critical of the way they have been ruled and abused, it is in the spirit of respect and affection.

In the course of writing this book, I am especially grateful to Bill Tarrant, Ralph 'Skip' Boyce, Martin Griffiths, Thongchai Winichakul, Joseph Liow, Priscilla Hayner, Kraisak Choonhavan, Kalimullah Hassan, David Harland and Rio Helmi, all good friends and colleagues who kindly agreed to read all or parts of the book as it made its way to completion.

Over many years of research, reporting, and professional mediation, I have greatly relied on advice and support from Southeast Asians in all walks of life. To list them all would constitute a small phone book. To name some of them may pose risks for their security. I owe a particular debt of gratitude to certain esteemed Southeast Asians of earlier generations who are no longer with us and who I would like to remember: Ali Alatas, Abdul Haris Nasution, Ong Hok Ham, Abdurrahman Wahid, L. B. Moerdani, Pramoedya

Ananta Toer, Mochtar Lubis and Slamet Bratanata in Indonesia; Chandran Jeshurun and K. Das in Malaysia, and Chao Tzang Na Yawnghwe in Myanmar.

As a reporter I learned a lot from colleagues, even if we were often competing and hiding as much from each other as we were sharing. I was fortunate to have worked with some of the finest journalists who have lived and worked in Asia over the last half-century, most of whom worked or wrote for the *Far Eastern Economic Review*. In particular: Philip Bowring, Nayan Chanda, David Jenkins, Hamish MacDonald, John McBeth, Bertil Lintner, Murray Hiebert, Michael Hayes, Lindsay Murdoch, Keith Richburg, Margot Cohen, Margaret Scott, David Murphy, Shawn Crispin, David Plott and Adam Schwarz. The late Derek Davies and Rodney Tasker were mentors without whom my journey in Southeast Asia would have ended shortly after I arrived.

I have worked for the Centre for Humanitarian Dialogue for a dozen years of my sojourn in Southeast Asia and would like to thank Martin Griffiths for giving me the opportunity to start a new career after the end of my happy one in journalism. My HD colleagues, notably David Gorman, Theerada Suphaphong, James Bean, Adam Cooper, Shienny Angelita, Katia Pappagiani and David Harland, have all been constant and stimulating companions on the long winding road towards peace in the region.

I owe an enormous academic debt to my undergraduate teachers of Southeast Asian history at the School of Oriental and African Studies at the University of London: Professor Merle Ricklefs and the late Dr Ralph Smith. However well they taught me, I take responsibility for any errors that may be found herein.

I am grateful to Alan Samson at Weidenfeld and Nicolson and his team for bringing this book to life. This book would not have been conceived or written without the tremendous help and sustained encouragement of my agent Kelly Falconer.

This book is dedicated to my family – Janick, Chloe and Stefan. Their love and affection is a constant source of strength and inspiration.

SELECT BIBLIOGRAPHY

CHAPTER ONE: JOURNEY INTO THE HEART OF SOUTHEAST ASIA

Michael Vatikiotis (1984) 'Ethnic Pluralism in the Northern Thai City of Chiang Mai', unpublished D.Phil Thesis, University of Oxford.

K. S. Maniam (1993) *In a Far Country*, Skoob; Kuala Lumpur.

J. S. Furnivall (1948) *Colonial Policy and Practice*, Cambridge University Press: Cambridge.

Michael Vatikiotis (1996) *Political Change in Southeast Asia: Trimming the Banyan Tree*, Routledge: London.

James C. Scott (2010) *The Art of Not Being Governed, An Anarchist History of Upland Southeast Asia*, Yale University Press: New Haven.

Anwar Ibrahim (1996) *The Asian Renaissance,* Times Editions: Kuala Lumpur.

CHAPTER TWO: LAND BELOW THE WINDS

E. H. G. Dobby (1950) *Southeast Asia,* London: University of London Press.

Maurice Collis (1936) *Siamese White*, Faber and Faber: London.

J. J. Clarke (1997) *Oriental Enlightenment: The Encounter between Asian and Western Thought*, Routledge: London.

Quote from Voltaire taken from his 1756 *Essai sur les Moeurs* cited in Maurice Collis (1961) *The Great Within,* Faber and Faber: London.

Anthony Reid (1988) *Southeast Asia in the Age of Commerce. Vol 1: The Lands below the Winds,* Yale University Press: New Haven.

Leonard Andaya (2008) *Leaves of the Same Tree: Trade and Ethnicity in the Straits of Melaka*, University of Hawaii Press: Honolulu.

Milton Osborne (2000) *The Mekong: Turbulent Past, Uncertain Future*, Allen & Unwin: Sydney.

George Orwell (2003) *Shooting an Elephant*, Penguin: London.

Norman Lewis (1952) *Golden Earth: Travels in Burma*, Jonathan Cape: London.

David K. Wyatt (1982) *Thailand: A Short History*, Silkworm Press: Chiang Mai.

Sarasin Viraphol (1977) *Tribute and Profit: Sino-Siamese Trade 1652–1833*, Harvard University Press: Cambridge, Mass.

Giles Milton (1999) *Nathaniel's Nutmeg: How One Man's Courage Changed the Course of History*, Sceptre Books: London.

Thant Myint-U (2006) *The River of Lost Footsteps: Histories of Burma*, Farrar, Straus and Giroux: New York.

Thongchai Winichakul (1994) *Siam Mapped: A History of the Geo-Body of a Nation*, University of Hawaii Press: Honolulu.

Benedict Anderson and Ruth T. McVey (1971) *A Preliminary Analysis of the October 1, 1965, Coup in Indonesia*, Cornell University Press: Ithaca.

M. Rajaratnam (ed) (1996) *José Rizal and the Asian Renaissance*, Institut Kajian Dasar: Kuala Lumpur.

CHAPTER THREE: DIVINE KINGS AND DARK PRINCES

Kershaw, Roger (2001) *Monarchy in Southeast Asia: The Faces of Tradition in Transition*, Routledge: London.

Pavin Chachavalpongpun (2013) 'Monarchies in Southeast Asia', *Kyoto Review of Southeast Asia*, Issue 13 (March 2013).

Paul Handley (2006) *The King Never Smiles. A Biography of Thailand's Bhumibol Adulyadej*, Yale University Press: New Haven.

Ong Hok Ham (2003) *Power, Politics, and Culture in Colonial Java*, Metafor: Jakarta.

Anthony Milner (2008) *The Malays*, Wiley Blackwell: London.

John Monfries (2015) *A Prince in a Republic: The Life of Sultan Hamengku Buwono IX of Yogyakarta*, ISEAS: Singapore.

J. M. Gullick (1989) *Malay Society in the Late 19th Century*, OUP:

Singapore.

Charles F. Keyes (1977) *The Golden Peninsula: Culture and Adaptation in Mainland Southeast Asia*, Macmillan: New York.

Peter Harris, Daguan Zhou (2007) *A Record of Cambodia: The Land and Its People*, Silkworm Press: Chiang Mai.

Shway Yoe [Sir George Scott] (1963) *The Burman: His Life and Notions*, The Norton Library: New York.

Thant Myint-U (2006) *The River of Lost Footsteps: Histories of Burma*, Farrar, Straus and Giroux: New York.

On Hun Sen of Cambodia and his mimicry of Khmer rulers: http://thediplomat.com/2016/08/the-state-and-the-cpp-cambodias-social-contract/

CHAPTER FOUR: ELEPHANTS AND LONG GRASS

Report on disappearance of Sombath Somphone: https://www.hrw.org/news/2016/07/15/laos-premier-should-account-disappeared-activist.

Report on disappearance of Billy Por Cha Lee Rakchongcharoen https://www.hrw.org/news/2014/04/20/thailand-prominent-activist-feared-disappeared.

Article about the Sarawak Report website, which has helped uncover a massive corruption scandal in Malaysia: https://www.malaysiakini.com/news/335350.

O. W. Wolters (2008) *Early Southeast Asia: Selected Essays*, Cornell University Press: Ithaca.

Lucian M. Hanks (1968) 'Entourage and Circle in Burma', 2:1 *Bennington Review*.

Report on Setya Novanto: http://www.nytimes.com/2015/12/18/world/asia/indonesia-corruption-setya-novanto.html.

Marina Mahathir was speaking at the Georgetown Literary Festival in Penang, November 2015.

On the 2009 Maguindanao massacre: https://cpj.org/blog/2014/11/maguindanao-five-years-on.php.

Fareed Zakariah (1994) 'A Conversation with Lee Kuan Yew' https://www.foreignaffairs.com/articles/asia/1994-03-01/conversation-lee-kuan-yew.

Data on Indonesian education levels, compared with Europe: http://

www.cgdev.org/blog/need-pivot-learning-new-data-adult-skills-indonesia

Anthony Reid (2015) *A History of Southeast Asia: Critical Crossroads*, Wiley Blackwell: London.

S. J. Tambiah (1976) *World Conqueror and World Renouncer: A Study of Buddhism and Polity in Thailand against a Historical Background*, Cambridge University Press: Cambridge.

David K. Wyatt (1994) *Studies in Thai History*, Silkworm Books: Chiang Mai.

Multatuli (1860) *Max Havelaar, or the Coffee Auctions of the Dutch Trading Company*, Penguin: London.

Syed Hussein Alatas (2010) *The Myth of the Lazy Native : A Study of the Image of the Malays, Filipinos and Javanese from the 16th to the 20th Century.* Routledge; London.

Pramoedya Ananta Toer (1980) *This Earth of Mankind*, Penguin: London.

Official explanation of Malaysia's New Economic Policy: http://www.epu.gov.my/en/development-policies/new-economic-policy

CHAPTER FIVE: BYGONES BE GONE

On UN Khmer rouge Tribunal: http://www.voacambodia.com/a/a-decade-later-khmer-rouge-tribunal-leaving-a-mixed-legacy/3384074.html

Pramoedya Ananta Toer (2002) *Jalan Raya Pos, Jalan Daendels (The Great Post Road, Daendels Road)*, Lentera Upantara: Jakarta

Komnas HAM declares 1965 purge a gross Human Rights Violation, *The Jakarta Post*, 24 July 2012.

The Findings of the Indonesian National Human Rights Commission on Human Rights Violations of 1965–66, 23 July 2012.

'Executioners' Confessions', *Tempo Magazine* special edition, 1–7 October 2012.

Indonesian Attorney General Rejects Komnas HAM Report on 1965 Massacres http://thejakartaglobe.beritasatu.com/archive/ago-rejects-komnas-ham-report-on-1965-massacres/

A. A. M. Djelantik (1997) *The Birthmark: Memoirs of a Balinese Prince*, Periplus: Singapore.

On the Indonesian people's tribunal in The Hague: http://www. abc.net.au/news/2016-07-21/1965-indonesian-mass-killings-were- 'crimes-against-humanity'/7647274

Assessment Report on the Conflict in the West Papua Region of Indo- nesia: An Overview of the Issues and Recommendations for the UK and The International Community (2016) University of Warwick https://www2.warwick.ac.uk/fac/soc/pais/research/researchcentres/ ierg/westpapua/papua_assessment_report_final_uk_pdf.pdf

Thongchai Winichakul interviewed by an exiled Thai journalist for the English language version of the Thai news portal Prachathai in November 2014: http://prachatai.org/english/node/4539.

Author's interview with Soedjatmoko, 31 May 1989 in Jakarta.

CHAPTER SIX: ORDERLY OPENING

Bertil Lintner (1990) *Outrage: Burma's struggle for Democracy*, Diane Publishing Company: Bangkok.

Clark D. Neher (1991) 'Democratization in Southeast Asia', *Asian Af- fairs* Vol. 18, No. 3 (Fall, 1991), pp. 139–52.

Michael Vatikiotis (1993) *Indonesian Politics Under Suharto*, Routledge: London.

Pasuk Phongpaichit and Chris Baker (1998) *Thailand's Boom and Bust*, Silkworm Books: Chiang Mai.

On CP Group CEO Dhanin Chearvanont's personal wealth: http://www.forbes.com/sites/forbespr/2016/06/02/cp-groups-che aravanont-brothers-top-2016-forbes-thailand-rich-list/#454baf 8ac9f6

Overseas Chinese Business Networks in Asia (1995) published by the East Asia Analytical Unit of the department of Foreign Affairs and Trade, Canberra.

Murray Weidenbraum and Samuel Hughes (1996) *The Bamboo Net- work*, Free Press: New York.

On Setiawan Djody purchasing Lamborghini: http://www. bloomberg.com/news/articles/1994-10-23/has-lamborghini-landed- on-its-wheels.

On the issue of slavery aboard Thai fishing vessels: https://www. theguardian.com/global-development/2015/aug/19/costco-c p-foods-lawsuit-alleged-slavery-prawn-supply-chain.

Pasuk Phongpaichit and Chris Baker eds (2016) *Unequal Thailand: Aspects of Income, Wealth and Power*, National University of Singapore Press: Singapore.

Chris Baker on Thailand's Assembly of the Poor.

http://www.redd-monitor.org/wp-content/uploads/2014/07/ae13.pdf

On the number of journalists killed in the Philippines since 1992: https://www.cpj.org/killed/asia/philippines/.

On poverty levels in Jakarta: http://www.thejakartapost.com/news/2015/01/29/jakarta-sees-rising-poverty-widening-income-gap.html.

CHAPTER SEVEN: DELUSIONS OF DEMOCRACY

News reports on the 2006 Thai coup: https://www.theguardian.com/world/2006/sep/19/thailand http://www.nytimes.com/2006/09/20/world/asia/20thailand.html

On the Thai referendum on the constitution, August 2016: http://asia.nikkei.com/Viewpoints/Viewpoints/Duncan-McCargo-Thailand-s-ambiguous-referendum-result?page=2

Anwar Ibrahim 'My Plea from Prison: Malaysia Must Choose Freedom over Repression', *Washington Post*, 12 October 2016: https://www.washingtonpost.com/news/global-opinions/wp/2016/10/12/my-plea-from-prison-malaysia-must-choose-freedom-over-repression/?utm_term=.696de00abcd5

On Abdullah Badawi: http://news.bbc.co.uk/2/hi/asia-pacific/2064535.stm.

Author's interview with Prime Minister Goh Chock Tong, March 2000.

'Thaksinomics': Keynote Address by Thaksin Shinawatra, Prime Minister of Thailand Organized by The Philippine Chamber of Commerce and Industry and the Philippine-Thai Business Council Dusit Nikko Hotel, Manila, 8 September 2003.

On Red Shirts in Bangkok: http://www.bbc.com/news/world-asia-pacific-13294268.

Jonathan Powell (2014) *Talking to Terrorists: How to End Armed Conflicts*, Random House: London.

On Myanmar elections: http://www.bbc.com/news/world-asia-

33547036.

Cherian George on Singapore: http://www.airconditionednation. com/2011/05/15/ge2011-aftermath/.

General Gatot Nurmantyo on doubts about Democracy in Indonesia: http://www.asia-pacific-solidarity.net/southeastasia/indonesia/in-doleft/2013/kompas_tniexpressesdoubtsaboutdemocracy_281013. htm

Tom Power on Jokowi: http://www.newmandala.org/cashing-in/.

On General Wiranto as a cabinet member in the Indonesian Government: http://www.thejakartapost.com/news/2016/08/04/why-wiranto-s-appointment-minister-controversial.html.

CHAPTER EIGHT: GREED, GRAFT AND GORE

Najib Razak: 'Please don't think I am a crook' quoted in https://m. malaysiakini.com/news/334426.

Joseph Stiglitz on the lessons of the Asian Financial Crisis: https:// www.theguardian.com/commentisfree/2007/jul/02/theasiancrisi s10yearslat.

Thai columnist Kong Rithdee on the culture of bribery in Thailand: http://www.bangkokpost.com/opinion/opinion/886684/taking-down-sorrayuth-no-graft-panacea.

Gallup Poll on corruption in Indonesia: http://www.gallup.com/ poll/157073/corruption-continues-plague-indonesia.aspx.

Perceptions of bribery and corruption in Malaysian business http://www.thestar.com.my/business/business-news/2014/01/18/ curbing-fraud-corruption-the-majority-of-respondents-of-a-kpmg-survey-believes-that-business-cannot/.

Edmund Terence Gomez (1994) *Political Business: Corporate involvement of Malaysian Political Parties*, Monograph of the Centre for South-East Asian studies, James Cook University of North Queensland.

Barry Wain (2009) *Malaysian Maverick: Mahathir Mohamad in Turbulent Times*, Palgrave Macmillan: London.

On the Missing Marcos millions: https://www.theguardian.com/ world/2016/may/07/10bn-dollar-question-marcos-millions-nick-davies.

The first blog report detailing the 1MDB scandal: http://www.
sarawakreport.org/2015/02/heist-of-the-century-how-jho-low-
used-petrosaudi-as-a-front-to-siphon-billions-out-of-1mdb-world-
exclusive/.

A subsequent Sarawak report blog post allegedly detailing
monies going to Najib's accounts: http://www.sarawakreport.
org/2015/07/sensational-findings-prime-minister-najib-razaks-pers
onal-accounts-linked-to-1mdb-money-trail-malaysia-exclusive/.

A long-form story detailing how the 1MDB scandal was leaked and
reported: https://www.theguardian.com/world/2016/jul/28/1mdb-
inside-story-worlds-biggest-financial-scandal-malaysia?CMP=
Share_AndroidApp_Tweet.

Malaysians reacting to the extent of corruption in the system: http://
asiapacific.anu.edu.au/newmandala/2015/11/30/wielding-the-pen-a
s-a-torch-for-freedom/.

News report on the Friday sermon demanding loyalty towards
leaders: http://m.themalaymailonline.com/malaysia/article/disloyal-
to-leaders-is-disloyalty-to-god-muslims-told-in-friday-sermon.

Danny Quah on Malaysia today: http://blogs.lse.ac.uk/inter-
nationaldevelopment/2015/08/06/malaysias-leaders-no-longer-
serve-the-people-danny-quah/.

Stories detailing China's investment in 1MDB assets: https://www.
malaysiakini.com/news/325170 http://www.freemalaysiatoday.com/
category/nation/2016/08/01/china-firm-denies-1mdb-bailout-plot/
http://www.scmp.com/news/china/diplomacy-defence/article/
1900056/chinas-investment-embattled-1mdb-throw-malay
sian-prime
http://www.sarawakreport.org/2016/07/outrage-najibs-secret-dea
l-with-china-to-pay-off-1mdb-and-jho-lows-debts-shock-exclusive/.

News report about the murder of AmBank Founder Hussain Najadi:
https://www.malaysiakini.com/news/318324.

News report about the death of DPP Kevin Morais: http://www.freema-
laysiatoday.com/category/nation/2016/04/15/pathologist-kevi
n-morais-was-killed-its-not-suicide/.

Global Witness report on Cambodian Prime Minister Hun Sen and
his family's business holdings: https://www.globalwitness.org/en/
reports/hostile-takeover/.

Comment by Cambodian Commerce Minister on Cambodia's ties to China: http://www.washingtonpost.com/sf/world/2015/09/05/the-push-and-pull-of-chinas-orbit/.

President Rodrigo Duterte on corruption: http://news-info.inquirer.net/793344/full-text-president-rodrig o-duterte-inauguration-speech#ixzz4Gjhjac2j.

CHAPTER NINE: SMALL WARS AND CONTESTED IDENTITIES

Statistics on internal conflict from the Asia Foundation: http://conflictstudy.asiafoundation.org/.

Ibrahim Syukri (1985) *The Malay Kingdom of Patani*, Silkworm Books: Chiang Mai.

Thant Myint-U (2011) *Where China Meets India*, Faber and Faber: London.

Lieutenant Colonel A. R. McMahon (1876) *The Karens of the Golden Chersonese*, Harrison: London.

http://www.bangkokpost.com/lite/topstories/355107/time-to-return-the-phaya-tani-cannon.

On the murder of a teacher by insurgents in southern Thailand: http://www.khaosodenglish.com/news/crimecourtscalamity/calamity/2016/10/28/teacher-shot-dead-pattani-school/.

James C. Scott (2010) *The Art of Not Being Governed, An Anarchist History of Upland Southeast Asia*, Yale University Press: New Haven.

C. T. Yawnghwe (1987) *The Shan of Burma*, Institute of Southeast Asian Studies: Singapore.

On exiled Papuan leader Benny Wenda: https://www.freewestpapua.org/.

Estimates of casualty rates in Southern Thailand conflict: http://www.newmandala.org/violence-thailands-deep-south/.

Joseph Chinyong Liow (2005) *Muslim Resistance in Southern Thailand*, East-West Center: Honolulu.

Duncan McCargo (2015) *Tearing Apart the Land: Islam and Legitimacy in Southern Thailand*, University of Cornell Press: Ithaca, NY.

On Thai government denials that Southern Thailand insurgents were responsible for national bombing campaign: http://www.nytimes.com/2016/08/15/world/asia/thailand-bomb

ings-police-investigation.html
http://prachatai.org/english/node/6471?utm

CHAPTER TEN: CLASHING BELIEFS AND THE NEW JIHAD

Author's interview with Fajrul Fallah, Jogyakarta, May 2004.

https://www.history.navy.mil/research/library/online-reading-room/ title-list-alphabetically/t/terrorism-in-southeast-asia.html#back ground.

Kamel Daoud (2015) *The Meursault Investigation*, Oneworld Publications: London.

Author's interview with Lee Kuan Yew, October 2002.

P. J. Vatikiotis (1987) *Islam and the State*, Routledge: London.

Source of one estimate of the amount Saudi Arabia has invested exporting Islamic education overseas: http://www.huffingtonpost.com/dr-yousaf-butt-/saudi-wahhabism-islam-terrorism_b_6501916.html.

Author's interview with Jallaludin Rakhmat, Bandung, 8 November 1989.

Taufik Abdullah and Sharon Siddique (eds) (1986) *Islam and Society in Southeast Asia*, ISEAS: Singapore.

Joseph Chinyong Liow (2009) *Piety and Politics: Islamism in Contemporary Malaysia*, Oxford University Press: Oxford.

Stephen Headley (2004) *Durga's Mosque: Cosmology, Conversion and Community in Central Javanese Islam*, ISEAS: Singapore.

https://www.hrw.org/news/2016/03/29/indonesia-persecution-gafatar-religious-group.

Setara Institute: http://setara-institute.org/en/english-religious-intoler ance-increases-in-indonesia-watchdog-says/

M. C. Ricklefs (2012) *Islamisation and Its Opponents in Java: A Political, Social, Cultural and Religious History, c. 1930 to Present*, NUS Press: Singapore.

Author's interview with A. A. Gymnastiar, Bandung, 20 November 2003.

Author's interview with Abdurrahman Wahid, Jakarta, 5 June 1990.

Interview with Dawam Rahardjo, Jakarta, 8 December 1990.

Rehman Rashid (1993) *A Malaysian Journey*, Rehman Rashid: Kuala

Lumpur.

Sidney Jones (2002) 'How the Jemaah Islamiyah network operates', International Crisis Group Asia Report No. 43, 11 December 2002.

Samuel Huntingdon (1996) *The Clash of Civilisations and the Remaking of World Order*, Simon Schuster: New York.

Author's interview with Syed Othman, Kuala Lumpur, 20 August 1993.

Anwar Ibrahim (1996) *The Asian Renaissance*, Times editions: Kuala Lumpur.

Anwar Ibrahim, Diary Extract, 7 September 2004.

CHAPTER ELEVEN: THE DRAGON APPARENT

C. P. Fitzgerald (1972) *The Southern Expansion of the Chinese People*, White Lotus: Bangkok.

Hillary Clinton's remarks on the South China Sea in Hanoi, 23 July 2010: http://iipdigital.usembassy.gov/st/english/texttrans/2010/07/2 0100723164658su0.4912989.html.

Ooi Kee Beng (2015) *The Eurasian Core and Its Edges: Dialogues with Wang Gungwu on the History of the World*, ISEAS: Singapore.

Yoneo Ishii (ed) (1998) *The Junk Trade from Southeast Asia: Translations from the Tosen Fusetsu-gaki 1674–1723*, ISEAS: Singapore.

Robert Kaplan (2012) *The Revenge of Geography: What the Map of the World Tells Us about Coming Conflicts and the Battle against Fate*, Random House: New York.

Bilahari Kausikan: 'Consensus, Centrality & Relevance: ASEAN and the South China Sea': Lunch talk at ASEAN Summit – 'Charging through the Complexities: Emboldening SMEs for the AEC' organised by RHTLAW TW, Singapore, 4 August 2016.

On levels of Chinese investment in Indonesia: http://www.thejakartapost.com/news/2016/01/25/china-likely-biggest-investor-indonesia.html.

Hong Liu (2006) *The Chinese Overseas: Vol. 4 Homeland Ties and Agencies of Interaction*, Library of Modern China, Routledge: London.

Jeffery Sng and Pimpraphai Bisalputra (2015) *A History of the Thai-Chinese*, Edition Didier Millet: Singapore.

Bill Hayton (2014) *The South China Sea: The Struggle for Power in Asia*, Yale University Press: New Haven.

Linda Jakobson (2014) 'China's Unpredictable Maritime Security Actors', Lowy Institute for International Policy, Sydney, December 2014

Michael Mazza on levels of Chinese influence: http://nationalinterest. org/feature/china-japans-battle-influence-southeast-asia-14006.

On the Chinese ambassador to Malaysia's visit to Chinatown in Kuala Lumpur: https://themalaysianinsider.wordpress.com/2015/09/25/china-envoy-visits-petaling-street-warns-against-using-violence/

Carlyle Thayer (2013) 'ASEAN, China and the Code of Conduct in the South China Sea', http://apjjf.org/2012/10/34/Carlyle-A.-Thayer/3813/article.html

SAIS Review of International Affairs Volume 33, Number 2, Summer–Fall 2013.

'Is Chinese influence re-defining Southeast Asia', *Straits Times*, 4 February 2016.

On attacks against Chinese immigrants in Laos: http://www.nytimes. com/2016/01/30/world/asia/laos-bombing-kills-chinese.html.

On the value of the Jade industry in Myanmar: https://www.globalwitness.org/jade-story/.

Brian Crozier (1965) *Southeast Asia in Turmoil,* Pelican: London.

CHAPTER TWELVE: THE ROAD AHEAD

On Indonesian food inflation see: http://pubdocs.worldbank.org/en/202891477357946101/IEQ-OCT-2016-ENG-web.pdf.

Freedom Map: http://www.independent.co.uk/news/world/the-map-that-shows-most-and-least-free-countries-in-the-world-a6869861.html.

On the Malaysian government calling Muslim liberals deviants http://www.thestar.com.my/news/nation/2016/03/17/liberal-muslims-being-monitored-parliament-told/.

On popularity of Prime Minister Prayuth Chan-o-cha: http://www.nationmultimedia.com/politics/Prayut-gets-high-marks-in-survey-on-confidence-30294000.html

Vietnam: Human Rights watch World Report 2017: https://www.hrw.org/world-report/2017/country-chapters/vietnam

James C. Scott (2010) *The Art of Not Being Governed, An Anarchist History of Upland Southeast Asia*, Yale University Press: New Haven.

Thai referendum results: http://asia.nikkei.com/Viewpoints/View points/Duncan-McCargo-Thailand-s-ambiguous-referendum-result.

On the Philippines claim on Sabah: http://philippineclaimoversabah.blogspot.com.

On the ASEAN Community 2015: http://thediplomat.com/2015/02/what-is-asean-community-2015-all-about/

Dr Veerayouth Kanchoochat (2017) 'Politics in Thailand: What to expect in 2017-8', Paper delivered at the 2017 Regional Outlook Forum, convened by the Yusof Ishak Institute of Southeast Asian Studies, Singapore, 9 January 2017.

On the impact of global warming on Bangkok: https://weather.com/science/environment/news/bangkok-sinking-subsidence-warming-15-years.

http://www.scmp.com/comment/insight-opinion/article/2044746/under-donald-trump-us-will-accept-chinas-rise-long-it-doesnt

Social Weather Station poll on Filipino's views on President Duterte's war on Drugs:

http://news.abs-cbn.com/news/12/19/16/8-in-10-pinoys-fear-dying-in-drug-war-says-poll

INDEX